A concise, clearly written, valuable tool for understanding and proclaiming the Thessalonian epistles. Written from the perspective of the Greek text.

—DR. ROBERT LIGHTNER
professor of systematic theology
Dallas Theological Seminary

The Thessalonian epistles are in many ways a primer to doctrine, and especially prophecy, written by Paul to a congregation of young Christians. Considering the letters' destination, it is an amazing revelation of many doctrines in answer to their questions. Prominent in the book is the doctrine of prophecy and that of the Rapture. This commentary is accurate, scholarly, understandable, and comprehensive.

—DR. JOHN F. WALVOORD
chancellor and former president
Dallas Theological Seminary

It is rare to find a detailed, expository commentary on 1 and 2 Thessalonians from a traditional dispensational perspective. Mal Couch and Ed Hindson have done a service in presenting Paul's two letters to the Thessalonians so that pastors, Bible teachers, and thoughtful Christians can more easily grasp and apply their valuable truth.

—DR. MIKE STALLARD
associate professor of systematic theology
Baptist Bible Seminary

the *hope* of CHRIST'S RETURN

the *hope* of CHRIST'S &RETURN

PREMILLENNIAL COMMENTARY ON 1 & 2 THESSALONIANS

MAL COUCH
Th.D, Ph.D.

Bible study outlines by
EDWARD HINDSON

foreword by
THOMAS ICE

AMG Publishers
Chattanooga, TN 37421

ISBN: 0-89957-362-2

Printed in the United States of America
06 05 04 03 02 01 –S– 7 6 5 4 3 2 1

Contents

Foreword

Dr. Mal Couch's commentary on the Greek text of Paul's Thessalonian epistles will be of great help to anyone interested in a deeper understanding of these New Testament letters.

This substantial work includes introductory material that addresses questions raised by critics. And although Dr. Couch exegetes the text from the original Greek, his information is presented in a way that will benefit students of the English text. Dr. Couch's analysis of the Greek text provides no superfluous data, but concentrates upon those key elements that are relevant to understanding Paul's message.

This commentary will be of special interest to those who wish to find exegetical support for dispensational, premillennial, pretribulational eschatology. These matters are often Paul's theme throughout both letters and they are the doctrines that Dr. Couch believes Paul taught in these epistles.

Dr. Couch's commentary on the Thessalonian epistles provides an extensive, clear, and satisfying treatment. He clarifies the intended meaning of the text, avoiding needless excursions into issues generated by the unbelief that is all too common, even in many of today's evangelical commentaries.

Maranatha,

—THOMAS D. ICE, PH.D.
Executive Director of the Pre-Trib Research Center
Arlington, Texas

■

Abbreviations

Alford	Alford, Henry. *The Greek Testament.* 4 vols. Chicago: Moody, 1958.
BAG	Bauer, Walter; William F. Arndt; and F. Wilbur Gingrich, eds., *A Greek-English Lexicon of the New Testament.* Chicago: University of Chicago Press, 1959.
EDNT	Balz, Horst and Gerhard Schneider. *Exegetical Dictionary of the New Testament.* 3 vols. Grand Rapids: Eerdmans, 1994.
PCH	Barlow, George. *The Preacher's Complete Homiletic Commentary.* 22 vols. Grand Rapids: Baker, n.d.
Calvin	Calvin, John. *Calvin's Commentaries.* 22 vols. Grand Rapids: Baker, 1989.
D&M	Dana, H. E. and Julius R. Mantey. *A Manual Grammar of the Greek New Testament.* New York: Macmillan, 1958.
Ellicott	Ellicott, Charles John. *Ellicott's Commentary on the Whole Bible.* 8 vols. Grand Rapids: Zondervan, 1959.
Barnes	Frew, Robert, ed. *Barnes Notes.* 14 vols. Grand Rapids: Baker, 1983.
EBC	Gaebelein, Frank, ed. *The Expositor's Bible Commentary.* 12 vols. Grand Rapids: Zondervan, 1978.
Gill	Gill, John. *An Exposition of the New Testament.* 6 vols. Grand Rapids: Baker, 1980.
NTC	Hendriksen, William. *New Testament Commentary.* Grand Rapids: Baker, 1983.
Lenski	Lenski, R. C. H. *The Interpretation of St. Paul's Epistles to the Colossians, to the Thessalonians, to Timothy, to Titus, and to Philemon.* Minneapolis: Augsburg, 1964.

L&S	Liddell, H. G. and R. Scott. *Greek-English Lexicon*. London: Clarendon, 1996.
Lightfoot	Lightfoot, J. B. *Notes on the Epistles of St. Paul*. 4 vols. Peabody, Miss.: Hendrikson, 1995.
NIGTC	Wanamaker, Charles A. "The Epistles to the Thessalonians," in *The New International Greek Testament Commentary*, edited by I. Howard Marshall and W. Ward Gasque. Grand Rapids: Eerdmans, 1990.
Milligan	Milligan, George. *St. Paul's Epistles to the Thessalonians*. Minneapolis: Klock & Klock, 1980.
NIC	Morris, Leon, ed. *The New International Commentary on the New Testament*. Grand Rapids: Eerdmans, 1979.
Nicoll	Nicoll, W. Robertson, ed., *The Expositor's Greek Testament*. 5 vols. Grand Rapids: Eerdmans, 1988.
Robertson	Robertson, A. T. *Word Pictures in the New Testament*. 6 vols. Nashville, Tenn.: Broadman Press, 1931.
TLNT	Spicq, Ceslas. *Theological Lexicon of the New Testament*. 3 vols. Peabody, Miss.: Hendrikson, 1996.
Vincent	Vincent, Marvin R. *Word Studies in the New Testament*. 3 vols. McLean, Va.: MacDonald, 1888.
BKC	Walvoord, John F. and Roy B. Zuck, eds., *The Bible Knowledge Commentary: New Testament*. Wheaton: Victor Books, 1983.
Ritchie	Stapley, T. and K. eds. *What the Bible Teaches*. 9 vols. Kilmarnock, Scotland: John Ritchie, 1983.

PART ONE

Introduction to the Thessalonian Letters

■

CHAPTER ONE

The Importance of the Thessalonian Letters

THE THESSALONIAN LETTERS contain some of the most interesting writings of the apostle Paul. While some scholars believe Galatians was Paul's first letter, a greater body of evidence indicates that 1 Thessalonians was written first in approximately A.D. 49.

The Thessalonian letters are important for their mix of doctrine, prophecy, instructions for enduring persecution, and the implications of the gospel for the Jewish, Hellenistic, and Roman worlds. Like the Thessalonians, Paul was suffering for the sake of Christ. Through it all, he gives strong words of encouragement, discipline, and spiritual insight. The two letters are alive with energy and personal concern, showing the heart of the apostle Paul, a former enemy of the Christian Church, now a loyal follower of Jesus. Paul is portrayed neither as a walking dictionary of theology nor as a whip, goading the believers without compassion or sympathy. Instead, Paul exhorted, encouraged, and implored each individual believer in Thessalonica "as a father would his own children" (1 Thess. 2:11).

The Thessalonian letters are also important because they illustrate how Christians should respond while living in a hostile spiritual environment. The truth of Jesus frightened the Thessalonian Jews, who feared they would again be persecuted if they were identified with Christ. Behind the writing of the letters is an environment of fear, compromise, and a willingness among the Jews to sacrifice, if required, the Christians in the city in order to keep the peace.

The letters highlight the work of Paul, Silvanus (Silas), and Timothy who belonged to the Christian social world with its distinctive beliefs about God and Christ, its ethical values, and its alternative social structures

INTRODUCTION TO THE THESSALONIAN LETTERS

centering on the community of faith, the Church. Through their preaching and Christian lifestyle, the missionaries went about making this world meaningful for their prospective converts and inducting them into it. At the same time, they symbolically destroyed the world out of which their converts had come.[1]

The Emphasis on Doctrine

Because the Thessalonian epistles contain no long doctrinal sections, some scholars do not view these letters as theological, preferring to classify them as useful only for practical instruction. But a careful analysis proves otherwise. These epistles can, to a limited degree, be classified as doctrinal because they contain a number of discussions and expositions on theological issues. For example,

1. Paul writes of God's divine choosing of the believer (1 Thess. 1:4–5; 2 Thess. 2:13–14) and discusses how the recipient should show himself or herself to be worthy of His calling (1:10).
2. When Jesus returns with His mighty angels from heaven, the Lord will deal out judgment and retribution on all those who do not obey the gospel (2 Thess. 1:8). Paul describes the terror of the Day of the Lord that will fall upon all those who walk about in darkness (1 Thess. 5:1–7).
3. The apostle writes about the deception of the man of sin and also reveals that in the future, because men will "not receive the love of the truth" (2 Thess. 2:10), they will be deluded and judged because they take pleasure in wickedness (vv. 11–12).
4. Besides retribution, Paul describes "the penalty of eternal destruction, away from the presence of the Lord and from the glory of His power" (2 Thess. 1:9). He thus places before the reader the doctrine of eternal separation from God.
5. He writes many verses about the struggles of the Christian life, about sanctification (1 Thess. 3:13; 4:3, 7), and the work of the Holy Spirit (4:8; 2 Thess. 2:13).
6. The doctrine of salvation and the blessedness of the gospel are referred to often in these letters. Paul mentions the gospel some eight times and writes in detail what Christ has done for the believer by His sacrifice.
7. The glory of God is also a major theme and is referred to five times in both epistles. The apostle also asks that the Thessalonian church pray

"that the word of the Lord may spread rapidly and be glorified" (2 Thess. 3:1).

Concerning these letters Walvoord concludes,

Their instruction had covered a wide gamut of doctrines, including election (1:4), the Holy Spirit (1:5–6; 4:8; 5:19), conversion (1:9), assurance and salvation (1:5), sanctification (4:3; 5:23), and many other doctrines related to the Christian life. They apparently understood also the doctrine of resurrection and the doctrine that some would be translated without dying.[2]

The Emphasis on Prophecy

While several prophetic themes are mentioned in both epistles—especially judgment, the Day of the Lord, and eternal punishment—the doctrine of the Rapture overshadows these other teachings. Quite possibly, Paul had introduced the subject of the Rapture in a previous letter or teaching session. Though disagreement may exist concerning specifics in regard to some of the following verses, the passages obviously refer to great prophetic truth:

1. Paul commends the Thessalonian church for serving God and exhorts them "to wait for His Son from heaven, whom He raised from the dead, that is Jesus, who delivers us from the wrath to come" (1 Thess. 1:9–10).
2. He adds, you Thessalonians are our hope "in the presence of our Lord Jesus at His coming" (2:19).
3. He writes, may your hearts be established in holiness "before [right in front of] our God and Father at the coming of our Lord Jesus with all His saints" (3:13).
4. Then Paul writes in detail about the Rapture in 4:13–18. In speaking of those "in Christ," Paul is clearly addressing the issue of—whether they are alive or whether they are part of the "dead in Christ"—Christians being given a resurrection body. He speaks of "you" and "we" "who are alive and remain [who] shall be caught up together" with those who have fallen asleep in Jesus (v. 17).
5. Paul continues to write of being joined with Christ in verses that follow 4:13–18. He says, "God has not destined us for wrath, but for obtaining salvation through our Lord Jesus Christ" (5:9).

6. Paul prays that the spirit and soul and body of the believer be "preserved complete, without blame at the coming of our Lord Jesus Christ" (v. 23).
7. Two other short phrases seem to refer to the Rapture:
    a. "Steadfastness of hope in our Lord Jesus Christ in the presence of our God and Father" (1 Thess. 1:3)
    b. "With regard to the coming of our Lord Jesus Christ and our gathering together to Him" (2 Thess. 2:1)

From 1 Thessalonians 4, it seems obvious that Paul had taught this doctrine to new believers in the few short weeks he was with them. They understood that the Lord was returning and that they would go up to meet Him in the air. Because they were new in their faith and had no written Scriptures to guide them, they totally depended on what Paul, Silas, and Timothy had taught. With no written Word and only brief exposure to the three evangelists, they would naturally still have questions.

Probably some of the believers had died since Paul had left them. Those who remained had new questions about the Rapture in relation to those who had died.

> What the Thessalonians did not understand, . . . was how the event of the resurrection of Christians who died related to the translation of living Christians. Their question, accordingly, was whether, if the Lord translated them before death, they would have to wait until a later time, namely, after the Tribulation, before those who had died would be resurrected.[3]

The Dispensational Importance

The Thessalonian letters deal exclusively with issues that are important to this current dispensation, that is, the Church Age. In these epistles, Paul focuses on those doctrinal truths that the early believers needed to know. Much of what was written in the letters covers practical theological matters that answered questions about the Christian walk.

The doctrine of the Church deals with "those in Christ" and what constitutes the body of Christ. The Church is neither the kingdom of God nor the kingdom of heaven so prominently mentioned in the Gospels. The Church is neither a replacement theologically for Israel, nor is the Church spiritual Israel. Paul in no way suggests such a correlation between the Church and Israel.

The Body of Christ

Through the Thessalonian writings Paul places these believers, and all believers in other locations, into the spiritual body of Christ. It must be remembered that the revelation of the Church Age was given to Paul exclusively. In Ephesians, Paul shows how the mystery of Christ was not given to past generations (3:5) but is now revealed to him (v. 3)—that Jew and Gentile are placed "in Christ Jesus" (2:13) and that the two groups are made into one (vv. 14–15), a "new man," reconciled together "both in one body to God through the cross" (v. 16). Referring specifically to the Gentiles, the apostle adds that they "are fellow-heirs [with believing Jews] and fellow-members of the body [with believing Jews], and fellow-partakers [with believing Jews] of the promise in Christ Jesus through the gospel, of which I was made a minister according to the gift of God's grace" (3:6–7).

Paul continues, "Through Him we both [Jew and Gentile] have our access in one Spirit to the Father" (2:18), made into God's household (v. 19), a "holy temple in the Lord" (v. 21), "built together into a dwelling of God in the Spirit" (v. 22), "Christ Jesus Himself being the corner stone" (v. 20).

The concept of salvation in Christ and the concept of the church, both local and as a universal body, continues in the Thessalonian letters:

1. "Our gospel came to you" (1 Thess. 1:5)
2. "The gospel of God" (2:2, 8–9)
3. "The churches of God in Christ" (v. 14)
4. "The gospel of Christ" (3:2)
5. "Exhort you in the Lord Jesus" (4:1)
6. "We shall always be with the Lord" (v. 17)
7. "We obtain salvation through our Lord Jesus Christ" (5:9)
8. "The church . . . in God our Father and the Lord Jesus Christ" (2 Thess. 1:1)
9. "With regard to the coming of our Lord Jesus Christ and our gathering together to Him" (2:1)
10. "He called you through our gospel, that you may gain the glory of our Lord Jesus Christ" (v. 14)

None of the above verses suggest that the Church is a replacement for Israel or that the Church is the fulfillment of the millennial kingdom that was promised in the Old Testament. The program in regard to the Church is different and unique. It is intimate and extremely personal. The Church is a new spiritual body made up of those who, for this particular dispensation, represent Christ here on earth—through the body of Christ universally and by the local assemblies of believers specifically. Yet another program for restored Israel will be fulfilled in the Davidic kingdom. But the Church is not the fulfillment of that program.

> The writers of the New Testament make such a distinction, seeing a difference between the Church, the Gentiles, and Israel. Paul states in 1 Corinthians 10:32, "Give no offense either to Jews or to Greeks or to the church of God." The same three groups are discussed in Ephesians 2:11–16, where he speaks of the Gentiles, Israel, and the "one new man," which is the Church. Also, in the book of Acts both Israel and the newly formed Church are mentioned numerous times and are always kept distant from each other.[4]

The Thessalonian epistles are part of the great body of New Testament church literature. The Church and the prophecies (e.g., of the Rapture) about it are central to these specific writings, which summarize what the Church is:

> First, the Church of Jesus Christ began on Pentecost. Until the Holy Spirit came that day with His new and expanded ministries, the Church did not exist. It could not exist until the Head of the body, Jesus Christ, had risen from the dead, ascended to heaven and had sent the Holy Spirit (Eph. 1:22–23). According to the apostle Paul, a believer enters into the Church, the body of Christ, through the Spirit's ministry of baptism (1 Cor. 12:12–13).
>
> Therefore, on Pentecost the apostles and all other believers in Jesus Christ were placed into the Church. Since this is the very first occurrence of the Spirit's work of baptism (placing individuals into the body of Christ) and since there is no other way of entering the Church, this is the beginning of Christ's Church.[5]

The Kingdom of God

Paul mentions the kingdom of God in each of these letters (1 Thess. 2:12; 2 Thess. 1:5), which some commentators interpret as an allusion to the Church as the kingdom, that the Church has replaced Israel and become that kingdom promised in the Old Testament.

Amillennial commentators offer nebulous generalities to support these beliefs, inadequately addressing a passage such as 1 Thessalonians 2:12. The following exemplifies the lack of a lucid and specific understanding within amillennial interpretations. Lenski writes,

> "His own kingdom" would mean the kingdom in general, "and glory" narrows down to the consummation of the kingdom when all the heavenly glory shall be ours. We should not conceive the kingdom in the common, earthly manner of kingdoms. . . . In the kingdom to come, the kingdom of glory, he rules with all his glory, the radiant effulgence of all his attributes. . . . We are called to be partakers of God's kingdom and glory, to inherit both, to share in the rule of God's glory, to be kings in this subjectless kingdom.[6]

Hendriksen also writes with uncertainty, saying that Paul exhorts the Thessalonians to walk in a manner worthy of

> . . . their relation to God, who, by means of preaching and pastoral care, was calling them into that *future realm*. . . . Where his kingship is fully recognized and his *glory* . . . is reflected in the hearts and lives of all his subjects.[7]

One is left to wonder if the kingdom is now and if it is the Church. Is the kingdom of God simply some sort of spiritual experience loosely labeled "the kingdom"? Godly men and Bible scholars such as those quoted above mean well but show their own confusion on the issue. They write in such general terms, the reader is left confused.

If understood dispensationally, however, the term *kingdom of God,* as used in the Gospels and later by Paul, always means the earthly, Davidic kingdom reign of Jesus, the promised Messiah of the Old Testament. With this understanding, the reader suffers no confusion. One must also pay careful attention to what Paul does not say. In both Thessalonian references to the kingdom of God, he does not say the Church is that kingdom. But all believers in all past dispensations will be resurrected to enjoy that one-thousand-year future kingdom reign of Christ, which occurs on earth at the second coming of Christ, following the horrors of the seven-year tribulation.

More discussion of these two Thessalonian kingdom passages is provided in the verse-by-verse commentary section.

Paul's Apostolic Authority

In many places in his letters, and especially in 2 Corinthians 10:1–12:18, the apostle Paul addresses his apostolic authority with strong arguments. With candor, he explains that he does not speak of his role as an apostle beyond what is right "but within the measure of the sphere which God apportioned to us as a measure, to reach even as far as you" (10:13). He adds that if he boasts about being an apostle he also speaks of his weakness (11:30). Too, he reminds his readers that God "knows that I am not lying" (v. 31).

In the Thessalonian letters, Paul also addresses the issue of his authority, saying that he does not seek personal glory. He likely did not have to touch upon these matters, because the majority of believers in that city were loyal to him and respected him (although a few may have had doubts). Nevertheless, Paul speaks to his authority in more than one passage.

He mentions, for example, that his gospel came not simply in word but also in power, by the Holy Spirit, and with full conviction (1 Thess. 1:5a). He adds "you know what kind of men we proved to be among you for your sake" (v. 5b) and you "became imitators of us and of the Lord" (v. 6). The exhortations spoken by Paul, Silas, and Timothy were not issued in error (2:3) but as having "been approved by God to be entrusted with the gospel, . . . not as pleasing men but God, who examines our hearts" (v. 4).

Paul reminds the Thessalonians that he did not seek glory from men, "either from you or from others, even though as apostles of Christ we might have asserted our authority" (v. 6). "But," he reminds them, "we proved to be gentle among you" (v. 7a). In 2:13 he adds, "we also constantly thank God that when you received from us the word of God's message, you accepted it not as the word of men, but for what it really is, the word of God, which also is performing its work in you who believe."

In 1 Thessalonians, Paul concludes the arguments that support his authority with "You know what commandments we gave you by the authority of the Lord Jesus" (4:2). In other words, what he is giving them actually comes from their Savior.

In 2 Thessalonians, Paul asks the brethren to "pray for us that the word of the Lord may spread rapidly and be glorified, just as it did also with you" (3:1). By the time this letter was written, it appears that any doubts about the authority of Paul, and of those with him, was abated. He adds "we have confidence in the Lord concerning you, that you are doing and will continue to do what we command" (v. 4).

Paul then punctuates that thought with "Now we command you, brethren, . . . that you keep aloof from every brother who leads an unruly life and not according to the tradition which you received from us. For you yourselves know how you ought to follow our example" (vv. 6–7a). This passage indicates that Paul had taught specific directives as to how believers should live, and he backed up what he commanded by his example when he was with them.

In contrast to those who are not working and are undisciplined, Paul points out how hard he labored to provide his own needs and not be dependent upon others (v. 8). Although, he adds, as one working for them spiritually, he could have requested help: ". . . not because we do not have the right [to request your aid], but in order to offer ourselves as a model for you" we did not do it (v. 9).

He further exerts his authority when he writes, we gave "you this order" (v. 10a), "such persons we command and exhort in the Lord" (v. 12a), and "if anyone does not obey our instruction in this letter, . . . do not associate with him, so that he may be put to shame" (v. 14).

Paul is the Lord's earthly agent to give His authoritative instructions to the Church saints. Regarding 1 Thessalonians 4:2, Lenski writes, "Paul means that we gave the orders, not 'through our own selves' . . . but wholly and altogether 'through the Lord Jesus.' For although we gave you the orders, . . . they were really given to you 'through the Lord.'"[8] As a final reference to Paul's authority, in writing to the Corinthians, he says, "I am writing these things while absent, . . . in accordance with the authority which the Lord gave me, for building up and not for tearing down" (2 Cor. 13:10).

CHAPTER TWO

The Canonicity, Authorship, and Date of the Thessalonian Letters

MANY SCHOLARS AND commentators believe that Galatians is the first epistle that Paul wrote, but the overwhelming evidence points to 1 and 2 Thessalonians as the first. The two letters are not only written to the same church, but they present basically the same subject matter. Both deal with the doctrine of the Rapture and end-time events. These two letters have, therefore, often been called Paul's eschatological epistles.

1 Thessalonians: Canonicity and Authorship

The external evidence for this letter is more than adequate. "It has been comparatively free from attack and is today accepted by practically all New Testament scholars."[1] It is alluded to in Ignatius' *Epistle to the Romans,* in *The Shepherd of Hermas,* in the Marcion Canon, and the Muratorian Canon. Irenaeus, Tertullian, and Clement of Alexandria ascribe it to Paul.

As to internal evidence of authorship, the writer twice calls himself Paul (1:1; 2:18). Harrison notes, "The personality of Paul is clearly etched here, and the teaching is fully consonant with what a newly formed group of Gentile believers would need."[2] And Hendriksen gives seven strong reasons for Pauline authorship as well as apostolic authenticity for 1 Thessalonians:

1. The epistle presents itself as a letter from Paul (1:1; 2:18).
2. Those who are represented as being with the author as he sends this letter are known (from the book of Acts) to have been with Paul on his second missionary journey.

3. The letter has the typical Pauline form as characteristic of Romans; 1 Corinthians; 2 Corinthians; Galatians.
4. The vocabulary is Pauline.
5. Not only the single words point to Paul as author, but so do many of the characteristic phrases that are found in his other letters.
6. The epistle expresses the character and thinking of the apostle Paul.
7. There is nothing in this letter which is not in complete harmony with the doctrine proclaimed in Paul's major epistles.[3]

But some modern liberal schools are not satisfied with the evidence. A few critics attempt to question Pauline authorship. They claim a lack of originality in the book and a supposed negative outburst against the Jews in 2:14–16, which some say is not in keeping with the needs of a newly established church. But Harrison replies, "Objections such as these could hardly be expected to carry sufficient weight to upset the accepted view of authorship."[4] Milligan points out that 1 and 2 Thessalonians stand together, and that one cannot attack the issue of authenticity and authorship of one without affecting the other. He writes,

> It is not necessary to carry the evidence further down, for, apart from the frequent references to the Epistles which are to be found in the writings of the Fathers from Irenaeus onwards . . . , the very existence of 2 Thessalonians, whatever its exact date, implies the recognition of the Pauline authorship of the First Epistle at a very early period in the history of the Church—a recognition moreover which it continued uninterruptedly to enjoy until the middle of the last century.[5]

2 Thessalonians: Canonicity and Authorship

Strong external evidence exists for the canonicity of 2 Thessalonians as well as its Pauline authorship. That its subject matter is so closely related to that of the first letter is strong evidence that Paul authored both. External evidence is found in the *Didache,* in the writings of Ignatius, Polycarp, Justin Martyr, Irenaeus, Turtullian, Clement of Alexandria, in the Muratorian Canon, the Old Syriac, the Old Latin, in the Marcion Canon, and elsewhere.[6]

But liberal critics try to destroy the validity of the letter based on internal, albeit contradictory, arguments. Harrison lists five arguments critics use as evidence that the epistle is not written by Paul.[7] First, it is thought unlikely that Paul would have penned two writings containing such similar subject matter and within such a short time. However, since the apostle was so emotionally and spiritually involved with this church, it is quite likely that he continued discussing and clarifying certain important issues. The Thessalonians asked for that clarification and he responded. He was not averse to saying the same thing more than once if he felt the situation required it.

Second, although critics claim the writings are too similar for both to be authored by Paul, they claim the issues about the Lord's return are too *different* from that found in the first epistle for it to be from the same writer. Yet Paul continues discussing end-time doctrines, he does not simply repeat himself. Paul shifts to a different aspect of prophetic truth, namely a discussion of the man of sin and the Day of the Lord. He deals with the Rapture in the first letter. It is obvious that in the second letter he extended the time-line of events and does not simply repeat his thoughts with additional words.

Third, since the man of sin is not mentioned in any other of Paul's writings, it has been concluded that 2 Thessalonians is not his letter but that of an imposter who is pretending to be Paul.

> This [argument] has been presented in it sharpest form by those who see dependence on the Nero legend, which maintained that this emperor was not really dead, but would reappear in the East and assert his old power. Some pretenders are said to have arisen to seek popular support on the basis of this expectation. . . . But this attempted tie-up between Paul's man of lawlessness and the Nero Recivivus tale is purely gratuitous.[8]

Fourth, it is alleged that the tone of the two epistles is too different to be authored by the same person. The first letter is considered warm and intimate and the second less so. Yet, it would be almost unnatural for a person to continue the same tone in the second letter, which apparently followed so closely behind the first. It would be normal to simply write more directly.

Fifth, some have pointed out that Paul described himself as both a nurse and as a father (1 Thess. 2:7, 11). However, Harrison argues that in the first letter the nurse's care was shown and in the second, the father's discipline.[9] The second writing declares itself to be composed by Paul (1:1; 3:17), and it mentions the same associates with whom Paul traveled (1:1). Also, the same percentage of Pauline vocabulary as is seen in his other epistles are used in this letter. Some argue that the percentage is, in fact, even higher.

Lenski concludes,

> The second letter advances all that the first contains. We have no details as to what intervened between the writing of the two epistles. All that we can say is that further information reached Paul, Silas, and Timothy who were now working with all ardor in Corinth and its environs. . . . The question of Christ's Parousia, however, is still very much alive among them. . . .
>
> Radical criticism of the two epistles offers so little as to be almost negligible for those who deal with their interpretation. The second letter has been subjected to the severest attacks: it is either a complete forgery or is so in greater part. These critical assaults have succeeded only in their negative way in more firmly establishing the genuineness of these two epistles.[10]

The Date of Writing

Almost all New Testament scholars place Paul on his second missionary journey—during which the Thessalonian letters were written—from about the end of A.D. 49 through the middle of A.D. 52. Some Bible teachers may vary, however, in their New Testament chronology by several years, with some placing the Thessalonian letters having been written as early as A.D. 50 or as late as A.D. 53–54. This present commentary uses the date followed by Boyer and others—A.D. 51.[11] During this period Paul spent eighteen months ministering in Corinth. First and Second Thessalonians were written during that time, with but two or three months between their composition. Barnes takes a similar view, but with some difference, and says that the first epistle

> . . . was written at the time supposed, at Corinth, it must have been about the 13th year of the reign of Claudius, and about A.D. 52. . . . It was the first epistle written by the apostle Paul, and, in some respects, may be allowed to excite a deeper interest on that account than any others of his. The Second Epistle to the Thessalonians is supposed to have been written at the same place, and probably in the same year.[12]

As with 1 Thessalonians, the second epistle was composed in Corinth. As far as can be determined, Timothy and Silas were not with Paul at any other time (Acts 18:5; 2 Thess. 1:1). Some have suggested Philippi and even Berea might have been the destinations of this second letter. Berea is not likely because of the unfavorable reception the Jews gave Paul there. Polycarp seems to think Philippi is possible because of several passages in 2 Thessalonians, but most New Testament scholars think it unlikely.

A. T. Robertson basically agrees on the A.D. 51 date and writes,

The Epistles to the Thessalonians were written from Corinth after Timothy had been sent from Athens by Paul to Thessalonica (1 Thess. 3:1f.) and had just returned to Paul (1 Thess. 3:6) which we know was in Corinth (Acts 18:5) shortly before Gallio came as Proconsul of Achaia (Acts 18:12). . . . The Thessalonian Epistles were written A.D. 50 to 51.[13]

■ CHAPTER THREE

Background to the Thessalonian Letters

History of the City of Thessalonica

When the Macedonians began their rise to power, they eclipsed all the other Greek states where the Greek language was spoken. At this time, the ancient city called Therma was given a new name as well as a new beginning as an important metropolis. As the story goes, a sister of Alexander the Great was named Thessalonica. Her name was given to Therma when the city was rebuilt and restored to power by her husband, Cassander, the son of Antipater. Through the generations, the city has retained this name with only minor modification.

During one period when Macedonia was divided into four divisions, Thessalonica was the capital of a province. But the Romans restored Macedonia as a united region and named Thessalonica as the metropolis of the entire area.

After it had conquered almost all of the Mediterranean lands, Rome went through a period of terrible civil wars. Antony and Octavius were in Thessalonica, and Cicero was exiled from there. Following the return of peace, the city was granted its freedom.

In the first century, the city was the most populous metropolis in Macedonia. And before Constantinople, Thessalonica was acting as the capital of Greece. With Ephesus and Corinth, it was an active trading center on the Aegean Sea. Thessalonica has been described as beautiful and strategically placed. It was located and cradled near a deep harbor, hosting a naval base and port of commerce for ships sailing the Balkan. The city was highly active in trade with scows plying the shores, carrying fruits and vegetables near the rivers Vardar and Vistritza. Wealth, administrative power, and commerce made Thessalonica an awe inspiring city of 200,000. Antipater the poet called it "Mother of Macedon."

The Jews lived in greater number in Thessalonica and were more aggressive than in other places such as Philippi. Philippi was but a Roman colony, containing a large mix of soldiers and retired legionnaires. But Thessalonica was cosmopolitan as well as commercial, and the Jews there would be less likely to live among and be intimidated by the Romans.

That a synagogue was located in Thessalonica was important for it was there that Paul would speak and it was there that the Jews would organize themselves against Paul. The Jewish citizens made protest and accused Paul and Silas—who claimed there is another king, "one Jesus" (Acts 17:7)—of acting contrary to Caesar's decrees.

Thessalonica During Paul's Day

Paul Arrives in the City

The apostle Paul did not come to Thessalonica by happenstance. During his second missionary journey to spread the gospel, the outer ring of witness was being expanded by the direct providence of God. One night in Troas, Paul was shocked awake by a vision from the Lord concerning a Macedonian begging him to "come over to Macedonia to help us" (Acts 16:9). Paul responded quickly and boarded a ship the next day. We know that this cargo vessel drove hard with the wind, for Paul's companion Luke records "we ran a straight course to Samothrace" (v. 11).

Within a short period of time, Paul and companions passed through the gates of the magnificent city of Thessalonica. Terrible times lay in store for the soon-to-be-converted (Acts 17). When Paul entered the city, he went straight to the local synagogue with an electrifying message of prophecy fulfilled and prophecy yet awaiting fulfillment. For at least three Sabbaths (or longer) Paul "reasoned" with his Hebrew brothers from Old Testament Scriptures, proclaiming that "the Messiah had to suffer and rise again from the dead" (vv. 2–3). In the Jewish understanding, his dogmatic message was "This Jesus whom I am proclaiming to you is the Messiah" (v. 3).

His speech's impact upon the city was both a blessing and a curse. Many Jews and God-fearing Greeks, along with prominent and influential women, were persuaded and quickly believed in Jesus. But jealous Jews fired up a restless and vagrant mob. They stormed the house of a leading Greek convert named Jason, who was dragged by force before the politarchs, who governed the city, and accused of following "men who have upset the world, [who] have come here also" (v. 6b). Many feared that if enough citizens trusted in a new king, Jesus the Messiah, the city would lose its free status. Rome would believe that Thessalonica's prominent citizens, noble-minded intellects, and leaders were turning the populace against the Empire.

Realizing that the situation was becoming inflamed, some of the Christian brothers sent Paul and Silas away by night (v. 10a).

The Issue of a King

As mentioned, Acts 17:7 is important because it bears dramatically on the background of Thessalonica. The reference in the verse to "the decrees of Caesar" catches the attention of the reader. In those days, the emperor was Claudius, who had expelled the Jews from Rome, thereby eliminating their influence in the capital city (18:2). History says he had ordered them to leave because of a riot started by one "Chrestus," who some feel might have been a misapplied reference to Christ.

As already shown, the Jewish population knew well how to play their own prejudices against the loyalties of Roman citizens by implying that Silas and Paul were planning insurrection by the rule of another king.

> Fearful that Roman vengeance would fall upon their city if they tolerated even the suggestion of rebellion, they quickly compelled Jason, a new convert, and the other believers to give bail for the good behavior of the apostles. The latter, realizing that their presence in the city was an embarrassment to the church, left immediately for Berea.[1]

Emperor Claudius knew well about revolt. In A.D. 48, his third wife, Messaline, fell in love with a nobleman named Gaius Silius, who plotted the emperor's death. Messaline and Gaius's plan was uncovered and they were executed. This event made Claudius alert for further plots. Thus any rumor of an uprising brought swift reprisal. According to history, Claudius was so fearful during his thirteen-year reign, he ordered the death of some thirty-five senators and two hundred knights. "Though the episode in Thessalonica was not large enough to create any general public alarm, contemporary conditions in the empire and the neurotic disposition of Claudius afforded ample cause for insecurity in Thessalonica."[2] Conybeare and Howson outline the political situation in Thessalonica:

> The privilege of such a city consisted in this—that it was entirely self-governed in all its internal affairs, within the territory that might be assigned to it. The governor of the province had no right, under ordinary circumstances, to interfere with these affairs; the local magistrates had the power of life and death over the citizens of the place. No stationary garrison of Roman soldiers was quartered within its territory. No insignia of Roman office were displayed in its streets. . . . There is no doubt that the magistrates of such cities would be very careful to show their loyalty to the Emperor on all suitable occasions, and to avoid every disorder which might compromise their valued dignity, and cause it to be withdrawn.[3]

Background to the Thessalonian Letters

1 Thessalonians

When Paul and Silas left the city, they ministered briefly in Berea (17:10) and then Athens (v. 15). Paul sent Silas and Timothy back into Macedonia on separate trips, Timothy to Thessalonica (1 Thess. 3:2) and Silas possibly to Philippi. They later joined the apostle in Corinth (18:5).

Timothy's response to what was happening in Thessalonica was positive, as determined by Paul's glowing comments in his first letter about the growth and zeal of his converts. Yet clearly they needed counsel on certain matters. Since persecution had broken out, Paul commends the Thessalonian church for their faith under fire (2:14; 3:1–4); but the letter also addresses criticism against Paul's leadership, probably inspired by Jewish opposition. This criticism forced Paul to defend his ministry, conduct, and motives (2:1–12).

The letter also indicates the existence of some moral problems, which Paul addressed (4:1–8). Also, some Thessalonian Christians had questions about the death of their loved ones. They were confused about the Resurrection and final salvation to be attained at the coming of the Lord (4:13–18). Finally, some were restless and inattentive to daily work, and they apparently needed Paul's rebuke (4:11).

The church experienced, too, some confusion about prophetic matters.

Many scholars suggest Paul had addressed the doctrine of the Rapture and resurrection while with the growing congregation. They may have misunderstood, needed additional reminders, or still required more clarification. The concept of the Rapture was something new.

2 Thessalonians

Nothing indicates that Paul had any fresh contact with the church that may account for his second letter. He must have heard about some problems among its members (3:11) and had apparently heard of an attempt to promote a different view about Christ's return, that view being propagated through a letter that he was supposed to have written (2:2).

The prophetic issue clearly prompted Paul to write. He desired to resolve the confusion in regard to the Rapture, the Tribulation, and the coming of the Man of Sin.

The Suffering of the Thessalonians

The church must have been undergoing wave after wave of torment, from both the Gentiles and the Jews. In 1 Thessalonians, Paul uses twelve different words, both nouns and verbs, for *affliction,* and he uses eight such words in the second letter. In one word, *suffer,* he describes his own labors in the ministry. Concerning the Thessalonians, one can only imagine the terror visited upon these young Christians. Their persecution could have included stoning, arrest, destruction of property, and ostracizing that kept them from being able to work.

Instead of seeing despair in persecution, however, Paul sees triumph. God is being glorified in the boldness and perseverance of the church's witness before their tormentors. Note the different words Paul uses.

1. **Opposition.** This word *agon* is used once (1 Thess. 2:2) when Paul writes that the gospel came to them "amid much *opposition.*" The word implies pain in a "contest" or "struggle." The English word *agony* comes from *agon.*
2. **Persecution.** *Diogmos* is related to the verb *dioko,* which means to "hasten, be behind something." From this use comes the idea of "to pursue, persecute." Paul says the other churches of God knew of the *persecutions* facing the Thessalonians (2 Thess. 1:4).
3. **To thwart or be thwarted.** The apostle writes that he had desired to come

to the congregation and comfort them "more than once—and yet Satan *thwarted* us" (1 Thess. 2:18), thwarted coming from *enkopto,* which carries the idea of "to be impeded, hindered, or restrained."

4. **Tribulation, affliction.** Using both the verb *thlibo* and the noun *thlipsis,* Paul commends the church for "having received the word in much *tribulation"* (1 Thess. 1:6). Timothy was sent, Paul says, so that no one would be disturbed "by these *afflictions"* (3:3). Paul says that he could speak proudly of the believers because of the way they maintained their faith in the midst of their *afflictions* (2 Thess. 1:4). The word is used two other times in these letters (1 Thess. 3:7; 2 Thess. 1:6).

5. **Labor under stress.** The verb *kopiao* and the noun *kopos* are used together more than almost any other word describing the church's troubles (1 Thess. 1:3; 2:9; 3:5; 5:12; 2 Thess. 3:8). The English word *cope* comes from this Greek word.

6. **Hardship.** This word *mochithos* carries the thought of "extreme difficulty, effort." It is used in 1 Thessalonians 2:9 and 2 Thessalonians 3:8 to describe Paul's own struggles for the sake of the gospel. The only other place Paul uses the word is in 2 Corinthians 11:27. In the Thessalonian letters, he writes of his own "labor and *hardship"* (1 Thess. 2:9) and how under this pressure he worked "night and day so that we might not be a burden to any of you" (2 Thess. 3:8).

7. **Suffer.** One of the most common words for *suffering* is *pascho,* which Paul uses twice (1 Thess. 2:14; 2 Thess. 1:5).

8. **Suffer previously.** *Propascho* is used only once and it refers to Paul's suffering: "But after we had already [previously] suffered . . ." (1 Thess. 2:2).

9. **Mistreat.** Also referring to Paul's abuse, *hubrizo* carries the thought of one being "insulted" (1 Thess. 2:2). The related noun is *hubris* and can be translated "arrogance, disaster, mistreatment."

By using some of these words to describe his own situation and suffering for the gospel, Paul made it clear that he could identify with what was happening to the Thessalonians. He probably also wanted them to realize that they were going through what he experienced. These things were coming upon all of them for the sake of Christ. They were united in a common walk of pain for a higher cause than their own existence or personal comfort.

Conclusion

Unger writes this interesting observation:

> Paul's synagogue preaching, together with his and Silas' personal work, resulted in the establishment of a strong church in the city. Much emphasis was placed upon prophecy both fulfilled in the Messiah at His first advent but especially unfulfilled in connection with His Second Advent. This appears strikingly in the first Thessalonian epistle, written evidently from Corinth not long after the founding of the Thessalonian church and also in the second epistle shortly after the first, probably while still at Corinth. The eschatological emphasis fitted into the general period of Paul's life (A.D. 51).[4]

CHAPTER FOUR

Outlines: 1 Thessalonians and 2 Thessalonians

1 Thessalonians

I. PAUL'S GREETINGS AND REMINDERS (1:1–3:13)
   A. Paul's Salutation (1:1)
   B. Paul's Words of Encouragement (1:2–10)
   C. Paul's Walk Before the Thessalonians (2:1–12)
      1. His Boldness (2:1–4)
      2. His Gentle Care and Labor (2:5–9)
      3. His Devotion (2:10–12)
   D. Paul's Care for the Thessalonians (2:13–3:13)
      1. His Desire to See Them (2:13–20)
      2. His Concern for Their Trials (3:1–8)
      3. His Consistent Prayers for Them (3:9–13)

II. EXHORTATION FOR CHRISTIAN LIVING (4:1–5:28)
   A. What it Means to Walk with the Lord (4:1–12)
      1. Sexual Issues (4:1–8)
      2. Brotherly Issues (4:9–10)
      3. Behavioral Issues (4:11–12)
   B. The Rapture: What It Means "to Meet" the Lord (4:13–18)
   C. What It Means to Escape the Day of the Lord (5:1–11)
   D. What It Means to be Sanctified by the Lord (5:12–28)

2 Thessalonians

I. PAUL'S GREETINGS (1:1–2)

II. PAUL'S ENCOURAGING THOUGHTS ABOUT SUFFERING (1:3–12)

III. PAUL'S DOCTRINAL CORRECTION ABOUT THE DAY OF THE LORD (2:1–17)
   A. "The Misunderstanding" (2:1–3)
   B. The Man of Lawlessness (2:4–9)
   C. The Delusion of the Unbeliever (2:10–12)
   D. The Security of the Believer (2:13–17)

IV. PAUL'S ENCOURAGEMENT AND WORDS OF DISCIPLINE (3:1–18)
   A. The Request for Prayer (3:1–5)
   B. The Resolve to Discipline (3:6–15)
   C. The Reminder of the Lord's Presence (3:16–18)

PART TWO

First Thessalonians Commentary

■

CHAPTER FIVE

Paul's Commendation of the Thessalonians

I. PAUL'S GREETINGS AND REMINDERS (1:1–3:13)

A. Paul's Salutation (1:1)

1:1 Paul and Silvanus and Timothy to the church of the Thessalonians in God the Father and the Lord Jesus Christ: Grace to you and peace.

Paul and Silvanus and Timothy. For a moment in history, these three men worked together to effect a strategy that initiated the worldwide spread of the gospel. In Acts 17, Luke brings their joint efforts to our attention. During Paul's second missionary journey (circa late A.D. 49 to early A.D. 50), they traveled through Amphipolis and Apollonia to Thessalonica (v. 1).

After three Sabbaths of speaking the message of Christ in the local synagogue, Paul and Silas witnessed a great response by some of the Jews and "a great multitude of the God-fearing Greeks" (v. 4).

Then the Jews stirred the crowds to a feverish pitch of hatred, shouting, "These men who have upset the world have come here also" (v. 6b). As a consequence of this outburst, Paul and Silas were swiftly sent away to Berea (v. 10). Timothy suddenly appears in the Acts narration when Paul called him and Silas (Silvanus) to join him in Athens (v. 15). It is generally accepted that Timothy previously had been in Thessalonica. Since Silvanus and Timothy are mentioned in the opening words of this letter, they must have been as familiar to the Thessalonians as Paul was. While laboring in Thessalonica, these three men had led people to the Lord, conceived friendships, and were now writing back to encourage their new Christian friends.

Paul. As the elder apostle, Paul's name comes first, as the other two men join him in a collective greeting. Paul may not have penned this letter himself, although he does make a point that he personally wrote the second epistle to the Thessalonians (2 Thess. 3:17).

Paul's Jewish name is Saul. "This Hebrew name was very appropriate because its bearer belonged to the tribe of Benjamin from which centuries earlier king Saul had arisen (Phil. 3:5; cf. I Sam. 9:1, 2)" (*NTC*). Paul's Roman name was Paul-us or Paullus and meant "little." Tradition said that he was truly a small man, bald, stooped, bow-legged but strongly built. Also, Paul appeared to be full of grace; he looked like a man but had the face of an angel.

Although the exact date is uncertain, tradition suggests that Paul was born the second year after the birth of Christ. Paul's birth place was Tarsus (Acts 22:3), the capital of Cilicia, a city founded by the Assyrians and an important crossroads during the first century. He was born with the privilege of Roman citizenship (22:25–28), and his father's ability to purchase this citizenship for Paul before he was born demonstrates that the family was wealthy. As the son of a wealthy Pharisee and a Hebrew of the dispersion (Phil. 3:5), Paul had a good heritage. Growing up, he had the advantages offered by orthodox Judaism coupled with a Hellenistic worldview. A privileged youth, he studied the Law in Jerusalem under the great Jewish scholar Gamaliel (Acts 22:3).

Because of his studies and his heritage, Paul was both a natural and authoritative leader of the Jewish people. As a Pharisee, he enjoyed both political and spiritual respect and believed in the coming of the Messiah. But he originally considered the early Christians as fanatics and heretics who were bringing harm to the people of Israel.

Chrysostom says that Paul died in the year 66 at the age of sixty-eight.

Paul first appears in Scripture in Acts 7:58 and 8:1, giving approval to the stoning and murder of Stephen. Later, he is seen zealously rooting out and persecuting Christians with the authority of the Jerusalem leadership (Acts 9:1–3). It was on his journey to Damascus to arrest more believers that he met Jesus Christ face to face. This miraculous encounter was needed to convince Paul of the reality of the Resurrection and of the person of the Lord Jesus. Afterward, Paul would never be the same.

Paul emphasizes in Galatians 1 that neither his apostleship nor his teaching came from men but, rather, it came from God. His new message was that the Messiah had come and had died for the salvation of the world. Paul would also be the person to whom the Lord revealed the mystery of this new work of God—the Church (Eph. 2:11–3:12).

Silvanus. As the older man, and out of respect, he is mentioned second in Paul's greeting. Silvanus is this missionary's proper name in Latin and originally meant "god of the forest or woods." His name in Greek is Silas, which is the name Luke uses in Acts. Silas is seen in a prominent position at the council of Jerusalem (Acts 15:22, 27, 32), and he journeyed with Paul to Antioch to give the council's decision to that city. In the dispute over John Mark, Barnabas ended up taking this young man on his trips, and Paul took Silas. Silas is always referred to in reference to Paul's second missionary journey. Seemingly in the background, he is seen as quietly serving Paul, carrying messages for him, and aiding the apostle.

Timothy. He is the youngest member of the missionary team and seems to have joined the group while the journey was in progress (Acts 16:1–3). "He is left unnoticed as being a junior subordinate, until the time comes when he can act as a useful agent of his leaders" (Nicoll). Through the years, Timothy's role in Paul's ministry may have had overall significance. According to Acts and 2 Timothy 1:5–6, this young man was the son of a believer and a disciple. At the very least, his Jewish mother trained him in the Old Testament Scriptures. We have no knowledge of his Gentile father (2 Tim. 1:5; 3:15).

Paul was a spiritual father to Timothy (1 Cor. 4:17), which may mean he was converted by the apostle on his first missionary journey. Paul certainly mentored him in the faith and the two developed a close-knit relationship based upon their faith and upon their trust in one another. Based on 2 Timothy 3:10–11, it is believed that Timothy may have accompanied Paul on at least part of his first missionary journey.

Timothy was loosely classed as an apostle with Paul and Silas, since he traveled with them (1 Thess. 2:6). He was with Paul at Ephesus on his third missionary journey (Acts 19:22) but is soon sent on his own trip for the apostle. He also traveled with Erastus and others (1 Cor. 4:17) to Macedonia and then on to Corinth. From Hebrews 13:23, it appears that Timothy was arrested at an early point: "You should understand that our brother Timothy has been released" (RSV). Because the author of Hebrews knew him, it would seem that he was not only well known to the readers but also probably to all the churches.

Following Paul's death in Rome, it is probable that Timothy escaped execution and was set free. Tradition says he died at Ephesus and was buried, like the apostle John, on nearby Mount Prion.

To the church of the Thessalonians. Some think that there was more than one assembly in each city and that these assemblies were collectively called "the church." No concrete evidence exists, however, for this claim. In this New Testament period, the assemblies (one in each city) were small and for the most part under persecution.

The Greek word *ekklesia* means "the called out ones" and is a word used even of the Jewish synagogues and assemblies. It also meant "any public assembly of citizens summoned by a herald" (Milligan). But in the New Testament the word carries a specific theological concept regarding those who have been spiritually "called out" of the world to be joined to Jesus in salvation and justification. One might say that one is called by God, and the herald is the Holy Spirit. This dispensation is a wondrous new work of God that radically distinguishes the Church Age from that of the Law.

> Sometimes *ekklesia* designates all Christendom and is a synonym for the body of Christ (Col. 1:18, 24). At other times it is a particular assembly in a particular location (Rom. 16:5; 1 Cor. 16:19; Col. 4:15). (*EBC*)

In God the Father and the Lord Jesus Christ. The church is grounded *in* (the locative case), as existing in the sphere and power of both the Father and Son (Robertson). By referring to the Father, Paul gives to the Thessalonians a sense of relationship with their God that they could never find in pagan religions. "A defining clause connected with *ekklesia*, the absence of any uniting art[icle] . . . helping to give more unity to the conception" (Milligan). "The *en*, as usual, denotes communion and participation in, as the element of spiritual life" (Alford). "The Apostle emphasizes that all Christians are locally united 'within the pneumatic [spiritual] body of Christ,' in so far as they together build up His body" (Milligan). "Other Thessalonians were 'in the world,' 'in darkness,' 'in their sins'" (Ellicott).

The word *Lord* (*kurios,* master) conveys Jesus' absolute authority over the life of the believer. In Pauline theology it likely means more, touching clearly on the divinity and messiahship of Christ. The apostle probably has in mind Psalm 110:1, which reads, "The LORD [*Yahweh*] says to my Lord [*Adonai,* my master]: 'Sit at My right hand, until I make Thine enemies a footstool for Thy feet.'" The Jewish leadership knew Psalm 110 was referring to the son of David. Quoting this passage to the Pharisees, Jesus then asks, "If David then calls Him 'Lord,' how is He his son?" (Matt. 22:45). The Pharisees had no answers but left Him alone and asked no further questions. Jesus baffled them because if the Lord addressed in the psalm was not already in existence, then how could David make this statement? Clearly, the Messiah is greater than David and preexistent. Even today some rabbis consider the Messiah as near deity, saying He existed in the mind of God from eternity past.

Robertson writes,

> In the very beginning of this first epistle of Paul, we meet his Christology. He at once uses the full title "Lord Jesus Christ" with all the theological content of each word. The name "Jesus" (Saviour, Matt. 1:21) he knew as the "Jesus of history," the personal name of the Man of Galilee, whom he had once persecuted (Acts 9:5) but whom he at once, after his conversion, proclaimed to be "the Messiah" (*ho Christos,* Acts 9:22).
>
> This position Paul never changed. In the great sermon at Antioch in Pisidia, which Luke has preserved (Acts 13:23), Paul proved that God fulfilled his promise to Israel by raising up "Jesus as Savior" (*sotera Iesoun*). Now Paul follows the Christian custom by adding *Christos* (verbal from *chrio,* to anoint) as a proper name to Jesus (Jesus Christ) as later he will often say "Christ Jesus" (Col. 1:1). And he dares also to apply *kurios* (Lord) to "Jesus Christ," the word appropriated by Claudius (*dominus, kurios*) and other emperors in the emperor-worship, and also common in the Septuagint for God as in Psa. 32:1f. (quoted by Paul in Rom. 4:8). Paul uses *kurios* of God (1 Cor. 3:5) or of Jesus Christ, as here. In fact, he more frequently applies it to Christ when not quoting the Old Testament as in Rom. 4:8. And here he places "the Lord Jesus Christ" in the same category and on the same plane with "God the father." There will be growth in Paul's Christology and he will never attain all the knowledge of Christ for

which he longs (Phil. 3:10–12), but it is patent that here in his first epistle there is no "reduced Christ" for Paul. . . . The Risen Christ became at once for Paul the Lord of his life. (Vol. 4, p.6)

Grace to you and peace. Although this was a common greeting of the day, as used in Paul's letters, it was not quoted as simply polite filler. Paul really meant these words. He intended "to evoke in his readers a sense of divine blessing upon their lives characterized by God's freely given favor and the sense of completeness or wholeness (the root idea of the Hebrew word *salom*) that results from reconciliation with God through Christ's death" (*NIGTC*).

The apostles ceaselessly exhort believers to seek and find peace between themselves, because peace is a distinguishing part of their religion. This is what gives *eirene* [peace] of the apostolic salutations its density of meaning; it includes peace with God, the benefits of salvation, harmony with all people, Christian blessedness, that is, peace of heart or calm in the soul, which is purified from its sins; an interior well-being that follows justification by faith and is the work of the Holy Spirit. In the secular literature, the . . . verb *eireneuo*, "be or live in peace," is always used in contrast to a state of war. (*TLNT*)

On verse 1, Calvin concludes,

A Church is to be sought for only where God presides, and where Christ reigns, and that, in short, there is no Church but what is founded upon God, is gathered under the auspices of Christ, and is united in his name.

B. Paul's Words of Encouragement (1:2–10)

> **1:2** We give thanks to God always for all of you, making mention of you in our prayers;

We give thanks to God always. *Eucharisteo* is a compound verb, *eu* (abundance, greatness) and *charisteo* (to grace, bestow favor, bless), which is related to *eucharist,* the noun originating from the verb and which relates to the Semitic expression "to say the table benediction." Thus, *eucharisteo* literally means "to good grace" and is interchangeable with the word *eulogeo,* which means "good word" (*EDNT*).

Pantote (always) carries the idea of "at all times" (*EDNT*). The apostle and his companions are continually thanking (present tense) the Lord for His work in the Thessalonian church. His "thanksgiving was not a spasmodic exercise but a habit of life (2 Thess. 2:13). He includes his fellow-workers by using the plural form. . . . 3:10 informs us that they engaged in thanksgiving and intercession night and day for them."

For all of you. Some in the Thessalonian congregation were living slothful and unproductive lives (2 Thess. 3:11–12), but Paul also includes them in his petitions to God. The preposition "for" (*peri,* "around") means "to encircle" around all of them, including each individual and the church as a whole (Robertson).

In our prayers. The preposition *in* (*epi*) has a local sense of "at" our prayers, or "when we engage in our prayers." Prayer (*proseuche*) refers to the act of praying and is used in the New Testament only of prayer to God (Milligan). Praying was serious business for the apostle Paul.

> **1:3** constantly bearing in mind your work of faith and labor of love and steadfastness of hope in our Lord Jesus Christ in the presence of our God and Father,

Bearing in mind. This can also be read, "unceasingly remembering" (Lenski). The apostle wants them to know that "on every occasion that reminds us of you," we are thankful to God for what He is doing through you.

Your work of faith. *Work* (*ergou*) carries the idea of industry, business, or task. Paul is not saying that faith is a work. Because two genitives are used with the word *work,* the idea is "the activity that faith inspires." "Almost equivalent to a very emphatic adjective—'faithful activity,' i.e., a work characterized by faith and prompted by faith, such as faith alone could have enabled you to accomplish" (Ellicott). Thus, we are justified by faith, but faith produces work (Robertson). With the genitive being subjective, the meaning is "practically, 'remembering how your faith works, and your love toils, and your hope endures'" (Milligan).

Labor of love. The word *love* (*agape*) is used as a descriptive genitive characterizing labor: "A love that comes from labor," or "a loving kind of labor." *Labor* (*kopos*) comes from *kopto,* which means "to cut, lash, or beat" as in pounding the flour dough. It can also mean to "shatter, slap, or be under hardship" (*EDNT*). Thus, the Thessalonian church's loving labor was a stressful and painful service to the Lord. Though it was motivated and characterized by love, it did not come easy; there was a price to pay. "This work is accomplished by the toil (*kopos*) that fatigues" (Lenski).

Steadfastness of hope in our Lord Jesus Christ. *Steadfastness* (*hupomone*) is often translated "perseverance." It is a compound noun meaning "being under [it] alone," with the idea of standing under persecution or pressure and taking it. The Thessalonian church's hope "was attended with patience, with a patient bearing of reproaches, afflictions, and persecutions, for the sake of Christ, and a patient waiting for his coming" (Gill).

The hope (*elpidos*) has to do with the coming of the Lord for His own in the Rapture, which subject Paul will address in more detail later. *Elpidos* would be better translated "anticipation," because it is not a wishful hope that may not happen; it is an assured expectation of something that will certainly take place. This hope of Christ's return is one of the main themes of 1 Thessalonians. In Titus 2:13, Paul also writes, "Looking for the blessed hope and the appearing of the glory of our great God and Savior, Christ Jesus."

Hope as a virtue—A feeling of confidence, hope resides in the heart (Jdt 6:9; Ps 28:7); it is a virtue infused by "the God of hope" (Rom 15:13) or the Holy Spirit (Rom 15:13; cf. 5:5)—the pledge of the world to come (2 Cor 1:22; 5:5)—and by means of the Scriptures (Rom 15:4). It is associated with faith and charity. (*TLNT*)

In this verse the three genitives (faith, love, hope), "may fittingly be translated as adjectives, respectively, *faithful, loving,* and *hopeful"* (D&M, p. 72).

In the presence of our God and Father. The word for *presence* (*emprosthen*) is composed of the prepositions *en* and *pros,* strengthened by the particle of direction, *then.* Thus, *emprosthen* carries with it both a local (or position) and a temporal (or time) element (*EDNT*). It can be translated "before [something happens]," or "before [as in front of something]."

Paul is likely saying that our anticipation (hope) of the return of the Lord is to be fulfilled soon; He will then take us into the presence of our God and Father. This is what Paul seems to be saying when he uses the word *emprosthen* in 2:19 and 3:13. The apostle asks, are not the Thessalonians his hope, joy, or crown of exultation "in the presence [*emprosthen*] of our Lord Jesus at His coming [*parousia*]"? (2:19). And he prays that God would establish their hearts unblamable "in holiness before [*emprosthen*] our God and Father at the coming [*parousia*] of our Lord Jesus with all His saints" (3:13).

All three verses are Rapture passages that anticipate his further detailed discussion in chapter 4. Although Robertson does not believe these three verses refer to the Rapture, he does agree that the verses are in reference to believers brought into the very presence of the living God. He writes, "The picture here is the day of judgment when all shall appear before God." "That is, in his very presence. When we think of God; when we reflect that we must soon stand before him, we are permitted to cherish this hope" (*Barnes*).

1:4 knowing, brethren beloved by God, His choice of you;

Knowing, brethren beloved by God. *Knowing* (*oida*) and *beloved* (from *agape*) are actually perfect tenses in Greek. And *knowing* is a passive participle. The passage might better read "having known [having learned from the past], brothers, and having been loved by God . . ." The perfect tenses give a sense of knowing something in the past with the resultant action continuing into the present, thus a causal participle (Robertson). Paul means, then, "You learned in the past (and that knowledge is still with you), you who have been progressively loved (and are still loved) by God, how He chose you." The participle shows the "exercise of God's love as already consummated and resulting in a fixed status of being loved (perfect tense)" (*EBC*).

Beloved (*agape*) is a typical Pauline expression that has to do with positional truth, that is, the salvation process whereby God's divine love chose them for eternity. The full meaning of *agape* is difficult to define. In the New Testament, *agape* certainly describes the highest form of care and affection. It is continually used by the biblical writers to express God's spiritual and divine love. It also describes the spiritual love believers should have for each other and that which a husband ought to have for his wife (Eph. 5:25–28).

Some commentators say that *agape* love expresses the most sober kind of charity and that it places the highest value upon another person, so that person is seen in the light of the greatest favor. But all these translations fail to convey the full, rich meaning of *agape*. In God's greatest show of love, *agape* brought His Son to earth to die for our sins (John 3:16). Nothing can overshadow this sacrifice of Christ for sinners and the commitment of the Lord for His creatures.

His choice of you. Although *His* is not in the better manuscripts, the choosing and election of a believer is of God. *Ekloge* means "election, choice" (*EDNT*). It is a divine act that causes salvation, the Lord actually bringing spiritually dead sinners to Him. The cause is not in man but is in God's mysterious providence. It is part of the work of predestination, "to before encircle," that is a sovereign work "through Jesus Christ to Himself, according to the kind intention of His will" (Eph. 1:5).

Ekloge is not found in the LXX but it occurs "elsewhere in the N.T. six times, and always with reference to the Divine choice" (Acts 9:15; Rom. 9:11; 11:5, 7, 28; 2 Peter 1:10) (Milligan).

The agent of election is the Holy Spirit, who so operates in the individual that faith and belief is initiated and consciously uttered. This work of the Spirit is the first cause of redemption with faith following as a result: "God has chosen you from the beginning for salvation *through* sanctification by the Spirit and faith in the truth" (2 Thess. 2:13b, italics mine). The sanctification of the Spirit and faith are but results of God's initial choosing.

One position on election holds that God's choosing is based on His foreknowledge, that is, on the basis of His foreseeing an individual at some point in the future responding by faith. In other words, He saves those He knows will believe. Others argue predestination and election are simply a corporate work, that is, God has determined to provide salvation to a group or body of people, the "elect."

The key verses often quoted are found in Romans 8:29–30: "For whom He foreknew [*prognosis,* 'to know before'], He also predestined . . . and whom He predestined, these He also called [*kaleo,* 'similar to chose']." But it must be noted that Paul says *whom* God foreknew not *what* He foreknew in reference to faith. Although it is true that God foresees all things, that is not the meaning of the word *foreknow*. This word refers to the Lord intimately knowing those whom He saves. He is bringing about a personal relationship with the redeemed.

The word *know* (*ginosko*) often refers to the bonding of a relation, such as that experienced by husband and wife. *Ginosko* is used, in fact, to describe the sexual union. For example, after Joseph was told the truth about Mary's pregnancy, the NASB says he *"kept her a virgin until she gave birth to a Son"* (Matt. 1:25). The Greek text actually reads "and he *knew* [sexually] her not until . . ." (italics mine).

> **1:5** for our gospel did not come to you in word only, but also in power and in the Holy Spirit and with full conviction; just as you know what kind of men we proved to be among you for your sake.

Paul is describing how the gospel changed those who accepted it. It did its work and transformed the Thessalonians into those who now live "with full conviction" concerning the Lord Jesus. Paul will also point out how they are now paying the price for their belief and their changed lives.

For our gospel did not come to you in word only. *Our gospel* might better read, "the gospel which we preach" (Milligan). Paul theologically describes the gospel (*euangelion,* "good news") in 1 Corinthians 15:1–8: "Christ died for our sins according to the Scriptures, and . . . was buried, and that He was raised on the third day according to the Scriptures" (vv. 3–4). To the Corinthians Paul noted, "so we preach[ed] and so you believed" (v. 11).

In a messianic prophecy that seems to clearly speak of the gospel and the deity of the Messiah, Isaiah writes,

> Lift up your voice mightily, O Jerusalem, bearer of *good news;* lift it up, do not fear. Say to the cities of Judah, "Here is your God!" . . . Like a shepherd He will tend His flock, in His arm He will gather the lambs, and carry them in His bosom. (40:9, 11, italics mine)

In Isaiah 40, the one who will "comfort" is God in the person of the Messiah. On these verses, Unger writes, "It was a *sine qua non* for the salvation the Messiah was to effect, the gospel of redemption He was to bring at His first advent, and for the deliverance He was to work at His second advent."[1]

By adding "not . . . in word only" Paul emphasizes that the converts did not simply hear some kind of new religious argument but that the gospel was attended by the dynamic power of the Holy Spirit that brought about changed lives and conversion.

In power and in the Holy Spirit. Probably in explanation, Paul means "in the power of the Holy Spirit" (Calvin). Though not mentioned, it is possible that miracles accompanied the message. The power of the gospel caused the Thessalonian Christians to break off from their sins, "to abandon their idols, and to give their hearts to God" (*Barnes*).

> [What changes lives is] the sharp sword of the word of God, clothed in the power of the Holy Spirit. It was also the trumpet sound of the herald with no uncertain note, but with the authority of God behind it. It was directed to the heart, mind and conscience of the hearers and demanded the response of the will. (Ritchie)

With full conviction. By adding *conviction* (*plerophoria*) and *full* (*polle*), Paul tells us how deeply convinced and committed these converts became. *Plerophoria* is a compound, *plero* (complete or completely) and *phoria* (clothed). The thought is having a wealth of assurance, "great fullness of divine working," or "inner confidence brought about by the Spirit" (*EDNT*). This divine working is the "'assurance' or 'confidence' produced by the Spirit's power of grace in the hearts of the Thessalonians through the gospel word" (Lenski).

You know what kind of men we proved to be among you. The Thessalonian believers knew how these apostles were fully devoted to the gospel. The church certainly had to realize these missionaries were unselfish in the cause for the truth and for the sake of the hearers. "'We got to know,' the writers say, 'regarding you,' and you, they say, now know in regard to us 'the kind of men we were among you . . . for your sakes'" (Lenski).

> **1:6** You also became imitators of us and of the Lord, having received the word in much tribulation with the joy of the Holy Spirit,

Not only did the Thessalonians accept the truth of Christ, they then attempted to live out what they saw in the apostles and in Christ.

You also became imitators of us and of the Lord. *Mimetes* as a verb means to "emulate, follow after," and it represents "the imitation of example" (*EDNT*). Paul uses the word eleven times in his epistles. In non-Pauline writings it refers to imitating "the good" (3 John 11), following the faith of leaders (Heb. 13:7), and being with those who through trust and patience inherit the promise (Heb. 6:12).

Having received the word in much tribulation. *You received* (aorist tense, a simultaneous action to their believing) seems to show that immediately they were thrown into tribulation (*thlipsis,* which implies "to press hard on"). They were instantly placed under pressure by the authorities, the Jews, and the general population. They were suspected of planning insurrection and revolt and were certainly not understood. That they bore up under the load is further proof that they were of the elect of God. The normal human reaction would be to run. It is not natural to stand so firm with such conviction, unless their belief had become a complete and vital part of their very existence.

With the joy of the Holy Spirit. Having such joy is a point of comparison even with Christ Himself. They experienced from the Holy Spirit a joyful endurance in spirit under sufferings. This is how they imitated the apostles and the Lord (Alford). Of Jesus it was said "for the joy set before Him [He] endured the cross, despising the shame, and has sat down at the right hand of the throne of God" (Heb. 12:2). This would become a pattern for other persecuted churches and for believers in general in the generations to come.

1:7 so that you became an example to all the believers in Macedonia and in Achaia.

So that you became an example. This church became a *typos,* a "pattern, model, impression" for the believers in a large area of the Greek civilization. The church's determination to "take it," even as their very lives were being threatened, would be spoken of throughout the region. "So complete a transformation rapidly accomplished happens only when God's elective purpose is at work in people" (*EBC*).

In Macedonia and in Achaia. Macedonia was a Roman senatorial province covering most of northern Greece. It was bordered on the north by Illyricum, Moesia, and Thrace, on the west by the Adriatic Sea, on the east by the Aegean Sea, and on the south by Achaia. Macedonia's rise came in the period 340 to 320 B.C. under Philip I and his son, Alexander the Great, both military geniuses. By Alexander's death (323), Macedonia had become the capital of a world empire.

When Paul visited the area, most of the major cities formed a thriving commercial Roman province. Sea lanes and overland highways veined this area, making it rich and strategically important. It was spiritually strategic as well; because of God's providence to establish churches here, thousands would hear the gospel.

Because of Thessalonica's strategic location, it would become an important crossroad of commerce and communication. Trading routes began at the various seaports of Dyrracium and Apollonia and extended across the mountains to the port of Thessalonica, and from there to a second port Apollonia on the Aegean, to Amphipolis, Philippi, and Neapolis.

Achaia. In early days when Greece was free, the word *Achaia* was applied to the entire region of Greece, although Achaia itself was small. From A.D. 15 to 44, the region was under the Caesarean legate of Moesia. Later, in A.D. 67, Nero suspended full Roman control of the area. In 1 Corinthians 16:15 Paul writes of the first Achaian converts, and he greets them in his second Corinthian letter (1:1). Although the believers in Achaia prospered materially, they were still growing spiritually.

> **1:8** For the word of the Lord has sounded forth from you, not only in Macedonia and Achaia, but also in every place your faith toward God has gone forth, so that we have no need to say anything.

The word of the Lord has sounded forth from you. *Sounded forth* (*execheo*) is a perfect tense indicating that the Word of the Lord is "resounding, ringing out" beyond Macedonia and Achaia and is even producing results. *Execheo* is used only here in the New Testament and carries the thought "to sound out" like a trumpet, thunder, or reverberating like an echo (Robertson). It shows "both the clear and the persuasive nature of the *logos tou Kuriou*" (Ellicott).

In every place your faith toward God has gone forth. Some commentators think Paul could mean that the Thessalonians had started their own missionary efforts. More likely, he means that the other Christian communities had heard of their struggles and of their bearing up under persecution.

Some scholars think that "in every place" is hyperbolic, but undoubtedly their witness had traveled far. We may never know how explosively the gospel traveled throughout the entire region, but it is fact that the gospel of Christ moved rapidly by sea and land, and Paul could be far more literal than we might imagine.

We have no need to say anything. Wherever Paul went, it was unnecessary to say anymore about the Thessalonians. The believing assemblies everywhere knew the undaunted testimony and staying power of this church under intense persecution. The gospel "was not kept to themselves, and lay hid in their own breasts; . . . they declared it both by words and by deeds, by making a profession of it, and by walking agreeably to it" (Gill).

> **1:9** For they themselves report about us what kind of a reception we had with you, and how you turned to God from idols to serve a living and true God,

For they themselves report about us. "*Gar* ['for'] elucidates the extent of the information thus spread throughout the provinces" (Lenski). How the apostles conducted themselves was vastly different from the way other charlatans behaved in attempting to subvert the confidence of the people. There were also Judaizers and fakes who soured religion and strongly opposed the new faith in Christ.

The Thessalonians accepted the truth and would not listen to any vilification that would turn them against the gospel. Their conversion was more dramatic because they had "turned to God from idols." We know that their salvation was a miracle and that they were divinely chosen of the Lord to respond to the truth. On the human level, however, what was happening within the hearts and minds of these converts that made their response in faith so sudden?

You turned to God from idols. Some commentators note that the "power" of the idols and false religion was wearing down. More and more Greeks were rejecting the powerless and human-like gods, but other factors may have come into play. Even though the Jews of the city would reject the gospel with such violent anger, could some of the truth about the One true God of heaven have through the years spilled out from the synagogue, and prepared the pagans for the message of Christ? We may never know. For certain, the conversion of these Gentiles was dramatic and apparently sudden, as seen by the aorist tense of the verb *epistrepho,* "to turn."

To serve a living and true God. *To serve* is an aorist infinitive of *douleuo* and could be translated "to be continuously serving," as a slave or bondservant. Formerly, these Thessalonians were enslaved to dead, lifeless heathen idols. Slave "is used of Christ Himself (Phil. 2:7) and of Paul (Rom. 1:1). The idea of a bondservant is probably taken from Exod. 21:1–6, which describes the voluntary slave motivated by love" (Ritchie).

God is said also to be "a living" (*zonti*) God. The Lord is the "genuine" (*alethinos*) God who is "not 'dead' like the idols from which they turned, but [He] is alive" (Robertson). *Zonti* includes "not merely the being, but the activity or power of God" (Milligan). He is real "as opposed to the phantom and senseless gods of the heathen" (Lightfoot).

> **1:10** and to wait for His Son from heaven, whom He raised from the dead, that is Jesus, who delivers us from the wrath to come.

And to wait for His Son from heaven. *To wait* (*anameno*) is also a present infinitive in Greek and reads as well "to be continuously waiting." It also carries the idea literally "to wait up," with the full meaning "to remain alert" or "expect" (*EDNT*). *Anameno* carries a linear connotation and could also read "to keep on waiting for" (Robertson).

The impact of the verb *to wait* must not be lost. It can be translated "to look forward to with patience and confidence." "It implies . . . being ready for his return. . . . The thought of his coming does not spell terror for the believer. . . . for it is this Jesus who rescues (is rescuing) us from the wrath to come (the coming wrath)" (*NTC*).

The Thessalonians were busy serving Christ in witnessing. They also "day by day . . . were in constant expectation of the Lord from heaven" (Ritchie). This report was spread about by the recently saved Greeks, yet they spoke correctly: "His Son" is the Son of God who also lives and is real. Christ's return is tied to His resurrection; The Lord raised Him and He is coming back.

The "wait[ing]" is for the Rapture, a point that Paul will develop later in this letter. The Rapture of the Church saints would be a mystery revealed primarily to Paul (1 Cor. 15:51–54), and it is a *now* expectation for the body of

Christ. The Rapture is to rescue the believers before the terror of the Tribulation begins. Some critics today see this doctrine as escapism, but the Thessalonians did not. They were serving *while* they were waiting; thus, they were doing both. The Thessalonians had been taught the doctrine of the Rapture, but they still had questions, as will be shown later.

Whom He raised from the dead, that is Jesus. The death and resurrection of Christ form the cornerstone of the gospel. It is not only the act of the Lord's substitution under the wrath of God for the sins of mankind, but it is the great proof that God has resolved the problem of sin in humanity. The penalty for sin has been suffered, and people must accept and believe this transaction in a personal way.

Who delivers us. This is a present active participle from *ruomai* that should be translated "the one who is rescuing." Some commentators have translated it as a timeless substantive (that denotes characteristics of the noun), "the Rescuer Jesus," or "Our Deliverer" (Alford). "He is our Saviour (Matt. 1:21) true to his name, Jesus. He is our Rescuer (Rom. 11:26, *ho ruomenos,* from Isa. 59:20)" (Robertson).

Ruomai actually comes from the Classical Greek word *eruo* but in Koine the *e* is dropped. In Classical Greek, *eruo* can be translated "drag, draw," implying force or violence as in "drag away the body of a slain hero," or "drag away, rescue friends" (L&S). Vincent translates *ruomai* with the force of the middle voice, that is, "to draw to one's self, with the specification [from] evil or danger." The present participle could have the force of a prophetic future: "The One who will drag us [to Himself]."

From the wrath to come. *Wrath* (*orges*) in the Thessalonian context, as a divine act, refers to the "coming" or "approaching" Tribulation. This wrath is not the divine wrath that hangs over the heads of mankind because of sin (Rom. 1:18), as in the final judgment, but it is the wrath of Daniel's Seventieth Week that purges Israel and also becomes a judgment upon the world (Rev. 6:12–17). The Church, the body of Christ, is rescued by Jesus before that day comes (1 Thess. 5:9): "For God has not destined us for wrath, but for obtaining salvation through our Lord Jesus Christ." Here Paul describes salvation as a rescue from the earthly wrath, the Day of the Lord (5:2), that comes upon the world. This wrath "is a title for the period just before Messiah's kingdom on earth, when God will afflict earth's inhabitants with an unparalleled series of physical torments because of their rejection of His will" (*EBC*). This truth "teaches that the Lord Jesus Christ will return to the earth, and leads the soul to wait for his appearing" (*Barnes*).

The wrath "coming" is a present active participle of *erchomai*. It is on its way. The present tense "is frequently used to denote the certainty and possibly the nearness, of a future event" (Lightfoot). Some say "the Wrath absolutely" (Vincent), or some translate it "the Wrath absolutely, the Coming!" or "which is already coming." Another translation is "the Wrath is on its way to the world, to appear with Christ from heaven" (Ellicott).

Some critics say the Thessalonians and others in the early church were fooled by Paul into believing that Christ *should absolutely* return at that very time. Some think He returned "spiritually" in A.D. 70 to be with His people in a spiritual and metaphorical way, but this belief does not hold up when tested by numerous biblical passages.

The hope of the Rapture is likened to a couple who has committed to getting married in the future; their union is certain though the date has not been set. The early church had great anticipation, but they certainly had no idea as to when the Lord would come for them. Believers still wait today because they know the "marriage" is certain, but "the when" is not known. The strong emotional desire of these believers to be taken home to Him in the Rapture should be prevalent among us today. Titus 2:13 from the Greek text could read, "[We are] excitedly expecting continually the joyous prospect, even [the] glorious appearance of our great God, even [our] Savior, Christ Jesus!" (author's translation).

> Rather than fearing this time, however, Christians find an incentive to persevere (cf. "endurance inspired by hope," 1:3), because for them it will mean rescue rather than doom. Not even the stepped-up persecution of Christ's followers that will mark this future period will touch them, for their deliverer will remove them from the scene of these dreadful happenings. (*EBC*)

Barnes adds,

> The hope of his return to our world to raise the dead, and to convey his ransomed to heaven, is the brightest and most cheering prospect

that dawns on man, and we should be ready, whenever it occurs, to hail him as our returning Lord, and to rush to his arms as our glorious Redeemer. It should be always the characteristic of our piety as it was that of John to say, "Even so, come, Lord Jesus [Rev. 22:20]."

Study Questions

1. Why do the three ministers of the gospel (Paul, Silvanus, Timothy) together write to the church at Thessalonica?
2. What do the apostles mean by "His choice of you"?
3. From what we know regarding the background of the city of Thessalonica, why did the church thus receive such mistreatment and tribulation?
4. From the human standpoint, what could have possibly brought about such rapid evangelism and open reception of the gospel in Thessalonica.
5. What were the two important things this church was doing since they had received Christ? Discuss.
6. In verses 9–10, what did Paul share with this church about the coming of Christ?

CHAPTER SIX

Paul's Care for the Thessalonians

C. Paul's Walk Before the Thessalonians (2:1–12)
    1. His Boldness (2:1–4)

In this chapter, the apostle Paul reminds the Thessalonians how he, Silas, and Timothy behaved before them. Paul points out that they had used no deceit or corruption, nor had they sought the praises of others. Additionally, the three had supported themselves and had not been a financial burden to the church. Thus, the new converts had been changed by the preaching of the Word of God and not by human cunning.

Paul reminds them that the opposition the missionaries received from the Jews was of the same intensity as that fostered in Judea. He points out, too, that the apostles were not seeking dictatorial authority and power; instead, their main task was to preach the gospel of Jesus Christ.

> **2:1** For you yourselves know, brethren, that our coming to you was not in vain,

Our coming to you was not in vain. *Kenos, vain,* carries the idea of "empty" or "without reason." It also can mean "fruitless," "without success" or "that which has no truth or reality to it." It can imply, too, that which is false or fallacious (*Barnes*). The apostles had a purpose in coming to Thessalonica, and it was to give forth the gospel (v. 2). The purpose of the apostle's statement was not so much to show how successful their work was but to meet head-on the argument from their opponents that they were impostors. Based on their own experience, the church knew that this was not so.

> **2:2** but after we had already suffered and been mistreated in Philippi, as you know, we had the boldness in our God to speak to you the gospel of God amid much opposition.

We had already suffered and been mistreated in Philippi. *Suffered* (*propascho,* aorist active participle) and *mistreated* (*hubrizo,* aorist passive participle) are strong words that show the intensity of the hatred against Paul preaching the gospel. *Hubrizo* means to treat insolently. "More than the bodily suffering it was the personal indignity that had been offered to [Paul] as a Roman citizen" (Milligan). The truth is not popular and satanic opposition against it is always bitter.

Philippi was one of the leading cities of the Roman province of Macedonia. Formerly, it was the Thracian city of Crenodes but was renamed by Philip of Macedon, the father of Alexander the Great, for himself. The city was on the Egnatian Way, the major highway through Greece, connecting Rome and Asia. It would have been one of the major trading centers since it was only ten miles from the port city of Neapolis. Some suggest that when Claudius expelled the Jews from Rome this colony city followed his example, which may explain why Paul finds only women praying by the riverbank when he arrives there. Living in a Roman city, the citizens enjoyed freedom from beatings and arrest, except in extreme cases. They also had the right to appeal to the emperor in crucial criminal cases.

Persecution followed Paul to Philippi. The epistle of Philippians shows the opposition to the gospel (1:28) and that Christians were truly suffering (2:17–18, 29–30; 3:10; 4:1, 5). In Philippi was found demonic activity (Acts 16:16), and the missionaries were imprisoned and beaten (16:23), a violation of their rights as Roman citizens. Roman law prohibited the proselytizing of Roman citizens, which is why the persecution came so strongly upon Paul and Silas (16:19–24). Whereas Judaism was somewhat accepted by the Romans, Christianity was seen as a cultish branch; thus it was forbidden to seek Gentile converts. The people were also hearing false doctrine from Judaizers (Phil. 3:17–19), among whom existed no unity of doctrine (1:27; 2:2; 4:2). Yet the church at Philippi was one of the most mature churches and it was very dear to the heart of Paul. Twice they sent gifts to him during his stay in Thessalonica to help in his work (4:15–16).

Lydia was the first convert in Philippi (Acts 16:14–15), and the apostles would later stay in her home. After being beaten and thrown into prison, Paul and Silas were released by the miracle of the great earthquake (v. 26) with the result that the jailer and his family came to the Lord (vv. 31–32). Leaving Philippi, Paul, Silas, and apparently Timothy, finally arrived in Thessalonica (17:1).

We had the boldness in our God to speak to you the gospel of God amid much opposition. The word for *boldness* (*parresiazomai*) means "to speak openly, freely, gain courage" with the thought of "frankness" and "confidence" (*EDNT*). Paul travels from one city to another and refuses to stop speaking the gospel regardless of the opposition encountered. "Uncowed by the fearful experience in Philippi, Paul and Silvanus freely and openly did their work in Thessalonica. They hid nothing of what they had suffered in Philippi" (Lenski).

"In our God" carries the thought of "union" with Him, "hence, by his help, they had summoned courage to continue the work. They had done what Jesus had enjoined" (*EBC*). As the Lord had told His disciples, so Paul practiced: "When they persecute you in this city, flee into the next" (Matt. 10:23).

In "amid much opposition" (*en pollo agoni*), the word *agoni* "refers first to a gathering, especially for games or contests; then the contest itself, and finally the agony (cf. the Greek word), anguish, or anxiety that is connected with it" (*EBC*).

> **2:3** For our exhortation does not come from error or impurity or by way of deceit;

For our exhortation. Paul reminds the Thessalonians that the three apostles came to them bringing the gospel with pure motives and methods. As they presented the gospel of Christ, they actually exhorted, "counseled" (*paraklesis,* "came alongside") or "appealed, entreated, comforted" them. No one could say by the manner of the apostles that they had forced themselves on the Thessalonians.

From error or impurity or by way of deceit. In New Testament days the world was full of tricksters and deceivers with evil motives and intentions.

False religion and witchcraft abounded; spiritual darkness was dark indeed. The truth of the gospel was certainly buried and hidden (Rom. 1:18; 2 Cor. 4:3–4) by those who could deceive.

But, Paul reminds the Thessalonian church, "our exhortation [or pleading] does not come"

a. out of error (*plane,* related to the verb *planao*), meaning "to lead astray, deceive, to wander, roam" (*EDNT*). The thought could carry the meaning of the deception of false teachers or self-deceivers.

b. nor out of impurity (*akatharsias*) or (sexual) uncleanness or immorality. Gentile religions were rife with sexual religious ceremonies. Many women attached themselves to the various pagan licentious cults and gave their favors away in the name of the gods. Some of Paul's antagonists were probably accusing Paul as belonging to such a group.

c. or by way of deceit (*dolos*). The apostles were accused of using "trickery, guile" to capture or fool their audience. "The world of that day was full of roaming 'philosophers,' jugglers, sorcerers, fakers, swindlers. In order to impress their audiences many tricks were used" (*EBC*).

Thus, Paul answers all three of these charges. He sets the truth over the lie and reminds his readers how they responded to the historical truth of the cross of Christ.

2:4 but just as we have been approved by God to be entrusted with the gospel, so we speak, not as pleasing men but God, who examines our hearts.

Just as we have been approved by God. *Approved* (*dokimazo*) means "to approve by testing," and it is a perfect passive in Greek that carries the idea "at some point in the past we were approved and that approval continues today." Further, with the perfect tense, Paul makes his claim that "being examined and approved by God, we study to please Him who constantly examines and approves us, not to court those to whom we are sent" (Ellicott). The word *approved* "signifies properly to examine an object with a view to its satisfying a certain test, and hence naturally glides into the meaning 'to approve'" (Lightfoot).

To be entrusted with the gospel. The word *entrusted* is an aorist passive infinitive of *pisteuo,* the root of which means "to believe." The thought as used here, with the passive voice, is "to be believed" with the responsibility of the gospel. Such is an awe inspiring task, that is, to be "trustable," to present the truth of Christ with accuracy, clarity, and honesty.

Not as pleasing men but God. Paul does not care the least about the criticisms or opinions of men. Elsewhere he writes, "I am conscious of nothing against myself, . . . but the one who examines me is the Lord" (1 Cor. 4:4).

[God] examines our hearts. Paul uses *dokimazo* (*examines*) with the idea that it is, again, God who approves by testing the motives of the heart. Paul is writing, then, "as God, who tests our hearts, has attested our fitness to be entrusted with the gospel." "The definite commission of the gospel excluded any weak attempt to flatter men's prejudices or to adapt oneself to their tastes" (Nicoll).

Some commentators translate *kardia* (*heart*) as referring to thought processes. More than likely, *kardia* is the ancients' way of referring to the affections and emotions. People could feel the pumping and pounding of the chest with anxiety or even the feeling of pulsing that comes with emotional love. They correctly attributed this physical response to the organ of the heart. Though feelings usually cannot be separated from some thought processes, emotions are more than likely the main idea in view. Human thinking surges forth into diminished, joyous, angry, excited, lustful, violent emotions. Thinking causes emotional responses; better thinking causes more productive emotional responses.

On this verse Calvin goes even further, perceiving conscience as playing a role along with the heart. He writes, "True ministers of the gospel ought to make it their aim to devote to God their endeavors, and to do it from the heart, not from any outward regard to the world, but because conscience tells them that it is right and proper."

2. His Gentle Care and Labor (2:5–9)

In a sense, Paul continues his thoughts from the previous verses, though he writes more specifically as to what he did among the Thessalonians that was so effective.

> **2:5** For we never came with flattering speech, as you know, nor with a pretext for greed—God is witness—

We never came with flattering speech. *Kolakia* carries the idea of "enticing, flattering." The Thessalonians knew well the behavior of the apostles, as is evident in Paul's writing the words "as you know." It is likely that the accusation was being spread by the Jews that Paul and those with him had schemed and tricked many citizens of the city into believing in Jesus. *Kolakia* is used only here in the New Testament. In Classical Greek the word also carries the idea "to fawn" over, "to soften" someone up, or to make them susceptible (L&S).

Nor with a pretext for greed. Being greedy was probably also another indictment against Paul. *Pretext (prophasis)* means to "have an actual motive, reason, valid excuse" (*BAG*), or "a pretext, a disguise, something used for appearance to conceal what lies behind it" (Ritchie). Paul's real motive, they said, was desiring more gain (*pleonexia*), seeking plenty. As masters of character assassination, the opponents of the apostles built argument upon argument to make them look evil.

Those who serve the Lord are always open to such abuse. But false accusations originate not only from the world but also from, it is sad to say, believers, who are jealous and want to destroy a valid ministry.

God is witness. "God is a witness," Paul is saying, "and He can testify [*martus*] of our character and intentions." The Lord also keeps good records. Here on earth His servants may not experience full justice, but they will be vindicated in glory and at the bema judgment. "The Thessalonians can only be appealed to as evidence for their own experience, the writers therefore call God Himself to witness" (Ellicott).

> **2:6** nor did we seek glory from men, either from you or from others, even though as apostles of Christ we might have asserted our authority.

Nor did we seek glory from men. These missionaries were not seeking the praise of people but of God only. Paul is reminding the Thessalonians of the characteristics of the apostles' ministry.

Traveling philosophers and orators were common in the Roman Empire. They itinerated from place to place, entertaining and seeking a personal following for fame and fortune. Paul and his companions had nothing in common with such men. (*BKC*)

As apostles of Christ we might have asserted our authority. Paul could have at any time called upon his Christ-given right to brandish his authority. The verb *dunamai, asserted,* carries the idea "to use strength," although it is often simply translated as "I can, am able." It is concessive in Greek and could be translated "though I can use [my] power, ability." Here, Paul adds "with weight" (*en barei*) as "with a burden." He is saying "we can (and could have) as apostles of Christ used our ability to be weighty," or we "could legitimately have claimed the dignity associated with" our apostolic office (*EBC*). One view holds that Paul is referring to his right to demand financial help from the church, but he covered that issue previously when he wrote about "a pretext of greed." Here, he is simply mentioning that he is not using "his great office for the purpose of placing himself at the head of churches, and giving them laws" (*Barnes*).

> **2:7** But we proved to be gentle among you, as a nursing mother tenderly cares for her own children.

But we proved to be gentle among you. *We proved* is a strong declarative indicative that is used in a statement of fact (D&M). It has profound meaning, however, in Paul's overall argument, which describes—in this verse as well as 8, 9, and 11—how he was gentle with the Thessalonians, that is, as a nursing mother tenderly caring for her own. He could not have claimed this in the letter if the Thessalonians were unable to confirm it with their own experience. He is thus only reminding them of facts they already know.

Paul, Silas, and Timothy were like spiritual parents, witnessing to the Thessalonian church until Christ was formed in them. The missionaries nursed them on the Word, tending them patiently as they grew and matured (Gill).

> **2:8** Having thus a fond affection for you, we were well-pleased to impart to you not only the gospel of God but also our own lives, because you had become very dear to us.

We were well-pleased to impart to you . . . the gospel of God. With great affection and a burning desire, the apostles gladly shared the gospel of Christ. This was their mission. Their lives were given to carrying out the Lord's commission, and none of these men ever seem to show regret for their sacrifice.

But also our own lives. "Paul declares that he was so disposed towards the Thessalonians, that he was prepared to lay out his life for their benefit" (Calvin).

Because you had become very dear to us. *Because* (*dioti*) begins a causal clause—because the Thessalonians were so dear to them, the apostles were ready to die for them. This is true love for the sake of someone else. *Dear,* *agapatoi,* means "beloved" or the "beloved ones," and "to be willing to communicate the knowledge of the gospel was in itself a strong proof of love" (*Barnes*).

> **2:9** For you recall, brethren, our labor and hardship, how working night and day so as not to be a burden to any of you, we proclaimed to you the gospel of God.

For you recall, brethren, our labor and hardship. *Labor* (*kopos*) and *hardship* (*mokthos*) are graphic words that demonstrate the extent to which the apostles fought. They were "coping" under extreme criticism, "wearied," "worn with toil," and "greatly distressed" by the opposition they were forced to struggle against (L&S). Although Paul mentions this labor, he does not go into details as to the extent of his struggles. The Thessalonians knew, however, what he was writing about.

How working night and day. *Working* (*ergozomai*) is a present participle, emphasizing Paul's continual practice while with the Thessalonians. Many commentators believe that Paul is saying that he began his labor before dawn and "no doubt began so early in order to be able to devote some part of the day to preaching" (Nicoll).

We proclaimed to you the gospel of God. In the phrase "we proclaimed [*kerusso,* aorist indicative] *into* [*eis*] you," "into" could be translated "into your midst." "The gospel of God" is an exclusive expression of the apostle Paul. He first used a similar saying when he spoke of "the gospel of the grace of God" (Acts 20:24). But he uses "the gospel of God" five times in his writings, probably in the ablative case, that is, "the gospel *from* God" (Rom. 15:16; 2 Cor. 11:7; 1 Thess. 2:2, 8, 9, italics mine). It is possible that Peter adopted the expression from Paul (1 Peter 4:17).

3. His Devotion (2:10–12)

These verses end Paul's primary defense of the methods the apostles used with the Thessalonians. He is not providing this defense for the church but is answering apparent charges and rumors that are being lodged against him. At no time, however, do the believers appear to believe the lie. Paul simply wants to remind them of the truth lest they become confused.

> **2:10** You are witnesses, and so is God, how devoutly and uprightly and blamelessly we behaved toward you believers;

You are witnesses, and so is God. In other words, "You can testify on my behalf, and so can the Lord!" Paul is not asking them to testify, but they could do so if it were necessary. His greatest comfort is that God knows his truthfulness and steadfastness as an evangelist and teacher.

How devoutly and uprightly and blamelessly we behaved toward you believers. Paul uses three adverbs to describe the missionaries' behavior:

- *Devoutly* (*hosios*) is related to *hagios* (holy). The apostles walked holy before the Thessalonian church.
- *Uprightly* (*dikaios*) means that they also were righteous in their dealings, or operated in a just manner.
- *Blamelessly* (*amemptos*) reminds the believers that no "fault" could be found in the apostles' practices or motives. They lived aboveboard before the assembly. "We behaved" is an aorist tense of *ginomai* meaning how they "lived, existed," or "performed" among the believers.

Calvin provides a summary:

> The servants of Christ cannot avoid calumnies, and unfavorable reports; for being hated by the world, they must of necessity be evil-spoken

of among the wicked. Hence, he restricts this [witness] to believers, who judge uprightly and sincerely, and do not revile malignantly and groundlessly.

Describing how the missionaries conducted themselves is amplified in verses 11 and 12.

2:11 just as you know how we were exhorting and encouraging and imploring each one of you as a father would his own children,

Just as you know. Paul is reminding them again what they know quite well. There is no question as to how Paul, Silas, and Timothy operated, and if anyone needs a verification, he or she can get it from the Thessalonian congregation.

We were exhorting and encouraging and imploring each one of you. Here, Paul uses a series of present participles that give the sense of a continual ministry: "We were continually exhorting and imploring." Paul personalizes this work by saying this effort was with "each of you." "Paul purposely stresses 'each single one of you' and then combines all of them in . . . , 'you.' He does this regularly with the singular and the plural, with individuals and with the whole group" (Lenski). Paul worked with the individual and the entire body of believers, that is, in "individual pastoral work, public admonitory preaching" (Lenski). "The three participles give three phases of the minister's preaching" (exhorting, encouraging or consoling, witnessing or testifying) (Robertson).

- *Exhorting (parakaleo)* is the same word used in verse 3, to mean "to call alongside, counsel."
- *Encouraging (paramutheomai)* has to do with "encouraging to continue in a course," whereas exhorting could mean "to exhort to a particular line of conduct" (Lightfoot). The thought carried by "encouraging" is "to move one to act freely, to do with pleasure."
- *Imploring (martureo)* is a present middle participle that could be translated "we ourselves are imploring." Its root, *martureo,* means "to witness," or better here, "summon to witness" (Milligan).

"Such a combination of appeals [in these participles] proved effective in moving the Thessalonians to action by the Holy Spirit's convicting power" (*BKC*).

As a father would his own children. The apostle again is reminding the Thessalonians how he behaved in their presence. He is likely specifically referring to his tone and speech as he taught, corrected, proved, and pleaded with them to accept Christ as Savior, and then to live for Him and leave their pagan habits behind.

In this chapter, notice how Paul repeatedly refers to his method of first winning their confidence and then patiently instructing them:

a. "We never came with flattering speech," verse 5.
b. "We did not seek glory," verse 6.
c. "We were gentle as a nursing mother," verse 7.
d. "We were well pleased to impart the gospel," verse 8.
e. "You became very dear to us," verse 8b.
f. "You are witnesses as to how we behaved," verse 10.
g. "We exhorted . . . as a father would his own children," verse 11.

> **2:12** so that you may walk in a manner worthy of the God who calls you into His own kingdom and glory.

So that you may walk in a manner worthy of the God who calls you. Here, Paul summarizes his arguments, finalizing everything he has previously said. The Greek actually reads, "exhorting and encouraging and imploring *into* the walk of you, worthy of the God . . ." *Walk* is a compound verb and present infinitive, *pateo* meaning "to set foot on, tread, trample" (*BAG*), and *peri,* to walk "around, about." *Pateo* is most commonly used in the New Testament to describe the whole range of a person's human activity as he or she goes about living. In a spiritual sense, *pateo* describes how one exists and what one makes of one's life while on earth. It may describe how the lost or how the believer should prioritize their living for Christ's sake.

Worthy (*axios*) is actually an adverb and should read "worthily" or "suitably" (Robertson). The Christian should be walking about in this life worthily of his or her mission and calling. "Now the object of all this fatherly exhortation was that the readers would walk (pass their lives) in a manner worthy of (in harmony with) their relation to God, who, by means of preaching and pastoral care, was calling them into that future realm" (*NTC*).

The God who calls you. With the genitive case, the passage actually reads "the God the One calling you" (*tou theou tou kalountos humas*). The verb *calling* (*kaleo*) is in a present active participle form and is similar to the compound noun (*ekloge*) *out-worded* or *spoken out,* thus the sovereign choosing, which indicates the election. The present tense expresses the idea that God is in the business, through time, of calling His own elect to Him. "This participle displays no duration but looks back to the initial call of these readers, which in Paul is always effectual" (Lightfoot). Election is the sovereign work of God in calling forth His own whom He marked out to be His redeemed. The believer should now live worthily of that divine appointment. "For as our salvation is founded upon God's gracious adoption, every blessing that Christ has brought us is comprehended in this one term [calling]" (Calvin). This calling is not simply an external one but an internal and effectual one by the powerful and efficacious grace of God. Since it is a call from darkness to light, the children of God must then walk in that light and away from the dictates of a corrupt nature (Gill).

Into His own kingdom and glory. Is this kingdom the Church? Robertson says Paul uses kingdom here for the present kingdom of grace but then, in apparent contradiction in the same paragraph, writes, "Kingdom (*basileian*) here is the future consummation because of glory (*doxan*)."

Lenski, in another contradictory paragraph, writes that the kingdom is here now, but he then writes that the kingdom in this passage "would mean the kingdom in general, 'and glory' narrows down to the consummation of the kingdom when all the heavenly glory shall be ours."

The New Covenant was ratified by Christ's death (Luke 22:20) and launched at Pentecost with the coming of the Holy Spirit (Acts 2), and is presently the dynamic of the Church dispensation (2 Cor. 3:4–9). This New Covenant will also be the spiritual force in the dispensation of the kingdom. That kingdom, however, with the earthly reign of the Son of David, the Messiah, reigning in Jerusalem is certainly not here today. It must be remembered that in the Gospels, the future Messianic Kingdom is called "the kingdom of God" (Luke 4:43), that is, "the kingdom belonging to God." Christ made it very clear that the kingdom of God is yet future, saying to members of the Laodicean church,

"He who overcomes, I will grant to him to sit down with Me on My throne, as I also overcame and sat down with My Father on His throne" (Rev. 3:21). Because of the New Covenant, the believer today enjoys many spiritual benefits such as salvation, forgiveness of sins, the indwelling of the Holy Spirit, peace, and joy. As for the one-thousand-year reign of Christ, the Davidic kingdom, "[the believer] looks forward to its full consummation in the manifested kingdom during the millennium, when righteousness shall reign and the manifested glory of Christ will fill the whole earth (Zech. 14:9)" (Ritchie). The "ultimate realization of the Messianic Kingdom with its future glory is in view here (cf. Acts 17:7) [in Thessalonians]. As frequently in the Thessalonian literature, those Paul is addressing are pointed to the bliss ahead as incentive to godly living now" (*EBC*).

D. Paul's Care for the Thessalonians (2:13–3:13)
1. His Desire to See Them (2:13–20)

In this section, Paul commends the Thessalonians in that they "endured the same sufferings at the hands of your own countrymen, even as [the churches of Judea] did from the Jews" (v. 14b). He continues by pointing out that those Jews who resist the truth are "hostile to all men" and attempt to thwart the message of the gospel from going forth, and he speaks to the wrath that will come upon them. Though not knowing God's timetable, the apostle was speaking of the coming vengeance that would fall on Israel in A.D. 70.

> **2:13** And for this reason we also constantly thank God that when you received from us the word of God's message, you accepted it not as the word of men, but for what it really is, the word of God, which also performs its work in you who believe.

And for this reason we also constantly thank God. The expression "for this reason" may look back at what Paul previously said or may look forward to the topic about to be introduced. "The latter seems the better interpretation: the *hoti* ('because') clause expresses the reason for thanksgiving to God" (*NIGTC*).

Some commentators think the words *we give thanks* and *we are continually giving thanks* (*eucharisteo,* "to good grace," present participle) are difficult to interpret. But the apostle seems simply to be thanking God repeatedly for His sovereign grace with this church. The believers were chosen of God to accept Christ (2 Thess. 2:13) and, according to all we know, that happened quickly with no apparent resistance.

When you received from us the word of God's message. This is what Paul is thankful for. *Received* is an aorist participle of *paralambano*. It generally denotes something received from someone else (*BAG*), but it can also have the force of "to take, draw to oneself" (*EDNT*). One might say, "They really received or took in the gospel with enthusiasm or relish."

This passage also touches on the inspiration of the apostles. What Paul, Silas, and Timothy gave was received as from the Lord. The noun *message* (*akoe,* from *akouo,* "to hear") carries the thought of "the act of hearing" or "the report" (*EDNT*). The form used here is probably a genitive of apposition and is translated "which you heard from us." "St. Paul [is] distinguishing himself and his companions, as mere publishers, from God, the great Source of the Gospel" (Alford).

You accepted it not as the word of men. *Accepted* comes from *dekomai* and normally means "receive" as "to take in." But here the idea of "accepted" seems to be the more specific. *Received* (*paralambano*) and *accepted* (*dekomai*) carry two separate meanings (Ritchie)": "The former verb denotes only the hearing, an objective matter of fact; the latter, the receiving into their minds as subjective matter of belief" (Alford).

But for what it really is, the word of God. *Really* (*alethos*) is an adverb modifying a verb (*BAG*). Related to the word *truth, alethos* can be translated "truly, actually, really." Paul is saying that what they spoke was authoritative and clearly from God. By saying "word" (*logos*) of God, Paul places the emphasis on the entire body of the message. The body of the written and spoken word that comes through the prophets and apostles is made up of words (plural). These words then form the concept and doctrine of "the Word," that is, all that God has to reveal to mankind in a package of truth or cluster of books that form our Bible.

Which also performs its work in you who believe. *Performs [its] work* is the present indicative of *energeo,* which expresses the idea that the Word of God causes things to happen. By using the present tense, Paul indicates that this activity of God's message is continuing and is even now operating in the lives of the Thessalonians—the results are continuing. The word *energeo* is either in a middle or passive voice. If it is a middle voice it could be translated "it is itself performing work." Or a better translation, as a passive it means "is set in operation" (Milligan). The idea, then, is that God's Word is set in operation in those who believe (Robertson).

This group of Gentiles in Thessalonica not only listened to the Word of God but accepted it with enthusiasm in a definite act of saving faith. The Word of God came with the authority of the apostles, and with the power of the Holy Spirit in the great work of regeneration. Thus, the doctrine of effectual calling can be seen as having obvious effectiveness.

> **2:14** For you, brethren, became imitators of the churches of God in Christ Jesus that are in Judea, for you also endured the same sufferings at the hands of your own countrymen, even as they did from the Jews,

For you, brethren, became imitators of the churches of God in Christ Jesus that are in Judea. In 1:6, Paul says that the Thessalonian church imitated the apostles and the Lord because of their receiving "the word in much tribulation." Here he points to the suffering churches in Judea, but that persecution actually began in Jerusalem. "Imitation 'of God's churches in Judea' differs, however, from imitating Paul and the Lord (1:6). Deliberate imitation of sufferings for sufferings' sake is an unworthy Christian objective, but imitation of a Christian life style is legitimate and desirable" (*EBC*).

Of God reminds the readers that these assemblies belong to God the Father; they are His personal possessions. By adding *in Christ* he speaks in technical language of the spiritual body of Christ, of which all believers are members. In regard to this spiritual unity, Paul later writes to the church at Corinth, reminding them that "all the members of the body, though they are many, are one body, so also is Christ. For by one Spirit we were all baptized into one body" (1 Cor. 12:12b–13a).

It is the believer united in the body of Christ that makes the dispensation of the Church unique. In Ephesians the apostle says that Jew and Gentile are two made into one new man (2:15b), and are reconciled "in one body to God through the cross" (v. 16). Paul adds that both groups are fellow citizens in God's household (v. 19), that the Church becomes a holy temple (v. 21), and united, the Church is built together into a dwelling of God in the Spirit (v. 22).

In his testimony to the Galatians (1:11–24), Paul reminded his readers how, in his "former manner of life in Judaism" he persecuted the church "beyond measure" and tried to destroy it (v. 13). It seems that because of his zealousness against Christianity, he was "advancing in Judaism beyond many of my contemporaries among my countrymen" (v. 14). But Jesus revealed Himself to Paul as Paul traveled from Jerusalem to Damascus in order to arrest more Christians and bring them to trial (vv. 16-17 cf. Acts 9:1-7).

It is almost implied in Acts 8:1–4 that Saul (Paul) was leading the persecution against the Christians, but his role may not have been so prominent. He certainly was a central figure in causing the torment that arose against the church and caused thousands to be scattered throughout Judea and Samaria (v. 1). The blessing brought about by God's providence, however, is that "those who had been scattered went about preaching the word" (v. 4).

You also endured the same sufferings. The verb *pasko* is translated "endured sufferings" (aorist indicative). *Same* is plural, that is, "the same things." These sufferings came from the hands of fellow Gentiles, just as sufferings came from Jewish hands in Judea. "The main point is that the Thessalonian believers accepted the Word of God (v. 13), that they thus entered the fellowship of the Judean churches, and thus 'suffered the same things'" (Lenski).

> **2:15** who both killed the Lord Jesus and the prophets, and drove us out. They are not pleasing to God, but hostile to all men,

Who both killed the Lord Jesus and the prophets. How far does Paul reach back with this statement about the prophets? Does he have some specific events in view or is he simply writing in a general manner? "The Jewish persecution extends far beyond the time of Jesus. Jesus himself mentions the killing of the prophets (Matt. 23:37), the Jewish prelude to the killing off of Jesus himself (Matt. 21:34–39)" (Lenski).

Luke referred back to Psalm 2 and applied the words of David to the hatred of the Gentiles toward the Lord, and against His Christ (Acts 4:26). Bringing this prophecy in the Psalms into his own times, Luke includes the Jewish people, and further writes that in Jerusalem "were gathered together against Thy holy Servant Jesus, whom Thou didst anoint, both Herod and Pontius Pilate, along with the Gentiles and the peoples of Israel, to do whatever Thy hand and Thy purpose predestined to occur" (vv. 27–28).

And drove us out. *Drove out* (*ekdioko,* aorist active participle) is better translated "to persecute vigorously" (*EDNT*). *Ekdioko* is an old verb, meaning "to drive out, banish," and it is used to describe chasing after a wild animal. It is used only here in the New Testament. "It is Paul's vivid description of the scene told in Acts 17:5ff. when the rabbis and the hoodlums from the agora chased him out of Thessalonica by the help of the politarchs" (Robertson). Similar things happened at Derbe and Lystra (14:6), Iconium (v. 1), and at Philippi (16:12ff) and Berea (17:13-14).

They are not pleasing to God. The persecutors have run amok emotionally and God is furious. They are venting blind anger against Jesus and all who believe in Him. Therefore, Christ warned of the vengeance to come (Luke 21:22), and alerted every serious listener that "there will be great distress upon the land, and wrath to this people, and they will fall by the edge of the sword, and will be led captive into all the nations" (vv. 23b–24a). Paul seems to have this warning in mind when he quoted the great judgment verse of Isaiah 6:10 to the Jewish leadership in Rome: "The heart of this people has become dull, . . . they have closed their eyes" (Acts 28:27). He then added, "Let it be known to you therefore, that this salvation of God has been sent to the Gentiles; they will also listen" (28:28).

[They are] hostile to all men. *Hostile* (*enantios*) can be translated as "opposite" or "contrary," as contrary winds blowing on the sea (*EDNT*). The Jews will stop at nothing nor flinch from anyone in their great tirade against Christ and those who trust Him. "The meaning is, that it was characteristic of them to persecute, and they spared no one" (*Barnes*). Barnes also quotes Tacitus who said of these Jews, "Cherishing hatred against all others."

> The spirit in which Tacitus so describes them may be inferred from the account given by Juvenal (xiv. 103, 104) of this unfriendly race, which denied even the commonest offices of hospitality to strangers. (Lightfoot)

2:16 hindering us from speaking to the Gentiles that they might be saved; with the result that they always fill up the measure of their sins. But wrath has come upon them to the utmost.

Hindering us from speaking to the Gentiles that they might be saved. Paul first went to the synagogue in Thessalonica to give the gospel to his fellow Israelites. When "a great multitude of the God-fearing Greeks and a number of the leading women" (Acts 17:4) came to Christ, the Jews became jealous (v. 5). Taking a wicked mob of Gentiles from the market place, they sought to drag Paul out of the house of one named Jason, but the mob could not find their prey (vv. 5b–6a). In blind rage the Jews "stirred up the crowd" with hatred (v. 8).

As with Paul before his conversion, the Jews were actually fighting against the Lord, whom they thought they were serving (Acts 26:14–15). Those who oppose God's own are opposing God and, at the same time, also hurting non-Christians. Often unbelief "hinders the salvation of others. Such people seek to extinguish the lamp of truth and in doing so cause others to stumble" (*BKC*).

They always fill up the measure of their sins. *Always* (*pantote*) probably means "at all times," "in every generation." "That is, to do now as they have always done, by resisting God and exposing themselves to his wrath. The idea is, that it had been a characteristic of the nation, at all times, to oppose God, and that they did it now in this manner in conformity with their fixed character" (*Barnes*).

But wrath has come upon them to the utmost. *Wrath* (*orges*) carries the thought that God is furious and angry with His own people. In this He is not a respecter of persons; He detests all sin. *Has come* (*phthano*, aorist indicative) indicates that the wrath has "arrived, come before" (*EDNT*), and has arrived upon them (*epi autous*), or "it now hangs over their heads"; "the Wrath has come upon them" (Nicoll).

The particular wrath Paul speaks of here is not the wrath of the Tribulation. That wrath the Church escapes by the Rapture (5:9), because that wrath is part of the Day of the Lord (v. 2) that comes upon the entire world. The wrath Paul writes about here in 2:16 comes crashing down suddenly upon the nation Israel, specifically for their rejection of Christ. The Lord called it the vengeance, the great distress "and wrath to this people" (Luke 21:22–23). As fulfilled in A.D. 70, the Jews fell "by the edge of the sword, and [were] led captive into all the nations." Jerusalem was "trampled underfoot by the Gentiles" (v. 24) and would be so "until the times of the Gentiles be fulfilled."

"To the utmost" is written simply *eis telos* in Greek "into, unto the end," probably meaning "but the wrath has come upon them at last" (Robertson). "At last" can mean "to the full extent," in "that the issue is now settled. The determination cannot be reversed, the obstinate blindness of the Jewish people furnishing obvious proof of this" (*EBC*).

> **2:17** But we, brethren, having been taken away from you for a short while—in person, not in spirit—were all the more eager with great desire to see your face.

But we, brethren, having been taken away from you for a short while—in person, not in spirit. The apostle makes it clear how much the three men miss the company of the church in Thessalonica. This church had not, however, been deserted. Paul is telling them "that he had been separated from them in appearance, not in heart, that they may know that distance of place does not by any means lessen his attachment" to them (Calvin).

Were all the more eager with great desire to see your face. [*We*] *were eager* comes from *spoudazo* (ingressive aorist active indicative) and carries the idea "to hasten" or "we became zealous." The hearts of the apostles are clearly seen in their love for the Thessalonians as the missionaries became eager just to look again upon the faces of the believers. This is not hyperbole; the attachments made with these people were genuine.

With great desire (en pollei epithumiai) can be translated "to run after, to yearn after" (Robertson). Paul is probably saying, "When [or although] we had been torn away from you for a short time only, we already endeavored all the more eagerly to return to you." Adding this to verse 18, Paul may mean that "the more Satan tried to effect a separation the harder we tried to effect a reunion" (*NTC*).

> **2:18** For we wanted to come to you—I, Paul, more than once—and yet Satan thwarted us.

For we wanted to come to you—I, Paul, more than once—and yet Satan thwarted us. Paul could be saying in a broad sense that Satan *hindered* (*egkopto,* aorist active indicative) their coming for a spiritual visit. In other words, resistance to our arrival is because of evil, and Satan is ultimately in charge of all wickedness.

But more likely the statement is meant in a specific sense in which Satan is personally attacking the ministry of Paul, who is, after all, the apostle of the gospel and of the revelation of the Church. It is certainly reasonable to envision Paul as being actually stalked by the Devil. Satan is not omnipresent, however, and cannot be at every place at all times. Thus, it is unlikely that he so personally attacks believers today on an individual basis. But Paul and the other apostles were especially chosen for unique tasks in the New Testament setting.

The word *egkopto* can be translated "hinder, prevent, delay, make weary" (*BAG*). Satan "can do nothing but by divine permission, nor can he hinder the will of God, and the execution of that, though he often hinders the apostle from doing what he willed and purposed, but he did not hinder the will of God, which was that Paul should be employed in other work elsewhere" (Gill).

> **2:19** For who is our hope or joy or crown of exultation? Is it not even you, in the presence of our Lord Jesus at His coming?

For who is our hope or joy or crown of exultation? Paul's love for this church comes to a climax in this most lyrical of passages. The church at Philippi is the only other assembly that received such emotional words of praise and love from Paul. Here he voices a rhetorical question that adds intensity to his enthusiasm. He asks what would be his greatest blessing at Christ's judgment seat. The answer—they would be!

> They were his *hope;* their development was what he lived for as a parent lives to see his children grow up to maturity, . . . They were his *joy,* they filled his life with sunshine as he thought of what they used to be, what they had become, and what they would be by the grace of God. (*BKC*)

"Crown of exultation." The word for crown is *stephanos.* Although still a symbol of honor, this word should be translated "wreath" in contrast to the bejeweled diadem (*diadema*) used by kings. The wreath was used as an expression of joy and consecration at public and private celebrations of the

Greeks and Romans. Because of pagan associations, the first century Christians avoided the use of such a heathen emblem, although they followed Paul and used the word in a figurative sense to look forward to heavenly rewards after death. The wreath was most significant in public life as the Olympic laurel and the victory wreath of Roman conquerors (*EDNT*). In secular use, as well as for the Christians, it is the "garland of victory" (Milligan).

Exultation (*kauchesis,* "to have pride, be boastful"), although often used in a selfish and negative sense, is here used by the apostle in the positive sense of having spiritual pride in how God so used this congregation for witness. Paul is also proud, in a positive sense, in the way these believers stood up under the onslaught of persecution and hate. No human bragging is intended here. Nor is Paul attempting to simply build the "self-esteem" of this church. From inner spiritual resources, not by the flesh, these Christians are standing for the truth.

Is Paul alluding to the "wreath of exultation" (or "wreath of pride") (*NIGTC*) as an established reward that other believers could receive if they, too, have so nurtured and matured new babes in Christ? Or is Paul simply applying this wreath to his own specific work with the Thessalonians? Is this a regular wreath that many could receive, or is it exclusive to the Thessalonian situation? A case could be made that all who so give themselves to reaching others for Christ will see those converts at the Bema and claim them as their own objects of joy and exultation. Though difficult to conclude from this passage, it may be that all who have been likewise persistent with the gospel shall be so rewarded.

Is it not even you, in the presence of our Lord Jesus at His coming? *Even* is the Greek word *kai* used in the emphatic sense and can be translated "Are not *in fact* [*kai*] you."

In the presence (*emprosthen*) can refer simply to a spiritual presence, such as in 3:9—"We rejoice *before* [*emprosthen*] God on your account—or "God sees (as if it is in front of Him) our rejoicing on your account." The second meaning, which probably applies here, denotes that one is actually standing before God following the Rapture and, thus, a literal encounter. But, since God the Father is Spirit and cannot be seen, it may refer to an actual presence before His almighty throne. It is more than likely, as John so often indicates in Revelation, we will be standing before Christ, but realizing we are actually in the presence of God. "It is the thought of presenting you to Him that thrills us with hope, joy, pride—at His coming" (Ellicott).

Coming is the word *parousia* that often causes much controversy. Some say it simply refers to one coming of Christ, whereas dispensationalists look more carefully at contexts and determine that the Bible clearly points to many "comings." So what does the word mean and in what contexts is it used?

Parousia is an unusual word with an unusual history. It is a technical term, having many applications in many texts. In Classical Greek, *parousia* is derived from a compound of the preposition *para* and the simple "to be" verb, *eimi,* forming *pareimi* (L&S). In the noun form, in both Classical Greek and Koine Greek, it is a feminine word. *Para* is "alongside" and *ousia* is the participle of *eimi.* It can freely be translated "the coming alongside of" or "alongside coming."

Examples abound of how *parousia* is used in Classical Greek literature: "we have no friends *present*"; *"arrival"; "*the *situation* of a planet"; "we have *property"; "contribution* of money"; "to be *present"; "*entertain them on their official *visits." Parousia* can also broadly refer to "possessions," and the active "presence" of law in a legal document. In Greek literature the *parousia* may denote the "presence" of the gods at mealtime.[1] Thus, *parousia* carries the idea of something transpiring, taking place, coming about, coming into being, being of substance, arriving, a special occasion. In the papyri the word is used in a specific sense, describing the arrival of a king or ruler who expects to receive his "crown of coming" (Robertson).

As in Classical Greek the verb in the New Testament is *pareimi* and is used twenty-three times, ten times by the apostle Paul. In simple terms, it has the idea of "to be present," or "he has come."

Several ways in which *parousia* is used in the New Testament are as follows:

1. In reference to the arrival of a person (4 times)
    a. "I rejoice over the *coming* of Stephanas" (1 Cor. 16:17)
    b. "God . . . comforted us by the *coming* of Titus" (2 Cor. 7:6)
    c. "And not only by his *coming* . . ." (2 Cor. 7:7)
    d. "Your confidence may abound in Christ Jesus through my *coming"* (Phil. 1:26)
2. In reference to the concept of simple "presence" (2 times)
    a. "You have always obeyed, not as in my *presence* only" (Phil. 2:12)
    b. "[Paul's] personal *presence* is unimpressive" (2 Cor. 10:10)
3. In reference to the appearance of the Antichrist (1 time)
    "[The lawless one] whose *coming* is in accord with the activity of Satan" (2:9)

4. In reference to the day of God (1 time)
   "Hastening the *coming* of the day of God" (2 Peter 3:12)

The next two categories of ways in which *parousia* is used relate to the coming of the kingdom and the Rapture appearance. Context indicates which is being referred to.

1. In reference to the coming of the King and the establishment of the kingdom (7 times)
   a. "What will be the sign of your [Christ's] *coming* and of the end of the age?" (Matt. 24:3)
   b. "So shall the *coming* of the Son of Man be" (Matt. 24:27)
   c. "For the *coming* of the Son of Man will be just like the days of Noah" (Matt. 24:37)
   d. "and they did not understand until the flood came and took them all away; so shall the coming of the Son of Man be" (Matt. 24:39)
   e. "The Lord will slay [the lawless one] . . . and bring to an end by the appearance of His *coming*" (2 Thess. 2:8)
   f. "We made known to you the power and *coming* of our Lord Jesus Christ" (2 Pet. 1:16)
   g. "Where is the promise of [the Messiah's] *coming?*" (2 Pet. 3:4)
2. In reference to the Rapture appearance (9 times)
   a. "Christ the first fruits, after that those who are Christ's at His *coming*" (1 Cor. 15:23)
   b. "You [our hope] in the presence of our Lord Jesus at His *coming?*" (1 Thess. 2:19)
   c. "At the *coming* of our Lord Jesus with all His saints" (1 Thess. 3:13)
   d. "We who are alive and remain until the *coming* of the Lord" (1 Thess. 4:15)
   e. "[You be] preserved complete without blame at the *coming* of our Lord Jesus Christ" (1 Thess. 5:23)
   f. "With regard to the *coming* of our Lord Jesus Christ, and our gathering together to Him" (2 Thess. 2:1)
   g. "Be patient, therefore, brethren, until the *coming* of the Lord" (James 5:7)
   h. "Strengthen your hearts, for the *coming* of the Lord is at hand" (James 5:8)

i. "[We shall] not shrink away from Him in shame at His *coming"* (1 John 2:28)

2:20 For you are our glory and joy.

For you are our glory and joy. The conversion of the members of this church gave Paul the grounds of his hope of future blessedness as he looked forward to seeing them in glory. He labored for the conversion and salvation of those he came in contact with. He gave himself totally to reaching the Gentiles for Christ. In so doing, he in no way neglected his own people, the Jews. In fact, he usually went to the synagogues first and presented the truth about their own Messiah before speaking to the Greek culture. "The passage suggests that there will be mutual recognition between the soul-winner and those he has led to the Saviour in his work for Christ here on earth. There will be both prizes and surprises at the *Bema"* (Ritchie).

Study Questions

1. Describe what happened to the apostles in Philippi (Acts 16:22–24).
2. Who were Paul and the other apostles trying to please (vv. 3–4)?
3. List at least ten ways the apostles tried to present themselves to the Thessalonians when they first brought the gospel (vv. 5–9).
4. What can we speculate was happening that made Paul work so hard to explain and defend himself before this church?
5. Why were the Jews of Thessalonica working so hard to slander the gospel and the witness of the apostles before the citizens of Thessalonica (vv. 13–16)?
6. In this chapter is Paul correcting or encouraging the assembly in Thessalonica? Or is he doing both? Discuss.

Chapter Seven

Paul Continues His
Words of Concern

2. His Concern for Their Trials (3:1–8)

It seems clear that Paul knew of his enemies' attempts to vilify his work and their accusation that he was a religious charlatan who cared only for himself. It is likely that Timothy informed Paul about the rumors that the Jews and others had circulated. Nevertheless, it seems obvious from what Paul writes that the Thessalonians in general were not accepting such claims. Overall, they had no such suspicions. This letter from the three apostles (Paul, Silas, and Timothy) corroborates all that Paul had already told the members of this church. They heard and felt the heart and emotions of this great man and his companions.

> **3:1** Therefore when we could endure it no longer, we thought it best to be left behind at Athens alone,

Therefore when we could endure it no longer. *Endure* is a satisfactory translation of the Greek word *stegos,* but it could also mean "to stand something," thus to endure. The present tense and participle conveys the idea "we were continually enduring, but . . ." Thus, we can "no longer be standing it without doing something about it." "It was a relief to act, to dispatch at least Timothy" (Lenski).

Since Paul's original purposes and plans were hindered (2:17–18), he could wait no longer in trying to see them, or at the least, he had to send Timothy to them. Paul really wanted to know how these new believers were faring. His own troubles meant little to him, and he was more concerned for those who were suffering in Thessalonica.

We thought it best to be left behind at Athens alone. Some of the Bereans had taken Paul to Athens (Acts 17:15). Paul had told them that they should then dispatch Silas and Timothy to him in Athens.

> **3:2** and we sent Timothy, our brother and God's fellow-worker in the gospel of Christ, to strengthen and encourage you as to your faith,

We sent Timothy, our brother and God's fellow-worker in the gospel of Christ. Timothy was chosen because Paul and Silas had been driven out of Thessalonica and Timothy had not. While in Athens, Paul had been moved by all the idolatry he saw in the city (Acts 17: 16). As a consequence, he entered the synagogue and reasoned with the Jews and the God-fearing Gentiles. He also went daily to the market place and held dialogue with whomever would listen (v. 17).

The Stoics and Epicureans took him to the public forum, the Areopagus, where he could continue presenting his apology. He closes his famous speech there by referring to Christ whom God "appointed, having furnished proof to all men by raising Him from the dead" (v. 31).

Paul does not refer to Timothy as "your brother" but instead, he sets him into a relationship with himself and with Silas as "our brother," because Timothy's job is to go to Thessalonica "to ease the anxiety of Paul and Silvanus" (Lenski).

To strengthen and encourage you as to your faith. The two aorist active infinitives (*sterizo* and *parakaleo*), introduced with *eis to*, are unusual in construction, and contemplate the result which Timothy was to achieve: "'to make you solid (to fix or make steadfast) and to encourage you in behalf of your faith,' i.e., so that no opposition should destroy this faith. Both aorists are effective" (Lenski). The need of the Thessalonian church would take precedence over the desires or needs of Paul (Nicoll).

> **3:3** so that no man may be disturbed by these afflictions; for you yourselves know that we have been destined for this.

So that no man may be disturbed by these afflictions. Although all Christians desire to escape the persecution exemplified in the cross, Paul teaches that we should not be caught off guard when such troubles come. Persecution is what God has designed for us. Peter agrees and writes, "Beloved, do not be surprised at the fiery ordeal among you, which comes upon you for your testing, as though some strange thing were happening to you" (1 Peter 4:12). But he adds that since you "share the sufferings of Christ, keep on rejoicing" (v. 13a), and remember, "you are blessed" to be reviled for the name of Christ (v. 14).

Disturbed (*saino*) is a present passive infinitive and is used only here in the New Testament. It might be translated "don't be continually wavering, upset, shaken" or even be deceived (*EDNT*); "these things are normal for you." *Saino* may also be taken in another way, such as "to be led astray, allured from the right path." It comes from *seio,* which originally meant "to shake or wag" as a dog wagging its tail. Paul is encouraging that "no one, in the midst of these troubles, desert the rough path of the truth, drawn aside and allured by the enticing prospect of an easier life" (Lightfoot).

Afflictions (from *thlipsis*) is that intense word for troubles that carries the thought "hardship" with the verbal idea "to press down on hard," to "crush," or "squeeze together" (*EDNT*).

> Because the affliction experienced in fellowship with Christ and in his service looks toward the future glory and the salvation of others, the believer can experience not only comfort in it, but can also experience joy because of the Holy Spirit (1 Thess. 1:3; 2 Cor. 7:4; 8:2; Col. 1:24; 1 Pet. 1:6–9; 4:13; James 1:2–4). (*EDNT*)

For you yourselves know that we have been destined for this. Peter says something similar when he writes, "Therefore, let those also who suffer according to the will of God entrust their souls to a faithful Creator in doing what is right" (1 Peter 4:19). *Destined* (*keimai,* present indicative) is an unusual Greek word that can have three different meanings: "to lie down," "to find oneself," or "to be destined" (*EDNT*). Here it carries the thought "to be destined" or "appointed" (Robertson).

It is a mistake to think that in this dispensation of grace—that is, in this Church Age—we should have it easy. Through the centuries, most of the pages of church history have been stained with the blood of martyrs. Only briefly, and only in some blessed locations, have the churches of God found peace. Often that tranquility comes with a price; the Church may forget its purpose and grow complacent.

For believers in Christ, Paul warns of a troubled existence. He warns that as servants of God we, as did those in his day, can expect afflictions, hardships, and distresses (2 Cor. 6:3–10). As well, we can be "afflicted in every way, but not crushed; perplexed, but not despairing" (4:8).

By God's divine providence, afflictions are, in their very nature and even duration, appointed for the saints of the Lord, and in turn, the saints are destined for such afflictions. This is the case of all who live godly lives, and particularly for those on the front lines, such as evangelists and missionaries. This persecution that fell upon the apostles, and then upon the Thessalonians, only confirmed their calling and should not have been seen as something strange. Persecution was an appointment from heaven, and by the will of God, that they should endure quietly and patiently what He laid upon them (Gill).

> **3:4** For indeed when we were with you, we kept telling you in advance that we were going to suffer affliction; and so it came to pass, as you know.

We kept telling you in advance that we were going to suffer affliction. It is not recorded anywhere that Paul told them of coming persecutions. But he was with them long enough to cover a variety of subjects and doctrines, and affliction was obviously discussed. Of course, the apostle had been on the front lines long enough to know of the troubles that would meet him on every side. He would certainly share this information with his friends.

And so it came to pass, as you know. The Thessalonians witnessed the onslaught of hatred that fell upon Paul, Silas, and Timothy. They also experienced the same rejection, both their own and that of the message of Christ. Peter reminds the churches "you have been called for this purpose, since Christ also suffered for you, leaving you an example for you to follow in His steps" (1 Peter 2:21).

> **3:5** For this reason, when I could endure it no longer, I also sent to find out about your faith, for fear that the tempter might have tempted you, and our labor should be in vain.

For this reason, when I could endure it no longer, I also sent to find out about your faith. This passage appears to be a pivotal verse because it reveals the ultimate fears of the apostle. He worried that the Thessalonian believers may have been tempted away from the truth. The persecution could have caused them to deny their beliefs before the eyes of their own community. At the very least, they may have become doctrinally confused and withdrawn their public witness. Such a tragedy would have rippled throughout the various regions of Greece. Paul's concern about the Thessalonians' faith also impelled him to send Timothy to them "to strengthen and encourage" them in the faith (v. 2).

For fear that the tempter might have tempted you, and our labor should be in vain. The verb *tempted* and the present participle *the tempter* both come from *peirazo* and can mean "to test" or "to try," and without question is referring to Satan, who tempts in order to cause one to fall. The Devil is also the believer's adversary (*antidikos*) or "opponent at court," who "prowls about like a roaring lion, seeking someone to devour" (1 Peter 5:8). It must not be forgotten that Jesus also experienced "the tempter" (Matt. 4:3) in His encounter with the Devil in the wilderness. In God's mysterious providence this trial was even promoted by the Spirit, in that Jesus was "led up . . . to be tempted" (v. 1). Being the Son of God, Christ did not fail, and so stands as an example for us. Would Satan be successful with the Thessalonians? No. By the hand of God and the Word of God, Timothy's work would be successful and have a happy outcome. The Devil, "who had successfully tempted our first parents in the garden of Eden, and had tried the same tactics on the Last Adam, our Lord Jesus Christ, in the Judaean desert, was still doing his nefarious work" (Ritchie).

Between verses 5 and 6, Paul seems to say, "We were in great anxiety, for fear you should have fallen away, and sent Timothy to see if all was well; but now, all anxiety is over" (Ellicott).

> **3:6** But now that Timothy has come to us from you, and has brought us good news of your faith and love, and that you always think kindly of us, longing to see us just as we also long to see you,

Now that Timothy has come to us from you, and has brought us good news of your faith and love. Some commentators have suggested that Paul shifts from a certain defensiveness to a more positive expression, although his consciousness of the continued opposition to the Thessalonian church never leaves him. The thought that "Timothy has come to us from you" seems to convey "Timothy was our representative to you. Now he has become your representative to us, revealing to us your very heart" (*NTC*).

"Has come" might read more strongly "has just come," which would indicate that Paul is replying immediately to the church. Reading between the lines, one might infer that Timothy was delighted to bring a positive report back to the apostle. A bit of good news amidst continual spiritual struggles would certainly pick up Paul's spirits.

Has brought good news is actually the verb *euangelizo* (to give a good message, report), from which we get the important word *gospel* (*euangelion*). *Euangelizo* is an aorist middle participle and can be translated "he himself good messaged" us about you, or he "has brought us the glad tidings of your faith and love" (*NTC*).

You always think kindly of us. Literally, "you are having [present tense] a remembrance concerning us good, always." Paul is not saying that the Thessalonians are having merely a "clear, vivid remembrance" but "a good, kind remembrance." "If the Thessalonians had been beginning to fall away, they would not have cared to see their teachers [so much]" (Ellicott).

Longing to see us just as we also long to see you. The feelings and responses are mutual, which uplifts and encourages the apostles. *Longing* (*epipotheo*) as a present participle probably indicates the continual character of their love for Paul and the others. That feeling is returned to them by Paul, Silas, and Timothy. Of the nine times *epipotheo* is used in the New Testament, Paul uses it seven, four times in noun form (2 Cor. 7:7, 11; Phil. 4:1; Rom. 15:23). He has marked it

> . . . and its derivatives with his personality, imbuing them with a lively sensibility. Sometimes they suggest an urge, an inclination; sometimes a fervent tenderness, an emotion that grips the heart; always love; always a favorable sense. (*TLNT*)

Such mutual attraction would make for strong supportive ties that would add strength to any ministry of the gospel carried out in the future.

3:7 for this reason, brethren, in all our distress and affliction we were comforted about you through your faith;

For this reason, brethren, . . . we were comforted about you through your faith. That is, "Because of the openness and love we have together, and because of your exemplary love observed by Timothy, we were comforted." *Comforted (parakaleo)* can mean "counseled," but here it is better translated "encouraged, uplifted." With the aorist indicative and passive voice, this encouragement may be seen as overwhelming the apostles. They held their breath, so to speak, and then were relieved when they found the Thessalonians unmovable in their confidence in the Lord, and their loyalty toward the apostles intact.

In all our distress and affliction. This indicates the state of the sufferings and troubles the apostles were experiencing. "The half may never be told" as to the degree that Paul experienced persecution—physical pain, mental torment, religious rejection, being socially ostracized. His letters probably just touch the surface. But he hints at what was happening by the use of two strong words, *distress (anagke)* and *affliction (thlipsis)*.

Anagke is, in Jewish linguistic thinking, almost equivalent to *thlipsis* (tribulation). The thought behind *anagke* is "perilous experiences" and being "under compulsion." In Classical Greek literature, *anagke* can mean a "constraint" under which humans exist that make decisions almost impossible. The word conveys the idea of laboring under a yoke and, as used by Herodotus (1.116), it could mean even torture (*EDNT*).

Thlipsis is the common word for *hardship* with the idea of being "pressed down, crushed, squeezed together" (*EDNT*). Extreme oppression or persecution is in view, but for the believer in Christ this affliction produces endurance, which in turn produces character (Rom. 5:3–4). The New Testament teaches that a close connection exists between afflictions endured by believers and those suffered by Christ Himself. The connection is inescapable and serves as comfort in order "that no one be disturbed by these afflictions" (3:3a), because Jesus also suffered.

"Through your faith" indicates that the apostles were clearly depending on the Lord for strength and help against terrible obstacles. Paul himself appears to be encouraged by watching the spiritual fortitude of other believers in Christ (Rom. 1:12; 2 Cor. 7:4, 13; Philem. 7) (*EBC*).

3:8 for now we really live, if you stand firm in the Lord.

For now we really live, if you stand firm in the Lord. *Now* carries the idea "now this being so." Paul uses the word *live* (*zao,* present active subjunctive [or indicative]) in an unusual way. He probably means "now we can be going on" or "we should be able to live once more." In his outward trials, Paul "died daily" (1 Cor. 15:31), but now the faith of his converts inspires him with new life (Lightfoot).

If you stand firm (*steko,* present active indicative, with the particle *ean*) connotes fixity. The *ean* with the indicative is an unusual form but probably alludes to "Paul's sense of well being continu[ing] as long as the Thessalonians continued to remain faithful" (*NIGTC*). "If you stand firm" is probably also a conditional clause with a hidden hortatory meaning, the construction "introduc[ing] a hypothetical condition" (D&M, p. 245). Paul speaks with some hesitation here—*"if* so be ye stand fast," reminding the Thessalonians that their faith was not complete (v. 10). "There was enough in the fact that they had been so recently taken, absorbed so entirely in the contemplation of the future state, to make the Apostle alarmed lest their faith should prove only impulsive and transitory. Such appears to be the connection of the thought with what follows" (Lightfoot). Thomas, however, takes a more positive view and says "Paul's choice of a present indicative rather than a more normal aorist subjunctive has the effect of expressing certainty that his readers will continue to stand firm from this point on" (*EBC*).

3. His Consistent Prayers for Them (3:9–13)

In verses 9–17 Paul concludes his discussion of the "problem." He has expressed his hopes and fears and his concerns that the Thessalonians might be outwardly influenced to shrink away from the stand for Christ. But Timothy's report tells him the church is standing tall.

3:9 For what thanks can we render to God for you in return for all the joy with which we rejoice before our God on your account,

For what thanks can we render to God for you in return for all the joy with which we rejoice before our God on your account. This long and seemingly complicated sentence seems to be fired by a great welling up of emotion in Paul. Actually, it is a rhetorical question that is not finished until verse 10. Paul is saying, "You have brought incredible joy to our hearts by your continual patience in these trials." The apostle could take no credit, however, in their actions; he is acknowledging that their endurance was a tribute to the providence of God working in their witness (Phil. 2:13). "He commended the Thessalonians, but also recognized and acknowledged the hand of God at work in their lives" (*BKC*).

In this verse Paul expresses a great vigor of life, a glowing return of emotion for God's favor. "Rejoicing before God" implies the very highest and best of joy, not a joy that comes from the world or from independent pride, but the kind that can bear the searching eyes of God (Alford). "Enter into Paul's emotion. . . . The intensity of feeling is augmented by this reversal from a great depth of depression to the loftiest height of jubilation" (Lenski).

> **3:10** as we night and day keep praying most earnestly that we may see your face, and may complete what is lacking in your faith?

As we night and day keep praying most earnestly that we may see your face. Paul's desire to return to Thessalonica is important in the apostle's long discussion. He really, "earnestly," wanted to return. "Most earnestly" means that his desire was expressed in more than ordinary prayer. The apostles were praying "constantly, exceedingly, abundantly." "He made [seeing their faces] a special subject of prayer; he urged it with earnestness, and without intermission" (*Barnes*). "Night and day" probably does not refer to simply praying twice daily; they were continually praying from dawn till dusk.

And may complete what is lacking in your faith? These words end Paul's rhetorical question that began "For what thanks can we render to God for you" in verse 9. The question, then, really answers itself and becomes an important point in this letter; although this church is so faithful in its witness, it is still growing in the Lord spiritually, and its trust in Him is yet immature. Thus, the best thanks that Paul could render to God for the Thessalonian church would be for him to complete the job of their spiritual upbringing. Maybe their spiritual immaturity is why Paul was hedging in verse 8 and so concerned about their testimony before the city. Would it falter? Would they deny Him who bought them?

May complete (*katartizo,* aorist infinitive) means "to put in order, put into proper condition" (*BAG*). The word can also mean "to mend, restore, equip." "Paul had been only a comparatively short time at Thessalonica, and naturally there were some points of doctrine which were not clear to the believers" (Ritchie). The things "lacking," some scholars have speculated, could refer to thoroughly understanding the apostles' teaching and more concerning the issues of moral behavior.

> **3:11** Now may our God and Father Himself and Jesus our Lord direct our way to you;

Now may our God and Father Himself and Jesus our Lord direct our way to you. Paul earnestly seeks the favor of God that he might be able to visit the Thessalonians. It is a distinct prayer whereby the apostle points to the Father specifically by adding *Himself* (*autos*). *Himself* is intensive, emphasizing and contrasting (*BAG*) "God Himself particularly and specifically" with "Jesus our Lord."

Lenski better translates, "Now may he, our God and Father and our Lord Jesus, direct our way unto you!" "May [He] direct" or "clear the way" (*kateuthuno,* aorist active optative, third, singular) seems to govern the two personal nouns God and Jesus. Thus, *autos* (singular) refers to the Father and to Jesus as one, just as the singular verb does. To so treat the two divine persons as one, as Paul appears to be doing here, is striking but offers no problem to those who recognize the deity of both and their unity of will and work (Lenski). Paul's construction here "can be understood in no other way" (*Barnes*). "Two persons viewed as one (cf. John 10:30) possess power to open the way to Thessalonica once again; 'our God and Father himself and our Lord Jesus' is the compound subject of [the] singular verb" (*EBC*). "The singular [verb] implies that God and Jesus count as one in this connection. The verb is common . . . in this sense of providence directing human actions" (Nicoll).

> The Lord Jesus is addressed equally in prayer with the Father. The fact that Jesus is God is further highlighted by Paul's use of a singular verb (trans. "clear") with a plural subject: "may He clear the way, even the Father and Jesus," not "may They clear the way." (*BKC*)

There can be no stronger way than with this passage that the apostle could have expressed the Lordship of Christ and His oneness with the Father. When Paul "thus speaks of both in the same terms, he teaches that Christ has divinity and power in common with the Father" (Calvin).

> **3:12** and may the Lord cause you to increase and abound in love for one another, and for all men, just as we also do for you;

And may the Lord cause you to increase and abound in love for one another. The "you" being first is emphatic. "You, may the Lord cause to increase . . ." The Lord "may apply to God, but in view of the general Pauline usage, and the application of the title to Jesus in the preceding clause, it is best understood of Him again" (Milligan).

Paul continues by using two aorist infinitives—*to increase, to abound*—that at first glance mean the same thing. But the connotations of the two words are significantly different. *To increase* (*pleonazo*) means "to become more, multiply, cause to become rich." Here, it can carry the thought, "May the Lord make you rich in love" (*EDNT*). *To abound* (*perisseuo*) goes further and implies "going beyond, to exceed, to have superabundance, to be extremely rich" (*EDNT*). Paul is saying "may the Lord cause you to become rich [yes], to go even further, to superabound in love." That is, "if love were diffused through their hearts they would abound" (*Barnes*) or "multiply you in love until you have enough and to spare of it" (Ellicott). "The latter verb is the stronger of the two, implying an overplus of love, and hence is often used by St. Paul in referring to Divine grace" (Milligan).

And for all men, just as we also do for you. Besides love for fellow Christians, the Thessalonians' love should also spill over to the lost. *All men* refers to the unregenerate of the world. Thus, believers in Christ should care for the souls of the unredeemed just as God does (John 3:16)—"So our love ought to go forth to the whole human race" (Calvin). Sometimes loving the lost is difficult, especially when they are tormenting and slaying the saints of God. But to be able to love the lost is to have the mind of Christ (1 Cor. 2:16).

> **3:13** so that He may establish your hearts unblamable in holiness before our God and Father at the coming of our Lord Jesus with all His saints.

So that He may establish your hearts unblamable in holiness. *That He may establish* (*sterizo,* "to support") is the articular infinitive of purpose with the preposition *eis,* also used in 3:2 (Robertson). If this were a present infinitive, as is used in the LXX, it would be a Hebraism translated "set one's face" (*BAG*). From *sterizo* comes the English *steroid* and *stereo,* carrying the idea "to make solid, strong." "The Lord by means of love strengthens . . . the inner purposes and desires. Hearts thus strengthened will be less prone to crave the unseparated life, the life of the world" (*NTC*).

Hearts (*kardia*), some commentators think, refers to the mind. But Paul is more likely speaking of the emotions, the affections. Christians are often swayed emotionally to sin, or they are misled in their feelings. The heart and the mind cannot be separated or forced apart; they operate together. Gill seems to agree and writes, hearts "are very unstable and inconstant in their frames, and in the exercise of grace, and have need to be established in the love of God, against the fears of men, the frowns of the world, the temptations of Satan."

Unblamable (*amemptos*) does not mean the Thessalonians will never sin again. Rather, "after they sinned they would deal with it as God requires and so be free from any unreasonable charge to their fellowmen" (*BKC*). Paul does not expect the Thessalonians to be perfect. That would be impossible. In Classical Greek, *memptos* connotes "to reject, to be contemptible, find fault, censure" (L&S). So with the negative *a,* it translates "not to reject, not to be contemptible, without fault, etc." Before the Lord, the church should be walking "in holiness" (*en hagiosune*) or "with holiness." Their hearts and their ways of life should be separated unto God. If Jesus came, Paul wanted them to be blameless before men but holy before the Lord. "[Mature] and settled sanctification in the eyes of God [as we stand before Him] is the object in view" (Ellicott). Stating succinctly his point in this passage, Paul

. . . sees the goal of his apostolic ministry as being "to strengthen and encourage" the faith of the disciples, to establish them solidly, without oscillation, to make them capable of standing fast without discouragement or doubt, notably in the midst of the physical, moral, and doctrinal calamities of the end times. (*TLNT,* 3:294)

Therefore, if the Thessalonians are to be established "without blame in holiness," this implies their moral conformity to the very character of God. That this was of fundamental importance for Paul can be seen in 4:3, where sanctification or holiness . . . is said to be the will of God for the Thessalonians. (*NIGTC*)

Before our God and Father at the coming of our Lord Jesus with all His saints. This verse clearly is a Rapture passage. With *emprosthen* (*before*) Paul uses the very same construction concerning "presence" as he does in 2:19. There, as here, His presence is used to mean a face-to-face encounter.

- *Before* (presence of) our Lord Jesus (2:19).
- *Before* (presence of) our God and Father (3:13).

Emprosthen "at times has non-local connotations, as in 1:3 and 3:9 of this epistle. Yet a judicial hearing requires actual proximity to the judge. So here the preposition requires a location before the Father in heaven" (*EBC*). When will this "before" the Father take place? By its context, the Great White Throne of Revelation 20:11–15 is a judgment concerning salvation in which all the participants are doomed. No unbeliever escapes because no one stands before the throne with the righteousness of Christ. Here then, this "before" in 3:13 has to be the *Bema* seat judgment when believers' works are judged in heaven. And that takes place sometime after the Rapture.

> The final accounting Paul alludes to will take place in the personal "presence of our God and Father." . . . Earlier, Paul has made "our Lord Jesus" the judge at this scene (1 Thess. 2:19). This is no contradiction. The unity of the Father and Son, just seen in v. 11, allows a joint judgeship. The *bema* of Christ (2 Cor 5:10) is also the *bema* of God (Rom 14:10), because Christ in his present session is with the Father in his heavenly throne (Rev 3:21; cf. Rom 8:34; Heb 1:3; 10:12). (*EBC*)

"The coming" with all His saints, then, is clearly the Rapture (for "coming," see 2:19). The "saints" are certainly not angels, as some commentators think, but the souls of believers who return with Him during that event. These saints would be the souls of those who return from heaven to receive their new glorified bodies. In all of his writings "not once does [Paul] employ [saint] to indicate angels, always the redeemed" (*NTC*). These are the dead in Christ (4:16) whom "God will bring with Him," that is, "those who have fallen asleep in Jesus" (v. 14). Those who are alive then join those in this resurrection, when the souls who come with Jesus are given a new body, and are caught up to meet the Lord in the air (v. 17).

When Jesus returns to establish His kingdom reign and rule on earth, He brings a host of angels (Matt. 24:31) who gather the elect, Jews and Gentiles who trust Him and have survived the Tribulation. This return is His coming (*parousia*) down to the earth to reign on the throne of David. The saints, or the elect remnant from the Tribulation, are gathered from under the four winds to enjoy His earthly rule. He comes as the Son of Man (25:31), the King (v. 34), to carry out an earthly judgment (v. 33), then reign on His glorious throne (v. 31) and inherit His earthly kingdom (v. 34). This return and reign is not the Rapture, which has taken place before the terrible seven-year period called the Tribulation.

On this verse, nonpremillennialist Hendriksen makes this interesting comment:

> One sometimes wonders whether the difficulty of conceiving the saints as coming with the Lord has led to an unnatural construction. Whether or not one happens to belong to the camp of the premillennialists, in all fairness to them one must admit that when they link "with all his saints" with the immediately preceding words, so that we get, "at the coming of our Lord Jesus with all his saints," they are entirely correct! (*NTC*)

Study Questions

1. For what were the apostles destined (v. 3)?
2. Did Paul have some honest doubts about this church holding up under pressure (v. 5)?
3. What kept Paul encouraged and persevering (vv. 6–8)?
4. In verse 10, is Paul mildly scolding, or is he simply and honestly pointing out that there were things that needed to be improved in their faith?
5. Explain in your own words what is the desire and hope of the apostle Paul for these believers.

More on Christian Living and the Rapture of the Church

II. EXHORTATION FOR CHRISTIAN LIVING (4:1–5:28)
    A. What it Means to Walk with the Lord (4:1–12)
        1. Sexual Issues (4:1–8)

Before Paul gets to the subject of the Rapture of the Church, he first deals with some urgent matters concerning Christian living. Though prophetic concerns are important, the apostle feels compelled to first discuss sexual matters that he and the other apostles had spoken about when they were in Thessalonica. In their view "walking with the Lord" comes before "waiting for the Lord."

Before the end of this letter, Paul includes a practical section (5:12–28). Prior to that, he exhorts the church about how to live ("Finally then, brethren"), and then returns to address, in more detail, the doctrine of the Rapture.

Lightfoot, however, presents another theory. He believes both chapters (4–5) are summary, including the good news about the Rapture. "In the passage before us this conclusion is extended over two chapters." He bases his theory on the first word, "finally."

> **4:1** Finally then, brethren, we request and exhort you in the Lord Jesus, that, as you received from us instruction as to how you ought to walk and please God (just as you actually do walk), that you may excel still more.

Finally then, brethren, we request and exhort you in the Lord Jesus. Robertson notes *Finally* (*loipon*) is an accusative of general reference. It does not mean, says Milligan, an actual conclusion but merely a colloquial expression pointing the way toward the end. Disagreeing, Lightfoot sees the "Finally" as "'Now' then as I wrap up," or "'For the rest' of what I have to say in conclusion," or "Now [*loipon*] then that I finished speaking of our mutual relations, it remains for me to urge upon you some precepts." *Loipon* (finally, for the rest), then, marks Paul's transition from the first narrative portion of the letter to this second and concluding part, which is also full of exhortations. If Lightfoot's view is correct, it still includes the positive and blessed information about the Rapture. It "points to all that remains to be said" (Lenski).

As he has done in the past, the apostle uses two words that are similar in meaning, *we request* (*erotao*) and [*we*] *exhort* (*parakaleo*), both written in the present tense: "We continue to request." "We request" has been noted by some as being almost like a question: "Would you please consider . . . ?" But others disagree on this usage. In Classical Greek, the word is used in the present tense, but in the LXX and in the New Testament the thought is "to request" (Ellicott).

Paul often uses "exhort," ten times in the Thessalonian letters (1 Thess. 2:11; 3:2, 7; 4:1, 10, 18; 5:11, 14; 2 Thess. 2:17; 3:12), five times with the translation "to exhort" (1 Thess. 2:11; 4:1, 10; 5:14; 2 Thess. 3:12). (For more on the meaning of this word, see 2:3, 11.)

Paul uses this second verb *to exhort* and then adds *to request* with a warm fraternal appeal to soften his admonition. Paul, Silas, and Timothy speak to the Thessalonians as the dearest friends who have shown the deepest of love and who have previously been admonished as a father would his own children (2:11–12).

In the Lord Jesus. The prepositional phrase with *en* reads better as "because of the Lord Jesus," in that they were to be responsible to Christ for their conduct. Yet they were also to be listening to the instructions given by the apostles, who were the authoritative representatives of the Lord Jesus Himself, and their lives were under His command.

As you received from us instruction as to how you ought to walk and please God. All of the commentary thus far presented on the text of 1 Thessalonians is built upon this statement. *You received* (*paralambano*, aorist active indicative) this instruction in the past. From this point, Paul sets forth two "as" clauses (*kathos*) with the verb *dei* (it is necessary). It can read "as you received from us [when we were with you], how it is necessary for you to be walking right now [*peripateo*, present active infinitive] and to be pleasing right now [*aresko*, present active infinitive] God." These ethical norms and patterns

> . . . constituted the distinctive Christian way of life that Paul required of his converts, as the words "how it is necessary for you to behave and to please God" indicate. The patterns of conduct Paul enjoined on his converts were intended to separate them from the pagan social world out of which they had come and to facilitate harmony and a common identity among the members of the newly formed community." (*NIGTC*)

(Just as you actually do walk). Paul uses a second "as" (*kathos*) clause, with a present indicative, to support the fact that his readers are now living this way, but he wants to make sure that they continue to follow these high moral standards.

That you may excel still more. This phrase seems almost redundant and even conflicting, but the apostles want to make sure that the Thessalonians do not stop their growth in Christ. The missionaries want them to go on!— *still more* (*mallon*) can be translated "more than ever." This translation can be improved upon because it actually reads with a *hina* clause, "in order that you might be [so] excelling [*perisseuo*, present active subjunctive] more than ever." Though things are going well, there is room for improvement in the Christian experience. We are continually learning, maturing, growing in Christ. And even though Paul commends this church with so much that was good, still some were struggling. Paul refuses to condemn everyone, but he does outline in the following verses some areas that might prove a moral hindrance.

4:2 For you know what commandments we gave you by the authority of the Lord Jesus.

For you know what commandments we gave you by the authority of the Lord Jesus. These commandments are given to the Church in the new dispensation of grace. They are moral imperatives, not simply repeated laws from the Mosaic covenant. Moral principles are eternal, but many directives are listed under the Law that are not for the Church Age. For example, the Church is not under the Sabbath, nor are believers required to bring sacrifices yearly up to Jerusalem. Yet many mix the Law system with legitimate commands given for the Church.

Dispensationalists are not antinomian; they teach that believers are given commands to follow. But obeying these commands is different than believing that one must remain under the Mosaic system in order to please the Lord. Paul writes, "You are not under law, but under grace" (Rom. 6:14), and he adds, "But now we have been released from the Law, having died to that by which we were bound, so that we serve in newness of the Spirit and not in oldness of the letter [of the Law]" (7:6).

Commandments (*parangelia,* instruction, proclamation) are directives that come from the apostles and are moral instructions to guide the church. *"Parangelia"* means "to give a message to, to give a charge, command." Thus, the commands are not suggestions nor are they optional. As an inspired prophet of Christ, Paul is telling us they are His rules.

> The word is military language, carrying with it connotations of weight and authority. . . . Paul is not giving orders on his own responsibility. They are following a chain of command, from the supreme commander, the Lord Jesus through Paul, His servant, to the embattled Christian soldier, fighting the battle of purity against the wiles of the wicked one. (Ritchie)

In the Greek text, "the authority" is not in the verse but is supplied by the translators. The verse simply reads "commandments we gave you by [*dia,* through] the Lord Jesus." Though the editors have taken reasonable liberty in supplying *authority,* the thought is more direct in meaning without it. The apostles' "commission ran to teach men all things whatsoever Christ commanded: . . . to engage them to obedience to them" (Gill).

> **4:3** For this is the will of God, your sanctification; that is, that you abstain from sexual immorality;

For this is the will of God; your sanctification. *Will* (*thelema*) is used several ways in Scripture. (1) It may refer to the absolute determination of

God in His providence to accomplish what He desires. *Will* used in this way refers to God's sovereignty, by which His plans are carried out and not thwarted. By the Lord's sovereignty, that is, "by the will of God" Paul became an apostle (1 Cor. 1:1). The election and salvation of the individual is certain by God's will: "He predestined us to adoption as sons through Jesus Christ to Himself, according to the kind intention of His will" (Eph. 1:5). In a strange and mysterious way believers in Christ even "suffer according to the will of God" and then must "entrust their souls to a faithful Creator in doing what is right" (1 Peter 4:19). Our very existence is determined by His will. No one can determine what will happen in his or her life one year from now, but what should be said is, "If the Lord wills [*thelo*], we shall live and also do this or that" (James 4:15).

Nebuchadnezzar stated well God's sovereign will: "And all the inhabitants of the earth are accounted as nothing, but He does according to His will in the host of heaven and among the inhabitants of earth; and no one can ward off His hand or say to Him, 'What hast Thou done?'" (Dan. 4:35).

(2) "Will" may also be an expression of the desire of God, although in His overall providence His plans are not blocked nor hindered, even by Satan. The Lord "desires" the salvation of all the lost but He has not worked to that sovereign end. God "who desires [*thelo*] all men to be saved and to come to the knowledge of the truth" (1 Tim. 2:4).

The will of God stated here in 1 Thessalonians 4:3 is the Lord's desire that the church be sanctified *experientially* and thus be strengthened by Him in order to avoid the terrible sin life of Thessalonica. In this verse Paul uses the noun *hagiasmos,* which means "to be set aside." Only this "work of God" can keep the Thessalonians from the "sexual immorality" (*porneia*) of the culture.

That you abstain from sexual immorality. *Abstain (apeko)* means "to stay away, to keep away" from something (*BAG*). As a present middle infinitive it may read, "to continually keep yourselves away from." Some commentators believe there were no problems with flagrant sexual sin among the Thessalonians, because Paul does not address how to be forgiven if they fell in this manner (Nicoll). If the apostle mentions such sins, it is likely that some in the church were either already involved or the danger existed that some would fall back into prior sinful practices.

To the Gentile Christians, the Jerusalem Council had already spoken and urged "that they abstain from things contaminated by idols and from fornication [*porneia*] and from what is strangled and from blood" (Acts 15:20). "It is scarcely less surprising here in [1 Thessalonians] to find that the Apostle needed to warn his recent converts, whose very adhesion to the Gospel involved a greater amount of self-denial than we can well realize" (Lightfoot).

Sexual immorality. Although often translated "fornication," *porneia* has a broader meaning and refers to illicit sexual intercourse. The word likely, too, includes all the grossly immoral practices taking place in the Roman and Greek cultures. Three thousand temple harlots practiced in Corinth. Because sexual sins were so common in each city, no one considered such acts as heinous sins against either God or against others. Sexual impurity was part of their cultic religious life and it surrounded and overwhelmed Christians as they attempted to live new lives in Christ. "Pagan religion did not demand sexual purity of its devotees, the gods and goddesses being grossly immoral. Priestesses were in the temples for the [sexual] service of the men who came" (Ritchie). Paul knew the Thessalonians could easily fall back into such a life. His words to the church at Ephesus are appropriate:

> But do not let immorality [*porneia*] or any impurity or greed even be named among you, as is proper among saints. (Eph. 5:3)

> And do not participate in the unfruitful deeds of darkness, but instead even expose them; for it is disgraceful even to speak of the things which are done by them in secret. But all things become visible when they are exposed by the light, for everything that becomes visible is light. (vv. 11–13)

> **4:4** that each of you know how to possess his own vessel in sanctification and honor,

That each of you know how to possess. *To know* (*oida*) caries the idea "to learn to know; for purity is not a momentary impulse, but a lesson, a habit" (Lightfoot).

Possess (*ktaomai*) can be translated "to procure for oneself, acquire, get," here, meaning to "gain control over his own body" (*BAG*). Almost all the Thessalonian readers would understand that Paul is referring to the matter of sexual sins and that he is expanding the prohibition that he began in verse 3.

Clearly, because of the temptations of the culture, the apostle is concerned lest any fall or even backslide into what they may have experienced before coming to Christ. "Self control in response to one's sexual desires, Paul taught, could and must be learned" (*BKC*).

His own vessel. *Vessel* (*skeuos,* "jar, dish") is used by many of the Greek writers (Philo, Plato) to describe the vessel as the instrument of the soul (Milligan). Some have thought Paul is here using the word to describe one's wife. Two verses may suggest that thought: "You husbands likewise, live with your wives in an understanding way, as with a weaker vessel, since she is a woman; and grant her honor" (1 Peter 3:7); "Let each man have his own wife, and let each woman have her own husband" (1 Cor. 7:2).

The majority of commentators, however, believe that it describes the believer's own physical body and that Paul is exhorting the Thessalonians to control it. That the vessel here is one's own physical being is supported by 2 Corinthians 4:7 where Paul writes about the great treasure of the cross of Christ: "We have this treasure in earthen vessels, that the surpassing greatness of the power may be of God and not from ourselves." "There can be no doubt that [Paul] employs the term vessel to mean body. . . . He would, therefore, have us keep our body pure from all uncleanness" (Calvin).

In sanctification and honor. "Sanctification" (*hagiasmos*) means "with holiness," considering the entire person as special for God's use. Paul speaks of sanctification as a positional truth that takes place at the moment of conversion: "Chosen you from the beginning for salvation through sanctification by the Spirit" (2 Thess. 2:13; also 1 Cor. 1:30; 1 Peter 1:2). Then he also teaches experiential sanctification, whereby the believer is to grow in cleanliness and holiness. In 4:3, he refers, in fact, to sanctification as including abstaining from sexual morality. In light of the over-sexed atmosphere of the pagan world, such abstention would be accomplished only by the miraculous power of God's Spirit: "For the fruit of the Spirit is . . . self-control" (Gal. 5:23).

Honor (*timee*) is related to *timios,* which is often translated as "precious," carrying the idea of being extremely valuable, such as marriage (Heb. 13:4), the blood of Christ (1 Peter 1:19), and the foundation stones of the new Jerusalem (Rev. 21:19). The body should not be debased or polluted, and "we should honour it as a noble work of God, to be employed for pure purposes"

(*Barnes*). Since the apostle is writing to the whole church, the directive in this verse is given to husbands and wives, and unmarried men and women.

Modern culture is slipping back into sexual openness in which anything is permissible and is displayed before the entire society. The impact upon young people is staggering.

4:5 not in lustful passion, like the Gentiles who do not know God;

Not in lustful passion, like the Gentiles. Regarding *in lustful passion* (*en pathei epithumias*), in this paragraph Paul uses three descriptions to paint a picture of sexual indiscretions: "sexual immorality" (v. 3); "lustful passion" (v. 5); and "impurity" (v. 7). The apostle knows the environment of Thessalonica and is doing everything he can to make the believers aware of the temptations surrounding them. He knows the destructive nature of sexual sin and how it can destroy marriages. The word *lustful* is sexual passion in the passive sense, an ungovernable force like a firestorm that begins all by itself. "Passion" is active desire that can be fed and further encouraged by the individual, "hence the combination: 'in passion of lust,' carried away by passion to which 'desire' (here in the evil sense of 'lust') eagerly consents" (Lenski).

In regard to Paul's use of the word *Gentiles* here, bear in mind that this assembly is made up mainly of Gentiles (*ta ethne*), but Paul now sees them as saints in Christ. Only a few times in his letters does he remind the believers they are Gentiles. Generally, he speaks to them as saints or with some other positive description. Romans 15–16, along with some other passages, stand as an exception. Here, Paul writes of the Macedonian Gentiles, who shared some material blessings with the poor saints in Jerusalem (15:26–27), and he writes also that the Gentile churches thanked God because he was spared from harm (16:3–4). Usually, Paul classifies humanity as (1) Jews, (2) Gentiles, and (3) believers in Christ.

Who do not know God. *Know* (*oida*) is a perfect active participle and could be translated "have [not] come to know" God or "have [not] arrived at a knowledge" of Him. The true God is foreign to the world as a whole. The divine revelation, coming through the Scriptures, was given first to the Jews. The nations were cut off from even being aware of the Lord of creation, and because of this, God gave them over to their sins: "And just as they [the Gentiles] did not see fit to acknowledge God any longer, God gave them over to a depraved mind, to do those things which are not proper" (Rom. 1:28 and vv. 24, 26).

4:6 and that no man transgress and defraud his brother in the matter because the Lord is the avenger in all these things, just as we also told you before and solemnly warned you.

And that no man transgress and defraud his brother in the matter. *Transgress* (*huperbaino*) and *defraud* (*pleonekteo*) might better be translated, with two present infinitives, "to infringe upon" (to go beyond) and "to take advantage of, outwit" (to take more, to overreach). Thus, "no one is to be infringing upon and taking advantage" of his brother in regard to sexual immorality. Can Christians wake up and find they are being dragged into a sinful situation that is about to ensnare them in deep and destructive sins, especially sexual? By using the present infinitives, it would seem that Paul is making such fraudulence a progressive action that has terrible consequences.

Paul also seems to imply here that a Christian may become a stumbling block to his fellow Christian and somehow bring about, and be at least partly responsible for, his or her temptation.

Because the Lord is the avenger in all these things. An "avenger" (*ekdikos*) is one who requites or brings about justice (*EDNT*). *Ekdidos* literally means "out avenge" and is related to the verb *ekdioko*, which means "to persecute vigorously." Both words are related to *dikaiosune*, translated "righteousness, justice." The context is still sexual transgressions. "Such sins are often practised in secret: the father or the husband does not know what is going on and his rights are being denied; he is being defrauded. But God knows, and he will prove to be the Avenger!" in both this life and at the bema judgment where the believer's works are to be tested (*NTC*).

We also told you before and solemnly warned you. This clause reveals clearly that Paul had spoken about these things when he had been with the Thessalonians. After their conversion, warnings in regard to sexual immorality were some of the first he gave. *Solemnly warned* (*diamarturomai,* aorist indicative) could also be translated "we completely testified" to you about this. "We do not know what prompted him to put in writing this admonition about judgment. Perhaps urgency required stern words" (*EBC*).

Robertson provides a summary: "The delicacy of Paul makes him refrain from plainer terms. . . . Modern men and women need to remember that God is the avenger for sexual wrong both in this life and the next" (Robertson).

4:7 For God has not called us for the purpose of impurity, but in sanctification.

For God has not called us. *Called* (*kaleo*), in its usual use by Paul, is the sovereign act of election whereby a believer is brought to salvation. Election relates to divine predestination, by which the Father draws unto Him those specifically called to salvation. Although He waits patiently for the "vessels of wrath prepared for destruction" (Rom. 9:22), they will not come to Him by their own will. Only the "vessels of mercy, which He prepared beforehand for glory" (v. 23) will respond and receive Christ. Although many today reject the doctrine of divine election, it has remained a glorious but mysterious truth of New Testament doctrine.

In the Thessalonian letters, Paul uses *called* to mean the divine, sovereign work of grace. In the early part of his Thessalonian letters, Paul writes that the believer should walk worthy of his or her calling (2:12). God, who calls us, is faithful, and He "also will bring it to pass" (5:24). In concluding his writing to the Thessalonians, Paul reminds them that "He called you through our gospel, that you may gain the glory of our Lord Jesus Christ" (2 Thess. 2:14).

For the purpose of impurity, but in sanctification. The apostle uses *sanctification* (*hagiasmos*) four times in these two letters (4:3, 4, 7; 2 Thess. 2:13). We are saved by the sanctifying work of the Holy Spirit but also are called to live a sanctified and pure life. Christianity is not only the final wondrous escape to eternal life, it is also the living of a life while here on earth. And that life should exemplify our Redeemer who bought us. "Holiness is to be the pervading element in which the Christian is to move" (Lightfoot).

Those who, having been called, have . . . not been inducted into a life of sexual impurity, but into a holy life (cf. 3:13; 4:3, 4). They now belong to a community with values different from those of "the heathen" (v. 5) among whom they formerly lived. (*EBC*)

4:8 Consequently, he who rejects this is not rejecting man but the God who gives His Holy Spirit to you.

Consequently, he who rejects this is not rejecting man. *Consequently* (*toigaroun*) is an unusual word, used only twice in the New Testament, here and in Hebrews 12:1. It introduces an inference from a preceding statement and can be translated "for that reason, then, therefore" (*EDNT*). With this word, Paul applies the logic of his case and brings to a conclusion with all of the best of his persuasion.

Rejects is a present active participle of *atheteo,* which is a compound word related to *tithemi,* (to place), and *"a,"* the negative. It may then read, "do not be displacing [or rejecting] what I am saying about impurity." Paul is thus using strong language, perhaps to stave off trouble before it develops. He sees the dangers, knows the temptations, and is afraid that lustful sins that are practiced in the dark may return and trap some of those in the Thessalonian church as it may have done before. He is fearful his converts will fall and then try to justify their licentiousness and not hesitate to set aside their God (Robertson).

The God who gives. The verb is a present active participle of *didomi* and is translated by some as "the Giver."

His Holy Spirit. The apostle reminds the Thessalonian church that if some are rejecting the truth about impurity and sanctification, they are not rejecting the teacher of the Word; indeed, their rejection is of the Lord. He then takes his persuasion a step further, reminding them that God has given them His Holy Spirit. This actually reads, "The Spirit of Him, the Holy One." Since God the Father is Holy, so likewise are the other two persons of the Godhead—the Son and the Spirit.

The Spirit takes up permanent residence within the believer at the time of salvation: "Having also believed, you were sealed in Him [Christ] with the Holy Spirit of promise, who is given as a pledge of our inheritance, with a view to the redemption of God's own possession, to the praise of His glory" (Eph. 1:13b–14).

But the indwelling Holy Spirit, by whom we are sealed for the day of redemption, may be grieved by our sins (4:30–32) and even quenched (1 Thess. 5:19) by our blatant and open transgressions. Uncleanness is the very opposite to the work of sanctification that is to be carried out by God's own Spirit.

He dwells within, as within a temple, and therefore we should be very careful not to defile it. Believers are "laid under obligations to live in the Spirit, and to walk after him, and not after the flesh" (Gill). "This gift of the Spirit leaves you in a different position with regard to God from that which you held before. It is a witness in your souls against impurity. It is a token that He has consecrated you to Himself" (Lightfoot).

2. Brotherly Issues (4:9–10)

In these verses Paul wants to return to the subject of maintaining love between the believers. Although mentioned earlier (3:12), Paul felt the subject needed revisiting. Because he knows of the trials the assembly is facing, he strongly exhorts them to close ranks and to not fall out of love with one another. Church factions soon developed in the early congregations. Carnality, with jealousy, envy, and bickering (1 Cor. 3:1–4; Eph. 4:30–32) would soon raise their ugly heads within the local church bodies. Paul understands Christian "human nature," realizing that lack of spiritual maturity would create divisions.

> **4:9** Now as to the love of the brethren, you have no need for anyone to write to you, for you yourselves are taught by God to love one another;

Now as to the love of the brethren, you have no need for anyone to write to you. In a sense, this sentence reflects only a slight concern and a gentle reminder. The apostle wants to keep this church on track concerning what they already know. *Now (de)* shows a clear shift in subject, while the flow of the thoughts of Paul's heart continues from the beginning of the letter.

Love of the brethren is actually a compound noun, *phila* and *delphia,* meaning, of course "brotherly love." The city by the same name was founded in the region of Lydia by Attalus II Philadelphus, sometime between 189 and 138 B.C., before his death. John addresses the Philadelphian church in Revelation 3:7–13.

By saying "no one needs to write to you" Paul probably means that this message does not need to be repeated, as if they had not heard it before. But he is likely demonstrating subtlety here because he *is* repeating himself on this subject. By being so tactful, "he is the better prepared to point out certain deficiencies. Let it be borne in mind that the man who is writing is the one who told others that their speech should ever be gracious, seasoned with salt

(Col. 4:6). . . . In Classical Greek [love of the brethren] means love to the brother by birth, in the New Testament [it] always denotes love to the brother in Christ" (*NTC*).

For you yourselves are taught by God to love one another. This reads literally, "For you are the Godtaught ones into the love of one another." "Taught by God" is a compound word (*theodidaktos*) apparently created by Paul and used only in this verse in his writings. In Classical Greek dozens of compound words begin with *theos* (God), so the practice of combining such ideas was not uncommon (L&S). This practice is also used in later Christian writings. "Godtaught" is a plural noun that demonstrates the close connection between the instructor and the pupil, that loving one another is God-originated teaching that instructed the Thessalonians about loving each other. "For you yourselves are divinely taught already" or "For you yourselves (as well as we) are taught of God" (Ellicott). "Godtaught" points to a divine communication. But even more, it points to a Godly relationship established between God and other believers (Milligan).

In "to love one another," *to love* is a present infinitive of *agapao*, expressing the result and issue of God's teaching, and carrying the thought "to produce mutual love" (Alford). Paul is saying, you "have been so schooled by God as to love one another" (Ellicott). Before the infinitive *to love,* and almost never translated, is the preposition *eis* meaning "into," which enforces the idea of results (Lenski).

> **4:10** for indeed you do practice it toward all the brethren who are in all Macedonia. But we urge you, brethren, to excel still more,

For indeed you do practice it toward all the brethren who are in all Macedonia. Paul is speaking about the Thessalonians' love one for another, but includes in their circle of brotherly love the churches beyond Thessalonica, and includes "all Macedonia," their neighbors living in Philippi, Berea, and other nearby cities.

In the period of the early church, members often traveled between congregations. They shared letters, exchanged teachings, and collected donations for those in distress. Traveling Christians knew believers in each town and stayed with them on their journeys. The assembly at Thessalonica, although under persecution, was hospitable to all living in the region (see 1:7).

But we urge you, brethren, to excel still more. Although the grammar is structured just slightly differently, the apostle is repeating what he wrote in verse 1b. Paul commends but then encourages the believers to mature spiritually beyond their present state. "Paul urges them to increase their feelings and expressions of love for their brothers and sisters, since Christian love should never become complacent, as though a certain level of love were sufficient to please God" (*NIGTC*). "There was still room for improvement, perhaps in the persistence and consistency of their love" (*BKC*).

3. Behavioral Issues (4:11–12)

Although not quite a summary, these verses offer in condensed form practical application of behavioral principles. Lenski calls this a further admonition that is in line with Paul's urgings in the verses above to abound more and more in love.

> **4:11** and to make it your ambition to lead a quiet life and attend to your own business and work with your hands, just as we commanded you;

In this verse the apostle uses four present active infinitives (two are deponent) to describe how the Thessalonians are to present themselves to the world.

To make it your ambition. A rare word, *philotimeomai* is used but two other times in the New Testament (Rom. 15:20; 2 Cor. 5:9) and means "to consider it an honor, make it one's ambition" (*EDNT*). The word is a compound, *philo* (to love, be fond of) and *time* (honor). In other words, "consider it an honor." Paul is attempting to lift the dignity of the Thessalonian church. They are not to grovel in the persecution coming upon them, but they are to lift their heads high in trust of the Lord.

To lead a quiet life. One word, *hesuchazo,* characterizes this phrase, and it means to live in "rest, peace, tranquility." Here and in 2 Thessalonians 3:2 it carries the idea of "assurance in eschatological expectations . . . , which make[s] one free for daily work" (*EDNT*). Although it cannot be proven, some commentators believe that the Thessalonians were unsettled because they believed the Lord's return was near. A better interpretation would be that Paul is urging them not to agitate the delicate balance of witnessing unashamedly while at the same time causing as little suffering as possible. They were to witness of the Lord but then go on minding their own affairs.

Attend to your own business. The word *prasso* means "to take care of, accomplish, be situated" (*EDNT*). Most Bible scholars think that Paul is saying "mind your own affairs" or "take care of your own business." Second Thessalonians 3:6–15 indicates that some Thessalonian Christians grew lazy in their daily work. Some commentators speculate that the church misunderstood or misapplied the truth of the Lord's return and began to simply sit down and wait for His arrival. Other commentators think the Thessalonian congregation took advantage of the generosity of the Macedonian Christians in their giving of financial aid and made no effort to support themselves (*EBC*). For whatever reason, the peace was broken and the name of Christ might possibly become tainted among the community of the Gentiles.

And work with your hands. If some in the assembly had been previously well off, this injunction to work may imply that they had lost their position of wealth and now had to perform manual labor in order to survive. Or the apostle may have been telling them to carry their own load and continue to do a fair day's work. "Christians must never evade their daily responsibilities under the pretense of proclaiming or preparing for Christ's return. To do so is to distort this great hope" (*EBC*).

Just as we commanded you. *Parangello* suggests "to command with authority." The instruction to work refers to charges that Paul had to mention previously, and he has no hesitation to repeat his injunction. "No man understands fully the blessings which God has bestowed on him, if he has hands to work and will not work" (*Barnes*).

4:12 so that you will behave properly toward outsiders and not be in any need.

So that you will behave properly toward outsiders and not be in any need. Paul's major concern was how the unbeliever would perceive Christians who were not laboring for themselves. He employs two present subjunctives to stress his point: "That you might be going about [*peripateo*] . . . and that you might have no need." The adverb *properly* (*euschemonos*) carries the thought of the noun "propriety, decency." It could even carry the idea of "noble, respectable, or proper." By adding *toward outsiders,* Paul, some commentators believe, is referring to business dealings with the Gentiles. The Christians should be self-sufficient and not dependent upon others. "[Proper behavior] includes honest financial transactions, but a good deal more. People outside the churches have a right to watch the conduct of professing Christians in business" (Robertson).

Though some believers may not have been able to work, Paul is urging, at the least, personal responsibility. He was not, however, trying to foster a fierce spirit of independence or false pride. "[Responsible] behavior also wins the respect of Christians; people appreciate those who do not take advantage of them" (*BKC*).

This verse dignifies manual labour. The Greeks despised manual work and had slaves to do it for them. But the Jews held it in esteem; every Jewish boy was taught a trade regardless of his family's wealth. There is nothing more honourable and commendable than a man doing a full day's work to provide for himself and his family, and dedicating any surplus of his earnings to God for His work and for helping the poor and needy. (Ritchie)

B. The Rapture: What It Means "to Meet" the Lord (4:13–18)

In this section, Paul gives more details about the Rapture of the Church than he does in any of his writings. It is apparent that he taught on this subject earlier in Thessalonica, but here he repeats some of his explanation and answers other questions that had arisen since he was with them. Most covenant or amillennial theologians assume this section is dealing with the second coming of Christ. Often they make no comment about the reference to the Church going up to meet Christ in the air, whereas the doctrine of His second coming pictures Him returning to earth to rule and reign. The Second Coming is not in view in 1 Thessalonians 4:13. Walvoord writes,

Nothing in the Old Testament encouraged any believer to anticipate translation at the time of the coming of Christ, or to expect reunion with loved ones with the comfort that this would afford by any imminent coming of Christ to take them to Himself. Once again the truth is given as a new revelation in the New Testament relating to the Church as the body of Christ.[1]

Walvoord shows eleven contrasts between the Rapture and the second coming of Christ (pp. 275–76):

- At the time of the Rapture the saints meet Christ in the air, while at the Second Coming, Christ returns to the Mount of Olives to meet the saints on earth.
- At the time of the Rapture the Mount of Olives is unchanged, while at the Second Coming it divides and a valley is formed to the east of Jerusalem (Zech. 14:4–5).
- At the Rapture living saints are translated, while no saints are translated in connection with the second coming of Christ to the earth.
- At the Rapture the saints go to heaven, while at the Second Coming the saints remain in the earth without translation.
- At the time of the Rapture the world is not yet judged and continues in sin, while at the Second Coming, the world is judged and righteousness is established on the earth.
- The translation of the Church is pictured as deliverance before the day of wrath, while the Second Coming is followed by the deliverance of those who have come to believe in Christ during the Tribulation.
- The Rapture is described as imminent, while the Second Coming is preceded by definite signs.
- The translation of living believers is a truth revealed only in the New Testament, while the Second Coming with its attendant events is a prominent doctrine of both Testaments.
- The Rapture concerns only the saved, while the Second Coming deals with both saved and unsaved.
- At the Rapture Satan is not bound, while at the Second Coming Satan is bound and cast into the abyss.
- No unfulfilled prophecy stands between the Church and the Rapture, while many signs must be fulfilled before the Second Coming.
- In neither Testament does any passage that deals with the resurrection of saints at the Second Coming mention translation of living saints at the same time.[2]

Some other comparisons can be added:

- At the Second Coming, Christ appears as the Son of Man (Matt. 24:30), which is a messianic kingly title, not a church title. At the Rapture, Jesus arrives as the Head of the Church to receive to Him those alive in the body of Christ (1 Thess. 4:15) and those who have fallen asleep "in Jesus" (v. 14), that is, the dead "in Christ" (v. 16).
- At the Second Coming, Christ appears in the clouds (Matt. 24:30) while at the Rapture, believers and those resurrected are caught up into the clouds (1 Thess. 4:17).
- At the Second Coming, the elect (Matt. 24:31), who are the faithful slaves (v. 45), are brought before the Son of Man, the King, who comes to reign on earth, and they are rewarded and put in charge of His possessions (v. 47). At the Rapture, those alive and the resurrected are "caught up" in the clouds to meet the Lord in the air (1 Thess. 4:17). Nowhere is He called "the king" on this occasion.
- At the Second Coming, the Lord returns to establish the reign of peace, the kingdom of God, at the end of the Tribulation (Luke 21:31). At the Rapture, the Lord comes back before the Day of the Lord, the Tribulation (1 Thess. 5:2).
- Before the Second Coming, cosmic events herald His return (Luke 21:25), whereas no such events occur before the Rapture.
- At the Second Coming, Christ sits on His earthly throne and gathers the nations for judgment (Matt. 25:31–32). At the Rapture, the Church saints are caught up with the Lord and go upwards into the clouds.
- At the Second Coming, the elect are gathered together by angels from the four corners of the earth. At the Rapture, there is no earthly "gathering" but simply a going up into the clouds to be with the Lord in heaven.
- At the Second Coming, a great trumpet sounds and many angels are employed for the gathering of the elect to the King on earth (Matt. 24:31), whereas at the Rapture, the voice of the archangel (Michael) is heard and the trumpet of God sounds (1 Thess. 4:16), calling the believers upward.
- Before the Second Coming, false christs will fool many (Matt. 24:24), but the Bible indicates no attempt prior to the Rapture to institute a false heavenly gathering. Such would certainly not be credible.

Thus, the evidence indicates a pretribulational rapture of the Church. All other readings confuse the text of Matthew 24–25 and try to place the Church in the Tribulation somewhere after Revelation 5. Other positions come and go, gain popularity for a period, then subside. A pretribulational rapture accounts for all the teachings revealed in Scripture.

Another important teaching that appears with almost all the rapture passages is that of imminence. All of the writing disciples teach their particular readers that the blessed Rapture could take them to glory. By definition, imminence means that there is nothing hindering the Rapture from taking place right now. And "now" could have come even upon those early Christians in the New Testament church. For them, the Rapture was a blessed anticipation.

In Titus 2:13, Paul almost shouts his excitement about the possibility of the Rapture. From Greek, the passage could read, "[We are] excitedly expecting continually the joyous prospect, even [the] glorious appearance of our great God, even [our] Savior, Christ Jesus!" (author's translation).

Excitedly expecting continually is often translated simply "looking for" (*prosdechomai*). And indeed, the present tense makes this "expecting" a continual hope: "This expectation [is] an abiding state and posture." The word also has the force of "welcome, wait for, expect." The "blessed hope" might be translated "the joyous anticipation." Thus, there is no question about this expectation. It is going to come about, and it produces a great joyousness that looks forward to ultimate redemption. "This describes the great expectancy which is the ruling and prevailing thought in the lives of men looking for their Lord's return."[3]

> **4:13** But we do not want you to be uninformed, brethren, about those who are asleep, that you may not grieve, as do the rest who have no hope.

But we do not want you to be uninformed, brethren. Paul uses a present tense verb *we want* (*thelo,* "to wish, desire, want") and a present infinitive (*agnoeo,* "to not know") to describe his concern in regard to their knowledge about what happens when the believer dies: "We don't want you to continue on not knowing." The wording of the text indicates that Paul had taught this truth some weeks or months earlier, but the Thessalonians, being new converts, evidently did not comprehend all that he said. Some commentators also believe that a number of believers had died and that this brought on the questions and concerns about what happens after death.

It must be remembered that, apart from a lot of mythology and superstition, the pagan world had no rational hope for eternal life. At the same time, because the gods were mortal-like and sinful, many thinking and educated people began to question the religion of Greece and Rome. Thus, the thought of death was frightening because pagan religions offered no reasonable answers in regard to the hereafter.

Paul, Silas, and Timothy gave solid, believable answers about the afterlife from both the Old Testament and revelation. The apostles had taught about the Day of the Lord and about the Rapture, but how did all this relate to the death of a saint and the issue of the resurrection?

Those who are asleep. Lightfoot translates the phrase as "lying asleep." The Greek word *koimao* (present passive participle) is used for *asleep* and can be translated "those who are being put to sleep." Sleep is a common way of picturing the death of a believer. To describe the death of the saints, Jesus used the word *sleep* on the occasion when He was called to the home of a young girl who was described as having died (Mark 5:35). But the Lord commented that she but slept and He raised her up before her parents and the disciples (vv. 41–42). Lazarus had clearly died and had been in the tomb four days, but Christ insisted "Lazarus has fallen asleep" (John 11:11). The Lord used the restoring of this friend, and brother of Mary and Martha, to illustrate the meaning of death and resurrection (vv. 24–27). The death of Stephen, the first recorded martyr, is also described as a falling asleep: being stoned by a wild crowd, Stephen called upon the Lord Jesus and "fell asleep" (Acts 7:60). Believers in Corinth who were disrespectful of the Lord's table were said to have been made weak, sick, with some of them falling asleep (1 Cor. 11:30).

This last example illustrates a general principle: Even those in Christ who willfully and continually violate known New Testament spiritual or moral principles, may be put to sleep and called home to glory. This doctrine, however, needs to be taught with great care, because the death of saints comes for a variety of reasons, only one of which may be a judgment of life style.

That you may not grieve, as do the rest who have no hope. *Grieve* (*lupeo*), as a passive, means "to feel pain, be sad" (*EDNT*). Here, the verb is a present subjunctive. Paul is writing, "You should not be going around griev- ing" as do the pagans. Several views are offered on the subject of grieving. Some commentators believe that "the survivors were distressed by the fear that these [who died] would have to occupy a position secondary to those who lived until the advent of the Lord" (Nicoll). Others believe that the Thessa- lonians were concerned that their relatives and friends might have to wait in an intermediate state before going to the Lord, a concern derived from pagan teaching.

A popular pagan belief, for instance, taught that souls are led by the god Hermes to the depths of the earth to await an answer concerning their eternal destiny. In Greek mythology, souls go to hades, from where they then cross the river Styx, conducted by the boatman Charon, and come to the court of judgment. The guilty are sent to the left, down a path that leads to dark Tartarus for punishment. The pious go to the right, to the Elysian Fields, a place of brightness and beauty.[4] Thus, shades of teachings from other religions and cultures placed a great gloom over the prospect of death. The Greeks had a saying that it is best not to be born and second best to die young. Clearly, then, Paul had much to explain and much to overcome!

"Who have no hope" would better read "the ones not possessing a hope." A great pall of hopelessness hangs over the hopeless and no revelation gives comfort except that of New Testament teachings.

> **4:14** For if we believe that Jesus died and rose again, even so God will bring with Him those who have fallen asleep in Jesus.

For if we believe that Jesus died and rose again. *For if* (*ei gar*) is a con- dition of the first class subjunctive that affirms reality. It should read, "Since we believe" or "Since this is true that we believe." The Thessalonian church believes in both the death and resurrection of Jesus. Unlike some at Corinth (1 Cor. 15:17–18), who questioned the Resurrection, the Thessalonians did not. "Paul assumes their faith in it and argues from it" (Nicoll).

Even so God will bring with Him those who have fallen asleep in Jesus. Actually, the article *the* is presented before God (*theos*) and makes His name emphatic—"Even so the God . . .." He "is the one true God who, as the raiser- up of Jesus, will raise up His people along with Him, cf. 1 Cor. vi. 14, 2 Cor. iv. 14" (Milligan).

Will bring is a future active indicative of *ago* that is normally translated "to lead." "The words 'God will bring' point to a continuing movement heavenward after the meeting in the air (v. 17), until the arrival in the Father's presence (3:13; cf. John 14:2, 3)" (*EBC*).

In Jesus can literally be translated (*dia*) "through" or "by means of" Jesus. It is amphibolous in position and can be taken either with "those who have fallen asleep" (that are fallen asleep in or through Jesus), or with "He will bring" (as through Jesus with God). The first reading is probably better (Robertson).

Those who have fallen asleep is an aorist passive participle of *koimao*. It could read "those who were made to sleep."

Putting it all together, then, it would read, "Those who have 'fallen asleep' in Jesus, God will bring with him (1 Thess. 4:14) through the resurrection (cf. v. 16), but at the time of the *parousia* of Jesus" (*EDNT*), or "stated in full the argument would run: 'so also, we believe that those who fell asleep through Jesus, and in consequence were raised by God through Him, will God bring with Him'" (Milligan).

The sleep the apostle writes about is the sleep "of the body in the earth until it is resurrected, changed into a glorious body, and reunited with the soul (1 Cor. 15:35–37; 2 Cor. 5:1–9)" (*BKC*). It is in 1 Corinthians 15:51–54 where Paul writes so much about the body being changed from perishable to imperishable, an event that occurs at the Resurrection/Rapture. Those asleep will be given their new bodies and those who are alive will be instantly transformed and also given their new bodies at the same time as those who had previously died. This instant change that takes place at the Rapture, Paul calls a mystery because it was not mentioned before in the Old Testament. He writes,

> Behold, I tell you a mystery; we shall not all sleep, but we shall all be changed, in a moment, in the twinkling of an eye, at the last trumpet; for the trumpet will sound, and the dead will be raised imperishable, and we shall be changed. For this perishable must put on the imperishable, and this mortal must put on immortality. But when this perishable will have put on the imperishable, and this mortal will have put on immortality, then will come about the saying that is written, "Death is swallowed up in victory." (1 Cor. 15:51–54)

> **4:15** For this we say to you by the word of the Lord, that we who are alive and remain until the coming of the Lord, shall not precede those who have fallen asleep.

For this we say to you by the word of the Lord. Paul reinforces what he is saying by claiming direct authority from the Lord. He restates his claim of apostolic powers in reference to this most important doctrine, the Resurrection/ Rapture. On this issue of authority he reminded the rebellious Corinthians, "In no respect was I inferior to the most eminent apostles, even though I am a nobody" (2 Cor. 12:11).

For (*gar*) "ushers in the explanation or elucidation," that is, "in order that you may fully understand" (Lenski).

This is a demonstrative pronoun, neuter accusative singular. Thereby, Paul places all he is about to say into a singular framework, forming a total package of truth.

By the word of the Lord. Paul claims divine inspiration when he adds "by the word [*logos,* singular] of the Master [*kurios*]." *Word* is also notably singular and may be translated "by the authority" of the Master who is in charge of all things!" The subject will be the Resurrection ("those who have fallen asleep") and the Rapture ("we who are alive") both of which subjects, for the Church saints, cannot be separated. Thus, they are, in a sense, treated as one. "It is generally concluded that Paul had received further specific revelation regarding the instantaneous transformation of the living without their first dying" (Lenski).

That we who are alive and remain until the coming of the Lord. This clause could read, "because [*hoti*] we the ones who are living [*zao,* present active participle]." This further supports the doctrine of the imminent return of Christ.

Without doubt, the early church and the apostles hoped for Christ's soon return. The use of the terms "we, you, and us" are proof that the Rapture could have happened in Paul's own generation. . . . since it did not come upon them, we do not question their hope nor the Lord's revelation about the doctrine itself. It simply means that it is yet to come.[5]

And remain (*perileipomai*) is also a present active participle and can be translated "remain behind" or "those who are left over" (Ellicott). Twice Paul uses *perileipomai,* here and in verse 17. The phrase may read "we, the living, who are left behind" (*EDNT*). The left behind are those who have not died. They are still here, though others have passed on into glory. All of us living today would be the left behind, the remaining, waiting for death to transport us into the presence of Christ. We would also be longing for the Rapture to change our bodies and remove us instantly from this earth.

Until the coming of the Lord. *Coming* is the controversial word *parousia.* (See the study of *parousia* in 2:19.) *Parousia* must be interpreted in context. The second coming (*parousia*) of Christ refers to His arrival upon the earth for the kingdom reign. But in the context of Thessalonians it is a reference to the Rapture coming. Christ's coming at the Rapture does not imply that He will remain upon the earth. The believers will suddenly be caught away, following the resurrection of those who lie in the grave.

Shall not precede those who have fallen asleep. *Precede* (*phthano,* aorist active subjunctive) is sometimes translated "prevent" in old English. The word is better translated "to come or go before, to anticipate." The idea here is that "those living won't go first," or "we shall certainly have no advantage over those who have fallen asleep" (*NIGTC*). "The dead in Christ shall have precedence. There are two distinct groups, those that are alive when the Lord comes and those that have died. . . . The raising and changing will all take place in a moment of time, but the order is that the dead will have priority, they will be raised first" (Ritchie). "From this clause we can see that the Thessalonians feared that their dead would lose out on the chance to be assumed to heaven at the time of the *parousia*" (*NIGTC*).

Ellicott summarizes, "'We shall certainly not get the start of them that sleep;' i.e., 'if anything, we shall be behind them; they will rise first.'"

> **4:16** For the Lord Himself will descend from heaven with a shout, with the voice of the archangel, and with the trumpet of God; and the dead in Christ shall rise first.

For the Lord Himself will descend from heaven with a shout. It is important to notice that, when Jesus comes, He comes to resurrect His own, "the dead in Christ." This dispensation is unique in that all believers of this age form the spiritual body of Christ. Though Christ's sacrifice will be applied to all past generations, in God's economic working of things the believers of this period have a different function and ministry. Contrary to the past, all who are saved now are baptized into one body, the body of Christ by one Spirit (1 Cor. 12:12–13). When this trumpet sounds, "the dead will be raised imperishable, and we shall be changed" (15:52b).

The personal pronoun *Himself,* (*autos*), is here used like a reflexive but the clause could read "Because He the Lord . . .." "Not by any intermediate agency, but in His own person He will come" (Lightfoot).

In the phrase *will descend from heaven, katabaino* (future active indicative) means "to come down." Heaven (*ouranos*) here is in the singular, but of the 274 times the word is used, 91 times it is in the plural, often with a preposition (*en ouranois,* in the "heavenlies"). Although not absolute, when in the plural, *ouranos* generally refers to the abode or dwelling place of God. This of course is but the humanlike way of describing the place of rule and enthronement of the heavenly Father. His presence is certainly not confined to any one location in the universe. Sometimes in the singular, *ouranos* may be referring to only the nearest upper region, the sky, thus, "Jesus will come down from the sky."

In *with a shout, shout* (*keleuo,* "summon") is a classical and a military term meaning to command, and is used for the purpose of gathering together. It has been used as a word of encouragement for rowers to keep up the pace. The word speaks of a "summons to all, both living and dead, to meet their Lord" (Lightfoot). Christ comes for His Church as a Conqueror.

In the present connection it is clearly the command of the Lord, as he leaves heaven, for the dead to arise. . . . Just as . . . now the voice of the Son of God is life-giving, causing those who are spiritually dead to be quickened . . . , so also when he comes back "all who are in the tombs will hear his voice and will come out" (see John 5:28). The command, therefore, is definitely his own, proceeding from his lips. It is not a command issued to him, but an order given by him. Leaving heaven in his human nature, he utters his voice, and immediately the souls of the redeemed also leave, and are quickly reunited with their bodies, which, thus restored to life, arise gloriously. (*NTC*)

With the voice of the archangel. *Archangel,* as has been mentioned, is probably a reference to Michael (Jude 9). "Scripture mentions only one archangel, namely Michael" (Lenski). Yet it may be noted that no article appears before the name in Greek. It could read "with [*en*] the voice of an archangel." As already shown, it is often speculated that Michael is the only archangel, but that may not be so. Michael is one "of the leaders of the heavenly host" (Lightfoot).

With the trumpet of God. As with *archangel,* there is no article before *trumpet.* It can read "with [*en*] a trumpet [belonging to] God." The absence of the article in the two phrases stresses the quality of the nouns (Lenski). Though the final goal of the Church saints is to be with Christ in His earthly kingdom reign, our joining to Him comes at the Rapture. Although 1 Corinthians 15 mentions the kingdom, the chapter actually focuses on the Resurrection and the "change" that takes place when "the last trumpet" is sounded (v. 52). At this trumpet, those who sleep in Jesus (v. 18) will be awakened and changed. This trumpet belongs to God, although the passage does not state who blows it. God will appoint an angelic being to sound it on that solemn occasion, but God Himself will not necessarily sound it (*Barnes*). But without question, it awakens and calls home the Church saints, those who belong to Him. Note how Paul emphasizes this event that closes the Church dispensation: "Those who have fallen asleep in Christ" (v. 18); in this life "we have hoped in Christ" (v. 19); Christ "the first fruits of those who are asleep" (v. 20); "in Christ all shall be made alive" (v. 22); "those who are Christ's at His coming" (v. 23); "the victory through our Lord Jesus Christ" (v. 57).

And the dead in Christ shall rise first. Some commentators speculate that the Thessalonians thought their loved ones would be left behind. Paul assures them that the saints who have already passed on actually rise in the Rapture before the living. Their souls are joined to their new immortal bodies and they are transformed to receive a body like Christ's. "We know that, if He should appear, we shall be like Him, because we shall see Him just as He is" (1 John 3:2b).

4:17 Then we who are alive and remain shall be caught up to-gether with them in the clouds to meet the Lord in the air, and thus we shall always be with the Lord.

Then we who are alive and remain. *We who are alive and remain* is re-peated from verse 15 with the same grammatical construction. Paul felt a rep-etition was needed to reinforce that the living saints follow the resurrected. For some reason the Thessalonians must have been expressing great fear over this issue. Either they did not understand the doctrine of the Rapture when they first heard it or, after the apostles left, questions occurred that called for clarification. Most commentators maintain that some believers must have died and this prompted the concern.

Shall be caught up together with them in the clouds. *Caught up* (*harpazo*) is a technical term that well describes the doctrine of the Rapture. The Latin word *rapio* is used to describe the word in English. Opponents of the doctrine of the Rapture argue that the word *rapture* is not in the Bible. Neither, however, is the word *trinity* in the Bible, yet both words apply to what the Bible teaches on these subjects.

Harpazo is a dramatic word that implies "to snatch, seize, take suddenly and vehemently" or "to steal, carry off, drag away" as by thieves or wild ani-mals snatching prey. It can also refer to rescuing someone from danger or snatching one out of a raging fire (*BAG*). Related words such as *harpage* and *harpax* refer in a negative sense to evil men who are like "ravening" wolves (Matt. 7:15), and also to "extortion" (23:25). Calvin translates the word "car-ried up."

Harpazo itself is used to describe violent men who take what they want "by force" (Matt. 11:12): the wicked one who "snatches away" the good seed (13:19); the wolf who "snatches away" the sheep (John 10:12); no one can "snatch" the sheep from the hand of the Son (v. 28) or from the hand of the Father (v. 29). Other uses of *harpazo* are the Spirit of the Lord "snatched away" Philip from the presence of the Ethiopian eunuch (Acts 8:39); Paul was "caught up" to the third heaven (2 Cor. 12:2) and "caught up" into Paradise (v. 4); some doubters God will have mercy on and will be "snatching" them out of the fire (Jude 23). And finally, *harpazo* is used to refer to the Messiah after His resurrection, called by John the "male child," as "caught up" to God and to His throne (Rev. 12:5).

For those who are resurrected and for those who are raptured, a real body is given. It is impervious to death and will last eternally, and yet it is an actual body. Some of the older commentators envision the new body to be "spiritualized" or immaterial (Ellicott). But this is not so. Because Christ is a life-giving spirit (1 Cor. 15:45), the new body will be spiritual (v. 46), energized and supported by Christ's resurrected power. "Spiritual" does not mean that this body is an apparition or ghostlike; it will, however, be imperishable and immortal (v. 53).

To meet the Lord in the air. Going up into the sky, into the air (*aera*), is an unmistakable description. Jesus is not coming down to establish His kingdom nor to judge men on earth. The Church saints are going upward. The reason seems to be clearly stated in 5:9—to escape the coming wrath or Tribulation that falls upon the earth. *To meet* is actually a prepositional phrase—"into [*eis*] a meeting" (*apantesis*) with the Lord. The word implies a nonhostile meeting, a civic, public welcome to rulers upon their arrival at a city (*EDNT*). It means also a "going toward."

And thus we shall always be with the Lord. With *and thus* (*kai houtos*) *and so,* Paul sets forth the results of the miracle of the Rapture. In Greek it reads, "And so always [*pantote*] together with the Lord, we shall ourselves be [*eimi,* present middle indicative]." "This rapture of the saints (both risen and changed) is a glorious climax to Paul's argument of consolation. . . . This is the outcome, to be forever with the Lord" (Robertson).

4:18 Therefore comfort one another with these words.

Therefore comfort one another with these words. *Comfort* (*parakaleo,* present active imperative) or "be calling alongside, be counseling, consoling" here, as in almost all of the Rapture passages, provides a practical, moral, and spiritual purpose for the teaching. Some commentators criticize the doctrine of the Rapture as encouraging escapism or a belief in "pie in the sky by and by." But such is not the case. Here, the apostle sees the Rapture as spiritual comfort for those who especially struggle through the heavy trials of life. Ellicott says the Rapture is balm for sorrow. "What bereaved Christian has not found this true?" (Ellicott). "Repeat these very words to one another, and you will find the comfort."

Study Questions

1. What potential problems could Paul be alluding to in verses 1–8?
2. Do you believe that these problems were already taking place in the congregation or that Paul is simply warning the Thessalonians of such temptations?
3. To what has God called believers (v. 7)?
4. How does Paul want this church to present itself to the world (vv. 11–12)?
5. Why were some in this church grieving (vv. 13–15)?
6. Discuss in detail how the Rapture of the Church is different than the Second Coming (vv. 13–18).

CHAPTER NINE

Reason for the Rapture

C. What it Means to Escape the Day of the Lord (5:1–11)

In this section Paul describes the importance of the Rapture. He argues that the Church will not face the horrors of the Day of the Lord. Prophecy scholar Arnold Fruchtenbaum characterizes the Day of the Lord:

> The most common biblical term for the seven years of Tribulation in both testaments is the *Day of Jehovah,* or the *Day of the Lord.* There are many who use the term, the Day of the Lord, to apply to both the Tribulation and the Messianic Kingdom. This is generally based on the assumption that the phrases, the Day of the Lord and "that day," are synonymous. While it is true that the expression, that day, has a wide meaning that includes both the Tribulation and the Messianic Kingdom, in those passages where the actual phrase, the Day of the Lord (Jehovah) is used, they never refer to the Millennium, but always to the Tribulation, . . .
>
> There are five passages [in the Old Testament] that directly relate the Day of the Lord to Israel. (1) Ezekiel 13:1–7 describes the Day of Jehovah in relationship to the false prophets in the tribulation. (2) Joel 2:1–11 describes the Day of Jehovah as a time of darkness and invasion for the people of Israel. (3) Joel 3:14–17 describes the Day of Jehovah as a time of refuge for Israel. (4) Amos 5:18–20 describes the Day of Jehovah as a time of darkness for the Jewish people. (5) Zephaniah 1:7–13 describes the Day of Jehovah as being especially severe for the city of Jerusalem.[1]

Pentecost outlines the horror of the Day of the Lord:

From these Scriptures it is inescapable that the nature or character of this period is that of wrath (Zeph. 1:15, 18; 1 Thess. 1:10; 5:9; Rev. 6:16–17; 11:18; 14:10, 19; 15:1, 7; 16:1, 19), judgment (Rev. 14:7; 15:4; 16:5, 7; 19:2), indignation (Isa. 26:20–21; 34:1–3), trial (Rev. 3:10), trouble (Jer. 30:7; Zeph. 1:14–15; Dan. 12:1), destruction (Joel 1:15; 1 Thess. 5:3), darkness (Joel 2:2; Amos 5:18; Zeph. 1:14–18), desolation (Dan. 9:27; Zeph. 1:14–15), overturning (Isa. 24:1–4, 19–21), punishment (Isa. 24:20–21). No passage can be found to alleviate to any degree whatsoever the severity of this time that shall come upon the earth.[2]

The Tribulation is revealed in the prophecy of Daniel's Seventieth Week, appearing in Daniel 9:24–27. The Lord told Daniel that there would be seventy weeks (calculated as four hundred and ninety years) in God's special dealings with the nation of Israel. An extensive and detailed study shows that four hundred and eighty-three of those years have been accomplished up to the week of Christ's final rejection and crucifixion. The final week of seven years (the seventieth week) is still to come and is commonly termed the Tribulation.

As history bears out, the sixty-nine weeks have run their course, the Messiah was killed, and Jerusalem was destroyed. But what has not taken place is the final seven years (one "week") of God's special dealings with Israel. These final seven years are yet future but will not begin until the covenant between Israel and the Antichrist is signed.[3]

Here in 5:1–3, Paul states that the Day of the Lord will strike the world suddenly and unexpectedly, just at a time when the earth is expecting "peace and safety" and living in a false security. But in 2 Thessalonians 2:1–4 the apostle emphasizes that before the Day of the Lord can actually come, a general falling away from God will occur and the Man of Sin will be revealed. Peter describes the Day of the Lord as a time of the burning of the earth (2 Peter 3:10–12), which is further portrayed in the fiery judgments contained in the seal, trumpet, and bowl judgments of the book of Revelation.

Again, the thrust of chapter 5 is that the Church will be raptured out of the earth and will not face the terrors of the Day of the Lord.

5:1 Now as to the times and the epochs, brethren, you have no need of anything to be written to you.

Now. *Now* (*de*) introduces a new subject, "concerning" (*peri*) the "times" (*kronos,* plural) and the "seasons" (*kairos,* plural). Paul is repeating the answer Christ gave to His disciples when they asked, "Lord, is it at this time You are restoring the kingdom to Israel?" (Acts 1:6). *Restore* (*apokathistemi*) means "to put something back into its original condition" (*EDNT*). As a present indicative in Greek it could read, "Are You presently going to again ordain" the kingdom to Israel? Jesus answered, "It is not for you to know times or epochs which the Father has fixed by His own authority" (v. 7).

The disciples had in mind the restoration of the Davidic reign with David's Son, the Messiah, on the throne. But Jesus clearly indicated that there was a postponement of that event.

The Lord then told His disciples they must wait for the Holy Spirit, who would impart power to them for witnessing (v. 8), and he then ascended to heaven (v. 11). Pentecost followed (2:1–13), during which the Spirit was poured out and the Church was launched and established. According to what Jesus said in the first chapter of Acts, then, it is clear that the Church is not the promised and anticipated Messianic Kingdom.

Times, epochs. "'The times' simply denote stretches of time while 'the seasons' (*kairoi*) refer to periods that are marked by what occurs in them. The former is a general expression to indicate the mere passing of the years, to which the second is added as being explicative of the years which include this and that that happened in them" (Lenski).

You have no need of anything to be written to you. Paul is saying that the Thessalonian church needed no explanation about the Day of the Lord mentioned in the next verse. They knew about the Tribulation and the earthly judgment coming. The Day of the Lord is another subject; it is not the Rapture. The Day of the Lord in the Old Testament

. . . is described as a time of judgment, ending in millennial blessing with Christ upon the throne of universal dominion. This is the vital distinction between the last paragraph of ch. 4 and the first paragraph of ch. 5. The joy of Rapture for the Church is followed after the Church has been raptured up to heaven by the period of unparalleled judgment on he that has rejected Christ.

The Church occupies a dateless, sign-less period sometimes called by prophetic students "the gap." For that reason we have been warned by the Lord of the futility of setting fixed dates for either the Rapture or the Appearing in glory. Our attitude should be that of waiting, watching, working and warning, in daily expectation of His return. (Ritchie)

> **5:2** For you yourselves know full well that the day of the Lord will come just like a thief in the night.

For you yourselves know full well. The Rapture is a blessing, but the coming of a thief is a dramatic and terrifying event. Because the Rapture is always described as taking the Church to glory, the Day of the Lord could not be that event. It describes wrath and judgment coming down upon the earth. "Full well" is not a good translation of the Greek word *akribos,* which is "a word of precision" (*EBC*). The word is better translated "accurately, carefully, precisely" (*EDNT*). Paul is not sarcastically alluding to the Thessalonians' own claim of knowledge, "but conceding that their previous learning on this subject had been adequate, definite, and specific, ultimately including even pertinent teachings of Christ" (*EBC*).

The day of the Lord. In the original Greek this phrase simply reads "a day of Lord" with no articles before *day* and *Lord.* The expression needs no articles because there is only one such day, and the omission of "the articles makes the expression a standard one although the articles could also have been added" (Lenski).

This day displays the sovereignty of God whereby He overthrows His enemies. Joel 2:31 calls this "the great and terrible day of the Lord" as distinguished from ordinary days. Since this is an ultimate day, it is often spoken of simply as "the day" (Rom. 13:12) and "that day" (2 Thess. 1:10), apart from the distinguishing words "Lord" or even "judgment."

Will come. This is a present indicative of *erchomai,* which would be appropriately translated as a kind of future present, because the force of the present tense is ongoing, linear, and into the future: "It is in the process of coming and will someday arrive." "The present tense denotes rather the certainty of its arrival, than the nearness. . . . It is akin to the prophetic present" (Lightfoot).

A thief in the night. Jesus told the Jews that His coming as the Son of Man to establish the kingdom would be like a thief coming in the night. Speaking to a future generation, He added, "For this reason you be ready too; for the Son of Man is coming at an hour when you do not think He will" (Matt. 24:44). The "you" is what is called a generic and prophetic you, and as such does not address solely those standing in front of the Lord, for "the coming" is yet to be fulfilled. Some Jews will be expecting His coming ("the faithful and sensible slave," Matt. 24:45) and some will not expect His arrival (the "evil slave," v. 48), His arrival referring to His coming to reign and to rule. But the illustration of a thief in the night is applicable for both occasions—both events will begin suddenly—that is, the Day of the Lord and the one thousand-year kingdom reign that follows. If Christ's earthly people, the Jews, are not prepared spiritually for His arrival, it will be a dark day of judgment for them.

This entire idea expressed in 5:12 should not, however, be taken too literally. "The point is that this day will come unexpectedly, not necessarily that it will take place at night" (*BKC*).

> **5:3** While they are saying, "Peace and safety!" then destruction will come upon them suddenly like birth pangs upon a woman with child, and they will not escape.

While they are saying, "Peace and safety!" *Saying* (*lego,* present active subjunctive) is indefinite. The subjunctive after *while* (*hotan*) refers to the expected future time (Lenski): "While at some future time they are saying. . . ."

Note in the Matthew 24:44 passage that Christ spoke about some future generation of Jews, though He addressed them as "you." Here, Paul writes about "they"—that is, the world that will be overtaken by the Day of the Lord—who think they are safe. In the New Testament *eirene* is the common word for *peace. Asphaleia* (safety) and its adjunct words are translated "security, certainty, reliability" (*EDNT*). "The blind world will remain blind to the last despite the great procession of signs during the course of the years, that advertise the Lord's day [coming]" (Lenski).

Then destruction will come upon them suddenly like birth pangs upon a woman with child. The apostle shifts from the illustration of the thief in the night to a woman suddenly gripped by birth pangs. He describes the destruction as "sudden" (*aiphnidios*), used here and in Luke 21:34, "referring to the unexpected in-breaking of eschatological events" (*EDNT*). In Luke 21:34, Jesus is reminding some future generation of Jews to "guard their hearts" so that they might not be likewise "suddenly" trapped. He adds that the day "will come upon all those who dwell on the face of all the earth" (v. 35).

And they shall not escape. With a double negative (*ou me*), this clause would read, "They shall in no wise escape" (Robertson). The entire world will be thrown into the horrors of the Tribulation. In the book of Revelation the events of the Tribulation are described as global happenings: "Peace is taken from the earth" (6:4); the earth and sea are harmed (7:2); the sea becomes blood (8:8); at certain times a third of mankind is destroyed at once (9:15); and, toward the end of the Tribulation, all the nations will drink of the immorality of the harlot Babylon (18:3). And Jesus said of that day,

> . . . for then there will be a great tribulation, such as has not occurred since the beginning of the world until now, nor ever shall. And unless those days had been cut short, no life would have been saved. (Matt. 24:21–22)

5:4 But you, brethren, are not in darkness, that the day should overtake you like a thief;

But you, brethren, are not in darkness, that the day should overtake you like a thief. "That the day" is a *hina* clause and should be translated "in order that the day," "[Giving] the purpose in the divine arrangement: for with God all results are purposed" (Alford). The Lord has made sure that this terrible day will not overcome the Church because of His provision in the Rapture. The Church will be snatched away.

With this passage, Paul departs from describing what will happen to "them" and gives a word of comfort and encouragement to the brethren (*adelphos*, brother) in Christ. Since being redeemed, the brethren are not living in spiritual darkness as is the world. Therefore, that day will not overtake (*katalambano*, aorist active subjunctive) them. Paul uses *katalambano* as "to grasp, catch, seize," with the idea "to lay hold of, to fall upon" (*EDNT*).

> "Brothers, that day will not fall upon you as a thief." "Brethren" helps to emphasize "you" in contrast with other men. The rest are "in darkness," in unbelief, in ignorance of the light of the Word, but not you. . . . The Lord's day will not catch the believers as a thief catches the sleeping owner of a house. (Lenski)

> **5:5** for you are all sons of light and sons of day. We are not of night nor of darkness;

For you are all sons of light and sons of day. We are not of night nor of darkness. In theology, this is a statement of positional truth. The believer's position in Christ is as a son. Paul includes himself and all future believers in the Lord as the "we" who are neither part of night nor of darkness. The apostle presents an image of the world stumbling about in unbelief, spiritual blackness, and unable to see the light of the gospel of Jesus.

The formula "sons of day" is not found anywhere else and must have been a Pauline neologism. "Sons of light" "clearly distinguishes those who belong to the community of faith from those outside, who are part of the darkness to be judged and condemned when the Lord Jesus comes" (*NIGTC*).

> **5:6** so then let us not sleep as others do, but let us be alert and sober.

So then let us not sleep as others do, but let us be alert and sober. *So then* (*ara oun*) is a conclusion, "introduc[ing] emphatically the necessary conclusion from the preceding statement" (Milligan). This combination is used especially by Paul in the New Testament (2 Thess. 2:15; Rom. 5:18; 7:3, 25). In an unusual grammatical construction, the apostle uses in this short verse three verbs in the present active subjunctive, first person plural: "let us [not] sleep," "let us be alert," "let us be sober." Since the believer belongs to the day and is not of the night, he or she must remain spiritually awake. "To be alert, in one's sober senses . . . , is more than to be merely awake. Here, as in verse 8, the Christians are summoned to live up to their privileges and position towards the Lord" (Nicoll).

With these three verbs, Paul is using a volitive idea: "Let us not go on sleeping," and "Let us keep awake," and finally "Let us not be drunk." He uses "drunk" only in the figurative sense in the New Testament as the opposite of "to be calm, sober-minded" (Robertson). Paul could be saying "Don't go into a spiritual slumber, stay awake as to what is happening around you, and don't loose your spiritual senses in a world of darkness, because you really belong to the day and not to the night."

As others refers to the lost and the unbelievers, "from whom ignorance of God, like a dark night, takes away understanding and reason" (Calvin).

Paul does not want the mind and the heart of the believer

> . . . overcharged with the cares of this world; for men may be inebriated with the world, as well as with wine; and the one is as prejudicial to the soul as the other is to the body; for an immoderate care for, and pursuit after the world, chokes the word, makes it unfruitful, and runs persons into divers snares and temptations, and hurtful lusts. (Gill)

> **5:7** For those who sleep do their sleeping at night, and those who get drunk get drunk at night.

For those who sleep do their sleeping at night, and those who get drunk get drunk at night. The world can do no other. In relation to positional truth theologically, the lost are depraved and cut off from the day and the brightness of God's Word. They do not hear nor understand spiritual truth. Here, Paul reminds believers how the lost exist spiritually, subtly saying that those in Christ are not to live this way. "While it is impossible for the day of the Lord to catch Christians unprepared, it is possible for them to adopt the same life style as those who will be caught unawares. Paul urges his readers not to let this happen" (*EBC*).

> **5:8** But since we are of the day, let us be sober, having put on the breastplate of faith and love, and as a helmet, the hope of salvation.

But since we are of the day, let us be sober. *Since we are* is a present active participle of the "to be" verb *eimi*. By using this construction, the apostle ties the Thessalonians' very being and personal existence to belonging to the day and not the night. They inherently are of the day because of their position in Christ—"Since you are existing as belonging to the day."

Let us be sober. Paul uses the same construction as in verse 6 (*napho*, present active subjunctive). Why does he repeat the same thought here? He is likely reinforcing in their minds that they have a new position and a different relationship. They now belong to Christ and have fellowship with the God of the universe! Therefore, they cannot fall into a spiritual or moral slumber and should "[Be] temperate, as men usually are in the daytime" (*Barnes*).

Having put on the breastplate of faith and love. *Having put on* (*enduo*, aorist middle participle) carries the idea "to dress, or clothe oneself." With the middle voice it could read, "having dressed yourself with the breastplate." A person is saved by faith and by means of the love of God. The love, however, could refer to the love that should be between the brothers in Christ, based on their new position in the Lord. Paul uses *enduo* in a specific parenthetic statement (*EDNT*), that is, this all happens at the new birth, at salvation.

Breastplate. The *thorax* covered the chest area and could be constructed from leather, iron plate, chain mail, or platelike scales. This armor was essential for close combat with swords and spears, because no one could survive hand-to-hand warfare without such protection. Paul draws on this imagery to remind believers of the protection they have been provided when they became servants of the Lord. Note that in Ephesians 6:10–17, Paul uses two imperatives: "Put on the full armor of God" (v. 11) and "take up the full armor of God" (v. 13). Because he uses imperatives, Paul is saying, "take hold of what you already have," or "implement and now use the armor you possess."

In comparing the two passages, Lightfoot notes that the metaphor in Ephesians (in regard to armor) is more fully drawn out. He writes,

> The differences between the two passages are such as to show that it would be unsafe to lay too much stress on the individual weapons in applying the lesson. Corresponding to the "breastplate of faith and love," we have in Ephesians "the breastplate of righteousness" and a little lower down "the shield of faith," love not being mentioned at all.

But Lenski goes further and notes that in the two passages Paul has created two different metaphors to illustrate two unique situations. Lenski writes, in 1 Thessalonians, Paul is making

> . . . only a contrast between men who are living in sodden drunkenness in constant night and Christians who are living in continuous light and day, awake and sober. The sober are not to fight the drunken, hence no sword or offensive weapon is mentioned.

Absence of battle is not the case in Ephesians. There, Paul speaks of taking up the "shield of faith" to extinguish the flaming missiles (arrows) of Satan (6:16) and of holding the sword of the Spirit, the Word of God, for offensive combat (v. 17).

> Faith and love are a unity; where the one goes the other follows. They are also not merely their own coat of mail, requiring no extraneous protection, but the sole protection of life against indolence, indifference and indulgence. They need simply to be used. . . . The transition to the military is mediated (as in Rom. xiii. 12, 13) by the idea of the sentry's typical vigilance. (Nicoll)

And as a helmet, the hope of salvation. In Ephesians 6:17 Paul writes about "the helmet of salvation." But here he describes it as "a helmet, the hope of salvation." Hope (*elpis,* "hope in anticipation") does not leave the door open for doubt—"Well, I *hope* this salvation will work out." Hope is an assurance that waits to come about, that is, "It is certain to take place, we are simply waiting for God's timing." But, because Paul has in mind delivery from the horrors of the Day of the Lord, *salvation* (*soteria*) here might better be translated as "deliverance," or "rescue." Spiritual salvation is not so much in view as the idea of eschatological salvation. And in this context, the salvation in view is the Rapture. It must be remembered that the Tribulation is God's wrath upon the world. His Church is not destined for such punishment (see v. 9).

Paul and the writer of Hebrews often use *hope* in connection with an eschatological anticipation: "We exult in [anticipation] of the glory of God" (Rom. 5:2); out of "the encouragement of the Scriptures we might have [anticipation]" (15:4); "The [anticipation] laid up for you in heaven" (Col. 1:5); "In [anticipation] of eternal life" (Titus 1:2); "Looking for the blessed [an-

REASON FOR THE RAPTURE

ticipation] and the appearing of the glory of our great God and Savior, Christ Jesus" (2:13); "The boast of our [anticipation] firm until the end" (Heb. 3:6); "The full assurance of [anticipation] until the end" (6:11).

5:9 For God has not destined us for wrath, but for obtaining salvation through our Lord Jesus Christ,

For God has not destined us for wrath. *For* (*hoti*) introduces the reason for the anticipation of deliverance. Believers in Christ are not "assigned" to the wrath that is on its way (see 1:10). *Destined* (*tithemi,* aorist middle indicative) can be translated "to place, position, firmly fix, determine, make something happen" (*EDNT*). The clause here might be translated, "God has [not] Himself assigned, appointed us for being recipients of His wrath." With the aorist tense and middle voice, the apostle is giving a firm, absolute soteriological promise, the keeping of which will be a sovereign act of the Lord. The promise is given without conditions: "God, according to His own good will and pleasure has decreed that we shall escape the outpouring of His wrath" (Ritchie). No idea of "sanctification" nor of a partial rapture is found here. No believer who belongs to the body of Christ will be placed under this wrath.

But what about those who become believers during the Tribulation? Though the blood of Jesus has bought their salvation, they are not technically a part of this present dispensation. They are not called members of the "body of Christ." Their earthly fate will be far different than what believers in Christ now face.

Some ask, "But what is the difference in regard to believers now suffering tribulations and the sufferings that will come during the seven-year tribulation?" Present sufferings are inflicted by the world. Likewise in the Tribulation, believers will suffer persecution, but those trials will produce far more martyrs. In the Tribulation, God's hand of protection will be removed, so to speak, as if the Tribulation saints are specifically called to a life of sacrifice and martyrdom. That entire tribulation generation will be living distinctly under the wrath of God being poured out. It is so terrible, no one would survive if it were not stopped (Matt. 24:22). Presently, the Church is existing in the period of grace.

This wrath (*orge*) is dramatically described in Revelation 6 with the breaking of the seal judgments, and is a traumatic time on earth following the

Rapture of the Church. The man on the white horse, whom many identify as the Antichrist, goes forth conquering (v. 2), and peace is suddenly taken from the earth (v. 4). In terms of economics, food becomes scarce and inflation begins to starve earth's population (vv. 5–6), with famine and pestilence coming quickly behind (v. 8). When the sixth seal is broken a great earthquake strikes, accompanied by terrible cosmic events that cause people of all classes to hide in caves and among the rocks of the mountains (vv. 12, 15). Then

> . . . they begin saying to the mountains and to the rocks, "Begin falling on us and hide us from the presence of Him who is right now sitting on the throne, and from the wrath of the Lamb; for the great day of their wrath has arrived and who right now is able to remain standing [under what has come upon us]?" (vv. 16–17, translation mine)

The wrath mentioned in 5:9 can be no other than the wrath described in Revelation.

But for obtaining salvation through our Lord Jesus Christ. *Obtaining* is the compound noun *peripoiesis*—*peri* (concerning, about) and *poiesis* (something made, provided, constructed, created), thus, "concerning [salvation] that has been provided" through our Lord Jesus Christ. *Obtaining* is seen "passively of the 'adoption' of (consisting in) salvation bestowed by God" (Milligan). It must be remembered that salvation is threefold: (1) The believer is saved from the guilt of sin by the death of Christ. (2) He or she is enabled to overcome sin by the indwelling Holy Spirit. (3) Final delivery from the presence of sin occurs at death or at the Rapture (Ritchie).

> **5:10** who died for us, so that whether we are awake or asleep, we will live together with Him.

[Christ] who died for us. *Died,* being an aorist active participle of *apothnesko,* ties the action close to the subject: "The One who died in behalf of us." Because of Christ's death on the cross believers are delivered from death. Apart from Him there is no hope. As shown, the preposition *for* (*huper*) is better translated "on behalf of," a preposition that indicates the vicarious nature of the Lord's work on the cross. The apostle makes it clear that He died and was not simply killed. He gave His life voluntarily; no man took it from Him (John 10:18). The substitutionary sacrifice of Christ is absolutely basic to Christianity, and no salvation or deliverance is possible without it.

That whether we are awake or asleep, we may live together with Him. Does the apostle have in mind "whether we are alive or dead," or "whether we are spiritually alert or lethargic"? (*BKC*). It appears likely that he means the latter because he uses the words for *awake* (*gregoreomen*) and *asleep* (*katheudomen*) the same way he used them in verse 6. Paul had in mind the necessity of being spiritually alert.

God's promises are to all the believers whether mature or spiritually carnal, whether spiritually watchful or not. All those in Christ will escape the wrath, whether walking in maturity or out of fellowship with the Lord (1:10). Paul is not, however, arguing for one to live one's life in carnality, nor is the promise an argument for taking the easy road as a believer, or saying that children of the Lord are free to live however they wish—just the opposite. Instead, the promise is a confirmation of the doctrine of justification by faith. All of our sins have been purged at the cross; our position in Jesus is based on His complete work of redemption. Thus, the promise says that, although our experience in Christ may be weak and may need strengthening, all believers should be longing for the return of their Savior. And if the trumpet sounds tomorrow, all who are physically alive, who belong to Him, will join the resurrected in meeting Him in the air.

Since future salvation has been so fully provided by Christ's finished work, it cannot be cancelled by lack of readiness. Moral preparedness or unpreparedness does not affect the issue one way or the other. In helping the Thessalonians, therefore, [Paul] had to calm their fears by convincing them of their participation in the *parousia* regardless of their degree of watchfulness. Every contingency has been met through the work done at Calvary by God himself. Christians need not fear missing the Lord's return, because they are "sons of the light and sons of the day" (vv. 4, 5). Their enjoyment of the future resurrection life in union with Christ is certain. (*EBC*)

"We may live together with Him" gives the ultimate assurance to all who trust the Lord. To see Jesus again face to face was also Paul's great personal longing, his burning and all consuming passion!

The *may* sounds optional, but *we may live* is an aorist active subjunctive of *zao* and can better be translated as a "constative aorist covering all life (now and hereafter) together with . . . Jesus" (Robertson). A constative affirms or verifies. But here, with *that* (*hina*), the force is toward the future and could possibly read, "[Christ] who died for us *that* (whether we are awake or asleep), we will live together with Him," or "so that we shall live with him," "with him who died we shall live," "died in our stead, together with him we shall live" (Lenski).

> **5:11** Therefore encourage one another, and build up one another, just as you also are doing.

Therefore encourage one another, and build up one another. *Encourage* is from the Greek *parakaleo*, "to call alongside" (see 2:11; 3:2, 7; 4:1, 10, 18; 5:14). *Build up* is from *oikodomeo*, "to erect, build up as constructing an edifice" (*EDNT*), as in to build up "as a temple for the Holy Spirit" (1 Cor. 3:16) (Lightfoot). Both *encourage* and *build up* are present imperatives and can be translated "be continually encouraging and building up."

One another (*allelon*) is formed by doubling the stem *allo to allo*, meaning "one to the other." The idea is that each "other" is to be mutually sufficient for every instance. Relative to theology, Christians in the community of believers are to have obligatory conduct toward each other that fulfills the commandment to love. In Paul's mind building one another up should have top priority (*EDNT*).

The second reference to "one another" is somewhat different in the Greek text. It is *"eis ton hena."* This is translated in various ways, such as "one in behalf of the one" (Robertson), or "edify the one the other," "edify yourselves into one body"; better, "into the one" (Ellicott).

> The most important factor, however, in ensuring that the norms of behavior taught by Paul were maintained was the sense of community fostered by the apostle among his converts. Group control and pressure are generally decisive in regulating the behavior of members of a group. (*NIGTC*)

Just as you also are doing. *Doing* (*poieo*) means practicing, as carrying out a task. It is also a present tense in Greek implying "as you are now practicing." Some commentators have seen this as a slight reminder or warning that the Thessalonians are to continue this habit (of building up each other), but also as a compliment. "But as we are slow to what is good, those that are the most favorably inclined of all, have always, nevertheless, need to be stimulated" (Calvin).

D. What It Means to Be Sanctified by the Lord (5:12–28)

5:12 But we request of you, brethren, that you appreciate those who diligently labor among you, and have charge over you in the Lord and give you instruction,

But we request of you. *We request* uses this common Greek word for "ask," *erotao,* and Paul's use of the word may demonstrate that he feels he need not demand or command. This church seems so cooperative in wanting to follow the apostles that Paul does not have to order them to follow a certain course of action. By putting *erotao* in the present tense he is almost saying "be thinking about this." No sense of urgency is suggested, as it would be if the Thessalonians are rebelling.

Brethren. Again, Paul appeals to the larger Christian community spirit and mutual camaraderie. The word *adelphos,* in the singular and plural, is used twenty-eight times in the two Thessalonian letters. Paul uses it one hundred and five times in all of his additional eleven epistles. On the average he applies this warm family reference to the Thessalonians more than to any other group. Truly, Paul had a special relationship with this church.

Appreciate. Actually *to know* (*oida,* perfect active infinitive), the idea is "to arrive at a realization [perfect tense] of how much others are laboring among you."

Diligently labor. This comes from *kopiao* (present active participle) and has the thought "to labor struggling under adverse circumstances," or to "toil even if weary" (Robertson).

And have charge over you. *Have charge* (*proistemi,* present middle participle) is a compound form, *pro* (before) and *histemi* (to stand). Leaders are those who "stand before" the group and lead, no matter what the personal cost. By using the middle voice, Paul may be saying "they are placing, positioning themselves" before you. This is why they are to be respected. *Proistemi* is a distinctly Pauline word, used one time in the Thessalonian writings (here), four times in 1 Timothy (3:4, 5, 12; 5:17), and in only three other occasions in two additional letters (Rom. 12:8; Titus 3:8, 14). It may be read "literally, those who stand in front of you, your leaders in the Lord, the presbyters or bishops and deacons. Get acquainted with them and follow them. . . . A thankless, but a necessary task" (Robertson). The entire discussion implies that such leaders had already been appointed. They may not have been fully seasoned or mature, so here Paul is urging the congregation in general to begin to listen to and rely upon these men.

In the Lord. The phrase could possibly read "with [*en*] the Lord," that is, along with Him these leaders are exercising authority. Another possible translation is "by His command, as if He were here," or "that is, by the appointment of the Lord, or under His direction. They are not absolute sovereigns, but are themselves subject to one who is over them—the Lord Jesus" (*Barnes*).

And give you instruction. This phrase is actually a present active participle, *instructing* (*noutheteo*). *Noutheteo* is a compound, *nous* (mind) and *tithemi* (to place, position). These leaders are to be continually shaping the mind of the assembly, or "brainwashing" them in a positive sense. *Noutheteo* always carries the idea "to admonish, to warn" (Milligan). Being a participle, the word could be translated "admonishers" (*NTC*). "It means to put in mind; . . . It is a part of the duty of a minister to put his people in mind of the truth" (*Barnes*), or "putting sense in the heads of people" (Robertson). If those who "have charge" refers to the elders of this newly formed church, they are the "spiritual guides to give practical advice to individual Christians" (Ellicott).

> **5:13** and that you esteem them very highly in love because of their work. Live in peace with one another.

And that you esteem them very highly in love. This clause is certainly not advocating self-esteem. In fact, the apostle calls for just the opposite: "Each of you regard one another as more important than himself; do not merely look out for your own personal interests, but also for the interests of others" (Phil. 2:3b–4).

Esteem (*hegeomai,* "to consider, regard, count") has here the idea "to regard with honor" (*EDNT*), and with the present infinitive means "to continually be regarding with honor." Another translation might be "regard them with a very special love for their works' sake," that work being so thorough and important (Nicoll). Yet another translation might be, "They should be honourably thought of, and be high in the affections of the saints, and others in the community" (Gill). Paul here seeks not merely a social affection. He desires that genuine godly love (*agape*) be shown to all, but especially to those laboring to serve the church and Christ. "The idlers in Thessalonica had evidently refused to follow their leaders in church activities" (Robertson).

Because of their work. Those in charge are struggling spiritually and emotionally to serve the congregation in very difficult circumstances. They are expending time and energy (*ergon,* "work") and possibly even placing their lives at risk for others and for the cause of the gospel. Thus, the esteem held toward them should be "a most extraordinary degree of love" (Ellicott). The ropes that bind Christians together should not be simply a nod of approval or casual recognition but a deep and meaningful holy affection. To harbor such feelings requires the work of the Holy Spirit within that brings forth honest appreciation.

Live in peace with one another. This is a strange clause that seems to be dropped into the middle of another subject. What brought on this thought in the mind of the apostle? Though he does not address it until the next letter, he seems to have in mind the confusion taking place regarding those who were lazy and not working (2 Thess. 3:6–15). Paul will attack this problem head on when he writes them again, but he seems to at least touch upon it in the next two verses when he writes, "admonish the unruly" and let "no one repay another with evil for evil."

Living in peace (*eireneuo*) is a burning concern with Paul. He uses the noun *peace* (*eirene*) forty-two times in his letters while the word is used only forty times in the rest of the New Testament. But it is interesting that he uses the verb here and in only two other places (Rom. 12:18; 2 Cor. 13:11). By using the noun so frequently, Paul has created a theological doctrine concerning peace: God is the God of love and peace (2 Cor. 13:11), providing peace through Christ (Eph. 2:14–15) by the gospel of peace (6:15). The Father is also called the Lord of peace (2 Thess. 3:16), and genuine spiritual peace only comes directly from God Himself (Titus 1:4).

So often peace is broken among Christian brothers. And when a congregation becomes carnal and spiritually callous, they take out their sinfulness on their pastors and leaders. Church splits follow quickly, and some of the saints never recover emotionally. Paul knew well the carnal nature of believers and realized problems could fester and burst forth quickly. "We see daily how pastors are hated by their Churches for some trivial reason, or for no reason whatever, because this desire for the cultivation of peace, which Paul recommends so strongly, is not exercised as it ought" (Calvin).

> **5:14** And we urge you, brethren, admonish the unruly, encourage the fainthearted, help the weak, be patient with all men.

And we urge you, brethren. Again, Paul speaks warmly by using the familiar family word *brethren.* "We urge" again is that word *parakaleo* that Paul uses so often in these Thessalonian letters (see 2:11). *Parakaleo* is a word of warmth but also of strong exhortation. Paul also uses the word in the present tense, "be exhorting continually, brothers."

Admonish the unruly. Paul has used *noutheteo* ("to place them in") before (see v. 12). The word is used here as a present imperative and can be translated "be putting some mental sense into." The *unruly* is a compound noun with the negative *a* and *taktos,* a verbal adjective from *tasso,* "to keep military order." It carries the idea to "put sense into the unruly mob who breaks ranks" (Robertson). Paul seems to be remembering the market-place idlers who were used against him when he first arrived at Thessalonica (Acts 17:5). Some of these may even have become Christians but still had rough edges.

Encourage the fainthearted. *Encourage* (*paramutheomai,* "to console") is a very strong word for "comfort" and is used concerning Martha's and Mary's friends, who attempted to calm them after the death of their brother, Lazarus. "Many of the Jews had come to Martha and Mary, to console them concerning their brother" (John 11:19, 31). The same word is used twice by Paul in this letter (2:11; 5:14). The *fainthearted* is also a compound, *oligos* (little, small) and *psuche* (soul), that is, the "small-souled," "little-souled."

The terrible conditions in Thessalonica caused many of the young Christians to lose heart and wish to drop from sight and be quitters. They had to be encouraged and kept in line.

When one becomes a believer in Christ one does not become instantly mature and able to handle all things. Although the majority apparently coped, others struggled to keep the faith. Paul was both sympathetic and firm.

Help the weak. *Help* (*antechomai,* "hold fast to, take an interest in, pay attention to") is a present imperative, "be continually paying attention to" the "weak, sick" (*asthenes*). Paul is referring to those who are spiritually sick or morally weak. "The brothers should 'cling to' them, rendering all the necessary spiritual and moral assistance" (*NTC*). "These disorderly elements try the patience of the leaders. Hold out with them. What a wonderful ideal Paul here holds up for church leaders" (Robertson).

Be patient with all men. *Be patient* (*makrothumeo*) is also a present imperative. *Makrothumeo* can be literally translated from Greek as "long-suffering." "Do not give way to a 'short' or 'quick' temper . . . towards those who fail, but be patient and considerate towards all" (Milligan). This long-suffering is an attribute of God Himself (Rom. 2:4, 9:22; 1 Peter 3:20). Some commentators think "all men" could include even those who are outside of Christ—the unbelievers. Others think the sentence is confined to the brothers in the Lord. Whichever, to show patience is called for in dealing with all people.

Because all of these imperatives are stated in such brief fashion, some scholars believe they do not represent burning problems within the congregation. In other words, the topics addressed here were not major concerns, but such cannot be proven. With the present imperatives, Lenski translates the verse, "Keep remonstrating with the disorderly, keep encouraging the fainthearted, keep supporting the weak, keep being longsuffering toward all."

5:15 See that no one repays another with evil for evil, but always seek after that which is good for one another and for all men.

See that no one repays another with evil for evil. Because Paul wrote this, we have an indication that some in the congregation were capable of doing such, or they were actually practicing this kind of revenge. *See* (*horao,* present active imperative) carries the thought that the Thessalonian church should be looking carefully or examining what was going on in this regard. They needed to be on guard against the subtleties of sin that could so easily come upon them (Gal. 6:1–2) and divide believers. "The natural tendency to retaliate and inflict injury for a wrong suffered must be strongly resisted, no matter what the injury" (*EBC*).

The preposition *for* (*anti*) carries the idea of equivalence, that is, a price paid or a balance made, as on the scales. "Fallen human nature acts on the principle of 'tit for tat,' but for the Christian it is not rendering evil for evil, or railing for railing, but contrariwise blessing, and that towards all men, whether believer or unbeliever" (Ritchie).

Repay (*apodidomi*, aorist active subjunctive) can be translated "give back, return, recompense" (*BAG*). Because of natural human depravity, small children quickly learn to hit back. Early on they find out how to retaliate with name calling. They are able to outdo the other and escalate the insult with increased verbal abuse. Paul does not want the believers to fall into such a trap and destroy the unity. It was enough to have the world so against this new body of believers, much less that they turn upon each other (see Rom. 12:17–21; 1 Peter 2:19–23).

But always seek after that which is good for one another and for all men. By saying *always* (*pantote*) the apostle makes no allowance for responding with insult for insult. *Seek after* (*dioko,* present active imperative) means "to pursue," or "keep up the chase . . . after the good" (Robertson). In the majority of times the word *dioko* is used, it refers to one being pursued by persecution. But Paul often uses it in the "sense of striving toward religious and ethical attitudes and goals" (*EDNT*).

In order to throttle human nature, the Law called for an "eye for eye, tooth for tooth" (Exod. 21:24). The Jews abused this letter of the Law and they used the Law to take revenge upon each other. But Christ set forth a higher standard when He said, "But whoever slaps you on your right cheek, turn to him the other also" (Matt. 5:39b).

5:16 Rejoice always;

Rejoice always. *Rejoice* (*kairo*, present active indicative) might be translated "be continually giving forth" as in joy. The word became a badge of greeting for the early Christians. Christ used it when greeting His disciples (Matt. 28:9), it is used in Acts 15:23 as a greeting, and by Paul as a word of farewell (2 Cor. 13:11). It must be remembered that rejoicing is not to be self-manufactured but to be genuine, it must be one of the fruits of the Spirit (Gal. 5:22). "The theme of 'joy' and 'rejoicing' is prominent in the epistle to the Philippians where the word and its derivatives occur about 16 times. God's redeemed people have every reason to be a joyful people considering their multiplied blessings, not only in this life but in that which is to come" (Ritchie).

By writing *always,* Paul is emphasizing that rejoicing should be done under all circumstances. Because to do so is, humanly speaking, almost impossible, the Holy Spirit must be working within to bring such a response.

5:17 pray without ceasing;

Pray without ceasing. *Pray* (*proseuchomai,* present active indicative) can be translated "be continually praying." Paul adds to this present tense imperative *pantote,* which may be translated "at all times," or under whatever painful thing may be coming upon us at the moment. "Not surprisingly Paul wished his converts to be people of prayer. He himself was devoted to prayer as a fundamental activity in his life (cf. 1:2f.; 2 Thess. 1:11; Rom. 1:10; Col. 1:3, 9)" (*NIGTC*). When Paul says without ceasing, he "does not mean some sort of nonstop praying. Rather, it implies constantly recurring prayer, growing out of a settled attitude of dependence on God" (*EBC*). By using these short, clipped clauses, the apostle is presenting a whole series of instructions that he wanted this church to follow.

5:18 in everything give thanks; for this is God's will for you in Christ Jesus.

In everything give thanks; for this is God's will for you in Christ Jesus. *Give thanks* (*eucharisteo,* present active imperative) is a compound, *eu* (good) and *charisteo* (to grace), reading literally that we "good grace" God or, in some other context, someone else. In this we recognize what He has done for us and give a word of cheer in His favor. *In everything* (*en panti*) refers to all circumstances.

By adding *this is God's will,* Paul justifies his short but urgent series of instructions: "rejoicing, praying, and giving thanks." "This is what God desires of you." He is not speaking of the Lord's mysterious sovereign work of providence whereby He causes all things, although that may not be far from Paul's intended thought. But his intended meaning here is that God desires that this be so. "We need to learn this secret of the happy Christian life—thankfulness. If everything actually conspires [together] to do us good, how can we do otherwise than always rejoice?" (Lenski).

5:19 Do not quench the Spirit;

Do not quench the Spirit. The Holy Spirit is always with the believer. He never leaves the child of God (Eph. 1:13–14; 4:30). By using *quench* (*sbennumi,* present active imperative) Paul has in mind, do not "extinguish, smother, suppress" the work of the Holy Spirit within. When using the present tense he may have had in mind that some believers in Thessalonica may have been continually doing things in their lives that were putting out the flame of zeal coming from God's Spirit. "With the present imperative [the word means] to stop doing it or not to have the habit of doing it. It is a bold figure" (Robertson). In a certain sense not fully understood, the Holy Spirit is the link between the believer and God the Father. The Holy Spirit is the Helper (John 14:16), the Pledge of the believer's redemption (Eph. 1:14), the Giver of gifts (1 Cor. 12:4), the Intercessor (Rom. 8:27). He carries out many other tasks for the sake of those in Christ.

Paul uses the illustration of a fire and the extinguishing of the influence of the Holy Spirit in our hearts. This may be an allusion to a fire upon an altar, which must be kept constantly burning. Fire here may be emblematic of devotion and zeal that must never go out. "The Holy Spirit is the source of true devotion, and hence the enkindlings of piety in the heart, by the Spirit, are never to be quenched" (*Barnes*).

5:20–21a do not despise prophetic utterances. But examine everything carefully;

Do not despise prophetic utterances. It seems as if these verses need to be connected in this way. *Despise (exoutheneo,* present active imperative) carries the idea of "to have a low opinion, scorn, reject contemptuously" (*EDNT*). As he has done through almost this entire section, Paul uses the present imperative: "Do not continually be rejecting." "Prophetic utterances" is actually one Greek word in the plural, *propheteias. Prophecies* then is actually placed first in the Greek text for emphasis: "Prophecies, do not be rejecting."

Outside of the apostles, there seems to have been a few prophets, such as Agabus, who could foretell the future (Acts 11:28). Most of those called prophets appear to have been "explainers" of truth because the full authoritative revelation was not in the hands of all of the church assemblies. The prophet "was one who pronounced or enunciated to men the will or command of [God] whose minister he was. Though he might at times be charged with the prediction of future events, as the manifestation of that will, and thus be a 'prophet' in the common acceptance of the term, still this was only an accident [limited event] of his office" (Lightfoot).

Agabus was used of the Lord to predict by the Spirit that a great worldwide famine was coming. He also predicted the arrest of Paul upon his going up to Jerusalem (Acts 21:11). At Tyre, some other disciples told Paul, "through the Spirit not to set foot in Jerusalem" (21:4). They were acting as foretelling prophets. Note that just prior to the words of Agabus in 21:11, Paul and Luke stayed with the evangelist Philip, whose four daughters were prophetesses (v. 9). If these women had forecasting powers, why didn't they make predictions over Paul, as Agabus would come and do? Since prediction was not the main emphasis of their ministry, it is likely they had no such abilities.

Prophecy was one of the important gifts given by the Holy Spirit to the body of Christ (1 Cor. 12:10). Many may have been given such a gift in order to set forth revelation to the local assembly. But was their gift absolute in that they could speak with inerrancy of message?

First Corinthians 14:29–32 indicates that prophets were teachers who explained spiritual truth not as yet having been revealed by the apostles. We must also remember that all the churches may not have had all the letters from the apostles. There was much to learn about church doctrine and the recorded messages had not been circulated to all. These prophets were something like "super" teachers, but they were not infallible.

In the assemblies, they had to speak by two or three, with the other prophets passing judgment (v. 29). The prophets must present their teachings in an orderly fashion "so that all may learn and all may be exhorted" (v. 31), a statement that suggests that prophecy was a teaching ministry and not primarily a forecasting one. In fact, the prophets' messages were subject to the scrutiny of the others (v. 32). The words of the prophets had to be tested against known doctrine as it was accepted and understood.

Other women, discussed in 1 Corinthians 11:5, had the gift of prophecy besides the daughters of Philip. Nevertheless, applying all the rules of Scripture, the prophetess or female teacher is not allowed to speak or teach in the mixed assembly (14:34–35; 1 Tim. 2:12). She would likely be an instructor of other women (Titus 2:4–5).

Paul lists what has been called the three communication gifts: prophecy, tongues (languages), and knowledge (1 Cor. 13:8). By communication gifts we mean those special gifts that helped move and explain the new dispensational doctrines of the Church. The apostles, especially the writing apostles like Paul, John, and Peter, were progressively setting forth Church revelation. Again, not all congregations had all the letters and if they did, what was their message?

These three unique gifts seem to have been given by the Holy Spirit in order to explain and make new revelations understandable. But these three communication gifts would end, probably when the canon of the New Testament was complete. "If there are gifts of prophecy, they will be made inoperative; if there are tongues [languages], they will in the future stop themselves; if there is knowledge, it will be done away with" (v. 8, translation mine).

Paul adds, "when the perfect (*teleion,* "the completion") should arrive, the partial will be done away" (v. 10). Some argue the *perfect* means the coming of Jesus. But such cannot be the case because the word *teleion* is in the neuter gender in Greek and could in no way refer to the Lord. Though Paul is not specific, it seems that such miraculous gifts ceased when the canon of revelation was completed (around A.D. 90–95) with the completion of the book of Revelation. There was then no more need for these dramatic communication gifts.

Examine everything carefully. This clause actually reads "test, prove" (*dokimazo,* present active imperative) all things (*panta*). And coming after "do not despise prophetic utterances" serves to warn that the words of the gifted prophets were not infallible. Though one had the gift, one did not teach with the same authority as those holding apostolic offices. The congregations had the right and the obligation to test the messages they heard. False prophets abounded and large numbers of believers were being seduced by doctrinal error. Paul is saying "Listen, but be careful!"

5:21b hold fast to that which is good;

Hold fast to that which is good. This clause "is best regarded as beginning a new sentence" (Alford). *Hold fast* (*katecho,* present active imperative) to the good (*kalon*), can be translated "Keep on holding down the beautiful (noble, morally beautiful)" (Robertson). *Katecho* is a compound verb consisting of *kata* (down) and *echo* (to have, receive, hold). What Paul says here can be considered a conclusion, in that once the standard has been set, and the message proven true, then it should be embraced. "The good should be accepted; every kind of evil (without any exception; hence, whether it be evil advice—given by a false prophet—or any other form of evil) must be avoided" (*NTC*).

5:22 abstain from every form of evil.

Abstain from every form of evil. The apostle now broadens his thought to go beyond evil or bad utterances or prophecies. Seductive evil may fool many young Christians who lack discernment. *Abstain* is the verb *apecho* (present middle imperative) and can have the meaning "to hold at a distance, be distant" (*EDNT*). With the middle voice, it could read "be always distancing yourself" from every form of evil. Paul seems to be setting forth a general principle that he wants the Thessalonians to live by. *Form* is *eidon* in Greek and refers to the "outward appearance, shape" of evil (*BAG*). Anything that smacks of evil must be resisted, that is, anything that men consider evil and that would give offense (2 Cor. 8:21) (Lightfoot).

The apostle uses the most diabolical and sensuous word for evil, *poneros* (miserable, bad, worthless, malicious, wicked), a word that describes the depth of depravity with a vivid picture of rebellion and sin. "An unhappy suspicion is left upon the mind, and fears are entertained, lest there should be some poison lurking" (Calvin). Even after making such a strong statement, Calvin confines Paul's statement to the problem of false doctrine, but it seems that the apostle has clearly broadened the base of his warning. Believers in Christ cannot toy with any hint of sin and evil. They must put it from their minds and feelings, especially if they feel in any way tempted by what is before them.

5:23 Now may the God of peace Himself sanctify you entirely; and may your spirit and soul and body be preserved complete, without blame at the coming of our Lord Jesus Christ.

Now may the God of peace Himself sanctify you entirely. *God of peace* probably means "the God who provides peace." "Paul addresses God as the giver 'of peace' (cf. 1 Cor 14:33), who has provided a harmonious relationship between himself and man through Christ's death" (*EBC*). Thus, Paul is making peace (*eirene*) a doctrine, an important element in salvation—the peace that is established between God and man. Peace might be defined in a practical sense as the "cessation of conflict and animosity." By using the pronoun *autos* Paul emphasizes that God Himself is performing the act—may "He Himself" sanctify you.

Positional peace is found at the Cross. "Having been justified by faith, we have peace with God through our Lord Jesus Christ" (Rom. 5:1). In regard to the position of the believer, the Father sanctifies those who come to Christ (John 10:36), the Holy Spirit sanctifies (Rom. 15:16), and the Son sanctifies also (Eph. 5:26). Thus, from our position in Christ should come experiential peace: "Being diligent to preserve the unity of the Spirit in the bond of peace" (Eph. 4:3). The apostle wants peace to spill over to the relationships in the body of Christ. The believer should also experience inner peace even though storms may rage without: "And the peace of God, which surpasses all comprehension, shall guard your hearts and your minds in Christ Jesus" (Phil. 4:7).

Sanctify, hagiazo (aorist active optative), in the Greek means "to set apart, make holy, make unique." In terms of salvation the word means "to consecrate, to separate" from things profane. The optative mood gives the idea of a wish for the future. Here, Paul is desiring that the Thessalonians progressively grow into sanctification.

Entirely (*holoteleis*) is a compound word, *holos* (entirely, completely) and *teleios* (completely, perfectly), that can be translated "through and through" or "entirely and completely." Paul is desiring that the believers progressively move toward greater maturity of character with the ultimate and final sanctification in mind. "Here it means the whole of each of you, every part of each of you, 'through and through'" (Luther), "qualitatively rather than quantitatively" (Robertson).

And may your spirit and soul and body be preserved complete. *Spirit* (*pneuma*) is the very essence of a human being. It is with the spirit that we communicate with each other: "For who among men knows the thoughts of a man, except the spirit of the man, which is in him?" (1 Cor. 2:11a). Then, after Christ redeems us, it appears that the Spirit of God communicates with the child of God through His spirit: "Even so the thoughts of God no one knows except the Spirit of God. Now we have received, not the spirit of the world, but the Spirit who is from God, that we might know the things freely given to us by God" (vv. 11b–12).

Soul (*psuke*) is the life of or the center of a human being. The soul is the moral and conscious part of man. Jesus said "I lay down My life (*psuke*) for the sheep" (John 10:15b). The soul can will—"doing the will of God from the heart (*psuke*)" (Eph. 6:6b)—and it is responsible—"There will be tribulation and distress for every soul of man who does evil" (Rom. 2:9). The soul can commit (Acts 15:26; 20:24), and it can be unstable (2 Peter 2:14). The Lord saves the soul (1 Peter 1:9), purifies it (1 Peter 1:22), and keeps it secure (2:25).

Body (*soma*) is obvious. This is the physical part of human beings.

All of the various "parts" of man actually work as a whole. Although the Bible describes us as having this makeup, we are a complete being. This tripartite division of the nature of man was not unique to Christianity. The Greek philosophers such as Plato, Plotinus, and the Stoics, as well as the rabbinical schools of Alexandria, recognize it. Even the pagan world was capable of recognizing the inner complication of the human species. Because of Pagan associations, some of the older theologians were fearful of humans being perceived as tripartite, feeling this was a Greek concept and not scriptural.

The early Church Fathers, however, also spoke of body, mind, and spirit. But in no way were the prophets and apostles simply copying worldly thinking. It is more likely that the Gentile world, in far off ancient times, had been touched by the truth of the Old Testament Scriptures.

Too, before one rejects what seems so plain in Paul's writing, one must remember that these descriptions of human nature are found in the Old Testament. The wisdom and revelation of ancient Hebrew Scripture probably spread out and influenced, even in a small degree, the Mediterranean civilizations.

Roo'ach is one of the most common words in the Old Testament and is translated "wind, spirit, breath," and even "mind." In many places it is even used to describe the "Spirit" of the Lord (Isa. 40:7; 59:19; 61:1; Ezek. 11:5). The Lord is said to be the God of all spirits (Num. 16:22), Job speaks of the troubled spirit (21:4), and David cries out that his spirit is overwhelmed (Ps. 143:4).

Neh'phesh is translated "soul" but also as "life." The psalmist asks God to preserve his soul (Ps. 121:7), the soul can be overwhelmed with life's problems (124:4), it must wait for the Lord (130:6), and must be quieted (131:2). One can sin against his own soul (Prov. 20:2), and it desires rest (Jer. 6:16). *Soul* is mentioned hundreds of times in the Old Testament.

Here, Paul makes it clear that being constituted of parts is a legitimate way of looking at mankind. To completely understand the makeup of people, heart and mind can be added, but Paul, under the direction of the Holy Spirit, conveys understanding by using the three words above.

Be preserved (*tereo*) is also an aorist active optative with a desire for the future. *Tereo* in Greek simply means "to keep watch over, preserve, keep" (*BAG*). It can also carry the thought of protecting. Paul adds the adjective *complete* (*holokleron*), which is a compound word, *holos* (whole) and *kleros* (a lot or a part of). He is arguing that all of the body's parts are to be kept complete, or that there should be no deficiency in any part.

> The spirit, which is the ruling faculty in man and through which he holds communication with the unseen world—the soul, which is the seat of all his impulses and affections, the centre of his personality—the body, which links him to the material world and is the instrument of all his outward deeds—these all the Apostle would have presented perfect and intact in the day of the Lord's coming. (Lightfoot)

Without blame. Paul adds *without blame* (*amemptos*) to further his argument. *Amemptos* is used in the New Testament only here in this epistle. It must be noted that the word *amemptos* has been found on sepulchral inscriptions discovered in Thessalonica (Milligan). This word became a goal for daily living but also a desire that one could live blameless before seeing Christ, the Judge of the believer.

> "Blameless" (*amemptos*, with no legitimate ground for accusation, cf. 2:10) is not sinless; sinlessness is not possible while still in the mortal body (Rom. 7:18–25). But by the power of the indwelling Spirit and God's preserving, keeping care, it is possible to live a life at which the world cannot point an accusing finger. It is for this that Paul prays. (Ritchie)

At the coming of our Lord Jesus Christ. This *coming* (*parousia*) is the Rapture, which Paul has already discussed in such detail. Depending on their view of eschatology, some of the older amillennial teachers saw the Rapture in one of two ways. Christ comes and snatches the believer away into heaven, and then a heavenly day of judgment begins. Or the Lord comes and snatches away the believer but comes right back down for an earthly period of judgment. Examining most of their writings one finds these venerable scholars in somewhat of a quandary. They do not address the details about how all of this works. They simply call the passage above the second coming of Christ and say very little else.

The great Baptist Calvinist John Gill seems to struggle in trying to determine the order of eschatological events. On 1 Thessalonians 4:17 he writes,

> He will descend, and will then clear the regions of the air of Satan, and his posse of devils, which now rove about there, watching all opportunities, and taking all advantages to do mischief on earth; these shall then fall like lightning from heaven, and be bound and shut up in the bottomless pit, till the thousand years are ended: here Christ will stop, . . . as yet he will not descend on earth, because [it is] not fit to receive him; but when that and its works are burnt up, and it is purged and purified by fire, and become a new earth, he will descend upon it, and dwell with his saints in it; and this suggests another reason why he will stay in the air, and his saints meet him there. (Gill)

5:24 Faithful is He who calls you, and He also will bring it to pass.

Faithful is He who calls you. Paul actually makes the word *faithful* (*pistos*) here a name or certainly an attribute of God, "impl[ying] that God will faithfully carry out the process of" sanctifying and keeping (Nicoll). The Thessalonians should have no doubt—"Assurance is assured!" The Lord will certainly complete what he has begun with respect to their salvation. He will surely sanctify and preserve them. He can be trusted (1 Cor. 1:9; 10:13; 2 Cor. 1:18; 2 Thess. 3:3; 2 Tim. 2:13).

Calls (*kaleo*) is a present active participle. The sovereign call of God is evidence of eternal grace that will be continually exercised toward us. "For he does not promise to be a Father to us merely for one day, but adopts us with this understanding, that he is to cherish us ever afterwards" (Calvin). As a participle, and with the pronoun *you,* this could read "your Caller" (Nicoll).

He also will bring it to pass. An alternative reading is "which also [*kai*] He will accomplish" (*poieo,* future active indicative).

The two phrases of 5:24 together, then, read "who besides calling you will also do it" (Nicoll). *Do it* refers to the sanctifying and preserving—He will carry this out! "Faithfulness is the characteristic of God that determines that he will do the very thing Paul has prayed for" (*EBC*).

5:25 Brethren, pray for us.

Brethren, pray for us. The apostle again uses the family expression *brethren*. He then includes Silas (Silvanus) and Timothy in his plea for prayers and intercessions before God. Paul often requested such prayers from the brothers and sisters (2 Thess. 3:1–2; Rom. 15:30–32; 2 Cor. 1:11; Col. 4:3–4), which may indicate that he saw some specific trials coming against them. If this is not the case, it was true that troubles were ongoing with them and constant prayer was the order of the day. Since he had a wish-prayer for them in verse 23, he may be alluding to it in showing the Thessalonians how they might reciprocate (*NIGTC*).

5:26 Greet all the brethren with a holy kiss.

Greet all the brethren with a holy kiss. *Greet* (*aspazomai,* present active imperative) means "to welcome" or even "bid farewell." The etymology of the word is uncertain, but it could come from *spao* that means "to attract." Without this word being uttered, two parties in Greek society could not begin to communicate. The encounter could remain hostile or even dangerous unless the salutation *aspazomai* was given (*EDNT*). Among believers in Christ, hostile encounters were not, of course, the case.

In many of Paul's letters he urges that greetings be given with a "holy kiss." He uses this salutation in reference to a holy kiss in three other places (Rom. 16:16; 1 Cor. 16:20; 2 Cor. 13:12). Kisses were typical forms of greeting in ancient days, demonstrating respect, love, reconciliation, and even the sealing of a contract. For Paul they show forth the warmth that should be in the family of God. By using the word *holy* (*hagios*), the apostle indicates that the kiss has spiritual meaning. It became a sign of the liturgical life in the community of the early church. More than likely the kissing of the opposite sex was not encouraged (*NIGTC*). Ellicott thinks this command for holy kissing was given only to the leaders of the church, and they were to pass on the kiss to the common members of the assembly. Such, however, cannot be proven.

It is noteworthy that Paul says to greet "all." Many in the congregation were very carnal, but they were not to be excluded from this warm greeting.

Since the holy kiss was a cultural practice, we are not expected to practice this today. Rather, friendly recognition and showing closeness would be a better pattern for our current generation. The true expression of love is more important than an antiquated cultural practice. Remember, a kiss of greeting was used by Judas to betray Christ (Luke 22:48). Although believers in a congregation may have some acute differences, they should not be divided in fellowship.

> **5:27** I adjure you by the Lord to have this letter read to all the brethren.

I adjure you by the Lord to have this letter read to all the brethren. *I adjure (enorkizo,* present active indicative) is used only here in the New Testament. In Classical Greek the word means "to make one swear" as in making an oath (L&S). *Enorkizo* is a form of a command and means that Paul wants to make sure that the letter is read. With this strong word we sense that Paul realized he was under the influence of God's inspiration and that he had the authority to give infallible instructions to the churches (*Barnes*).

Why is the apostle so adamant about having the letter read?

> The explanation is perhaps to be sought, not in any supposed differences existing between the Elders and the laity of the Thessalonian Church . . . which might lead to the suppression of the letter; but in a sort of presentiment or suspicion, which St. Paul may be supposed to have entertained, that a wrong use might be made of his name and authority. Such a suspicion was entirely justified by subsequent occurrences . . . , and doubtless sufficient grounds for it had already appeared. Hence it was of infinite importance that his views should be known to all. (Lightfoot)

Further, Paul wants the letter read "by the Lord" or "with the authority of the Lord." He is very concerned that his instructions be passed on to all the believers. Because of this verse, many commentators believe this epistle first went to the leadership. This was probably true, but without question it was intended as a letter of instruction for all. Doctrinal and discipline problems did develop later, or were in the making, that Paul may have anticipated (2 Thess. 2:2; 3:6–15).

Writing "have this letter read" may suggest that those receiving it could not themselves read. Someone else, the "reader" in the assembly, may be called upon to read it out loud. The "angels" of the book of Revelation may have been the reading "messengers" or couriers of those seven congregations the Lord addresses through John the apostle. Only one other time did Paul want to make sure his letter was read, and that was to the church at Colosse (Col. 4:16).

Some of the wayward brothers in the church at Thessalonica may not have desired to be present when Paul's letter arrived and was read. By stressing *all*, the apostle made sure everyone must be present. When he writes *by the Lord*, that authority may have implied a threat of divine punishment if this were not done (*NTC*). In saying "all brethren," however, his letter moderates the command by expressing appropriate warmth and endearment toward everyone.

5:28 The grace of our Lord Jesus Christ be with you.

The grace of our Lord Jesus Christ be with you. This closing is similar to Paul's opening greeting. He began this letter by mentioning the name of the Lord Jesus Christ and then writing *Grace to you and peace* (1:1). He closes almost all his letters by writing *Grace to you* (Rom. 16:20; 1 Cor. 16:23; 2 Cor. 13:14; Gal. 6:18; Eph. 6:24; Phil. 4:23; Col. 4:18; 2 Thess. 3:18; 1 Tim. 6:21; 2 Tim. 4:22; Titus 3:15; Philem. 25).

By using the preposition *with* (*meta*), Paul means "Let this be . . . , in company with you!" (Lenski). The *you* is plural (*humon*), that is, "in company with all of you."

"The sacred Scriptures, neither one part nor another, nor the whole of them, are to be kept from private (individual) Christians, but may be read, and heard, and used by all" (Gill).

The grace of Christ with all its redemptive power and all the heavenly benefits summarizes everything.

Study Questions

1. What is the Day of the Lord?
2. Who are "they" in verse 3?
3. Explain and discuss the difference between those who are of the day and those who are of the night (vv. 2–11).

4. Is the wrath of verse 9 the daily troubles of Christians or is it the wrath of the Day of the Lord—the Tribulation? Discuss.
5. From the context, what does Paul mean by "obtaining salvation" (v. 9)?
6. Read carefully verse 10 and explain and discuss what it means.
7. Were these problems of a serious nature (vv. 12–15) or were they festering sores that Paul was concerned about? What is his tone in these verses?

■ CHAPTER TEN

Bible Study Outline of
1 Thessalonians

Edward E. Hindson

THE THESSALONIAN LETTERS are as ideally suited to special Bible study as they are to expository preaching. They contain a balance of doctrinal truths and practical advice. Written early in Paul's ministry, they express his heart as a pastor and an evangelist. In each letter we see his personal concern for the young believers' spiritual well-being. He depicts himself as both a nursing mother (2:7) and a caring father (v. 11). In both cases, the Thessalonians are depicted as his spiritual children.

The teacher who approaches the Thessalonian letters would be wise to assume the same care and concern as the original author. One cannot read these letters without noticing the tender compassion of the apostle toward this fledgling congregation. His tone is kind and fatherly. His concerns are basic. He deals with such matters as salvation, sanctification, spiritual growth, evangelism, and future hope.

Paul's letters in general combine explanations of doctrinal truths with exhortations to practical Christian living. First Thessalonians, in particular, ends with a series of admonitions in the form of practical commands: rejoice, pray, give thanks, quench not, despise not, prove, abstain (5:16–22). Preparing to teach or study this epistle, one should pay close attention to the apostle's original intention as he poured out his heart to his spiritual children in general and to this local church in particular.

The outline of 1 Thessalonians can be divided into five points that roughly correspond to the five chapters of our English text:

Considering each section individually, note several key areas for teaching from 1 Thessalonians. In chapter 1, Paul commends the believers at Thessalonica for the example of their lives and their evangelistic impact on Macedonia, Achaia, and "every place" where their faith was known (vv. 7–8). Paul opens the chapter commending their (1) work of faith, (2) labor of love, and (3) patience of hope (v. 3). His list is similar to that of 1 Corinthians 13:13. He acknowledges the assurance of their salvation based on their "election by God" (1 Thess. 1:4). Paul also observes the transforming power of the gospel (v. 5), which resulted in these new converts turning to God and away from their idols (v. 9). *Key words* in this chapter include *faith, love, hope, election, gospel, power,* and *example.*

Chapter 1 could be approached in this manner:

I. EXAMPLE OF THE BELIEVERS IN TRUE EVANGELISM (1:1–10)
   A. Divine Election (vv. 1–4)

   What makes the church unique? The Greek word *ekklesia* means an "assembly," and was used in a variety of contexts. What makes the New Testament Church unique is that it is "in God . . . and the Lord Jesus Christ" (v. 1). Although the Thessalonian church was still relatively young, Paul was convinced of its stability and perpetuity because of its foundation—in God and in Christ.

   The basic Christian graces (faith, hope and love) are the result of being chosen by God (vv. 3–4). Election is not cause for self-centered pride, but the cause of humility, holiness, and spiritual assurance. These evidences of the activity of the Holy Spirit were proof of the Thessalonians' relationship to God. He was at work in their lives, and the spiritual transformation they were experiencing was because of divine grace, not human self-effort.

   B. Power of the Gospel (vv. 5–6)

   The preaching of the gospel (Greek, *evangelion,* "good news") is the means by which God's truth is communicated by human messengers. Our response to the gospel determines our salvation. And the power of the gospel results in our personal transformation.

The force of its operation in our lives points to the power of the gospel. But it is not a message simply about power. The gospel is power. And its power is seen in the evidence of God working in the lives of those to whom it is preached.

The fact that the gospel comes with "much assurance" indicates that the assurance of our salvation is a work of God in our hearts and not some device of self-effort by which we attempt to persuade ourselves that we are saved. We know that we are saved by the assurance of the divine witness of the Holy Spirit in our lives. He convinces us that we indeed belong to God and have been changed by the gospel of Jesus Christ.

C. Example of their Faith (vv. 7–8)

The example set by the apostles was reproduced by the believers at Thessalonica. The Greek word for *example* is *tupos,* or "type." In Greek usage it refers to a stamp or design imprinted on something and came to mean an image or pattern. Collectively, the church was a pattern or model community that stood as an example to secular and pagan society.

How can the Church make a difference in society? First, by setting an example of holiness and righteousness that gives evidence to the transforming power of the gospel. Second, by "sounding forth" the Word of the Lord (v. 8). We cannot expect the watching world to believe our message until they respect our lives. On the other hand, we cannot expect their respect to turn to belief if they don't hear and understand the gospel message. The bottom line for all Christians is the same: Live it and tell it!

D. Evidence of their Transformation (vv. 9–10)

The changed lives of the believers spoke so loudly to the community that everyone was continuously telling others of what God had done for them. It is this spontaneous communication of the testimony of changed lives that captures the heart of the secular soul and speaks to the unbeliever of the reality of God. It is not just the preaching that leads to evangelizing the lost, but it is the spontaneous spreading of the story of what God has done in the lives of the believers that speaks powerfully to unbelievers.

New believers quickly become "trumpeters" of the Word. God's truth "sounds forth" from their lips and their lives. As they turn from the "idols" of false religion and surrender their allegiance to God they find themselves in a whole new relationship to God and His people. In the meantime, we are to serve the Lord faithfully until He returns. It is our unique position in Christ that gives meaning to our lives here and now and hope for our eternal future.

Believers are promised deliverance "from the wrath to come." This will occur when we are raptured to heaven prior to the tribulation period when the wrath of Christ (Rev. 6:16) will be poured out on an unbelieving world. The fact that Jesus is coming again assures us that history is moving toward a specific and definite conclusion. Jesus Christ the King is coming to take His bride home to the Father's "house" in heaven and then, after the marriage of the Lamb (Rev. 19:6–8), He will return, with His Bride—the Church, to establish His kingdom on earth.

Chapter 2 is a recitation of Paul's exhortations to encourage the believers in their walk with the Lord. Paul, as the apostle (the sent one) of Christ (vv. 4–6), reminds them that his exhortations were not insincere (v. 3), but were an expression of his responsibility to God to proclaim the gospel (good news). He reminds them that he cared for them as a nursing mother (v. 7) and a spiritual father (v. 11). Paul also observes that they believed the gospel as the "Word of God" (v. 13) and became part of the "churches of God," which are "in Christ Jesus" (v. 14). Because their salvation has made them members of God's eternal family, Paul refers to the believers as his "hope," "joy," and "crown of rejoicing" (v. 19). *Key words* include *trust, glory, gentle, gospel, worthy, joy,* and *rejoicing.*

Chapter 2 could be further outlined like this:

II. EXHORTATION OF THE BELIEVERS IN GENUINE SINCERITY (2:1–20)
   A. Sincerity of the Gospel (vv. 1–6)
      The integrity of the apostles was key in the successful evangelization of the pagan world. These missionaries were free of selfish ambition or financial exploitation. People respond to the gospel when they are convinced of the sincerity of our message. They want to know if we believe it and live it ourselves.

The early evangelists hoped the memory of their preaching and the impact of their lives would compel their converts to remain steadfast. So we, too, must set the example for those who hear us that they might see Christ in us. While salvation is received by faith, it is demonstrated by how we live. Therefore, the power of the gospel results in a personal spiritual transformation that proves the sincerity of the gospel message.

B. Sacrifice of the Apostles (vv. 7–12)

The apostles literally paid their own way to reach the people of Thessalonica with the gospel. They were so committed to the truth of their message, they spared no expense to spread it far and wide. Paul's constant emphasis in these verses amounts to, "I paid my own way." That got their attention. It reminds us that we must give ourselves to the work of evangelism because we believe it, not just because we can make a living off it.

The ultimate incentive is to live lives "worthy of God" (v. 12). This is the least we can do in light of all that God has done for us. God's people should display His glory in their daily lives. How we live reinforces what we preach. Personal holiness is the ultimate apologetic against which there is no valid argument.

C. Suffering of the Believers (vv. 13–20)

The Thessalonians responded to the gospel quickly and graciously. They became a model to other Christian communities despite their personal suffering. Years later, Paul referred to the "severe test of affliction" that the churches of Macedonia were experiencing (cf. 2 Cor. 8:1–2). Despite their personal suffering, they remained steadfast in their faith.

The Christian Church has always faced opposition, but when it has remained radically Christian, it has endured and prospered. Generations of sincere believers have followed the example of the apostles. As gentle nurses they have nurtured new generations of converts who, despite their challenges and difficulties, in turn have passed the gospel message on to others. And so must we.

Chapter 3 focuses on the sanctification of the believers. Because Paul's visit to Thessalonica was brief, he was anxious to know how they were doing and sent Timothy to follow-up on their progress (v. 2). The apostle was greatly

encouraged when he heard of their continued faith and that they were standing firm in Christ (3:8). His prayer for them was that they would be grounded
in holiness in light of the coming of Christ (v. 13). Paul then defines this holiness as living to please God (4:1), by abstaining from sexual sins (v. 3), and
treating each other with brotherly love (v. 9). *Key words* include *establish,
faith, love, stand firm, holiness, sanctification.*

First Thessalonians 3:1—4:12 could be outlined like this:

III. ESTABLISHMENT OF THE BELIEVERS IN SANCTIFICATION (3:1–4:12)
    A. Report of Their Faith (vv. 1–8)

      Paul sent Timothy to Thessalonica to encourage the believers there
and, in turn, he was encouraged by the report of their faith. The
need for encouragement is an integral part of the Christian faith.
While our salvation is produced by God and sustained by the Spirit,
it is often encouraged and helped by fellow believers.

      The New Testament pictures the Church as a caring community of
believers who nurture each other. Paul, himself, emphasized the
need for such fellowship. Christianity is meant to work in the relationships of a believing community of caring members. It was never
meant to be lived in isolation from one another. As we see God at
work in the lives of our fellow believers, we ourselves are encouraged to trust God more in our own journey of faith.

    B. Request of the Apostle (vv. 9–13)

      Paul longed to return to Thessalonica to further encourage the be-
lievers there. He had planted the church in a few short weeks and
now it was growing even under persecution. The entire enterprise
was the work of God, not man. Yet the apostle longed to see them
again to rejoice with them over what God was doing.

      In his prayer for them Paul prayed that they would increase and
abound in love toward one another. Paul made no references to the
size of the church but measured its success by the quality of its
members' lives. Loving each other and living in holiness are the
keys to a successful church.

    C. Requirement of Holiness (4:1–12)

      The life that pleases God is a life of holiness. This is especially true
of a believer's relationship to the opposite sex. Paul makes it very
clear that sanctification involves abstinence from sexual immoral-

ity. The believer must "possess his own vessel" (literally, control his body) in sanctification and honor (v. 4). How we behave toward one another indicates the depth of our relationship to God. Those who reject such ideas, actually reject God.

The root word for *sanctification* is *hagios,* meaning "holy." Thus, to be sanctified is to be holy (see 1 Peter 1:15–16). In the Bible, holiness is related to usefulness. Holy people and holy things are "set apart" for God's use. There is nothing normal about the Christian life. It is a supernatural rebirth created in us by the Holy Spirit and results in a changed lifestyle that makes us useful for God's service.

One of the underlying themes of 1 Thessalonians is the second coming of Christ (1:10; 2:19; 3:13; 5:1–9). This truth is especially highlighted in 4:13–18, where Paul describes the return of Christ "in the clouds" to snatch us up to meet Him "in the air" (v. 17). This passage parallels similar promises to the believers in John 14:1–3 and 1 Corinthians 15:51–58. The Rapture of believers is described by the Greek word *harpazo* (caught up, or snatched away).

Several aspects of the Rapture are clearly distinguished in this section:

1. Jesus returns in the clouds (v. 17).
2. Spirits of departed saints return with Him (v. 14).
3. A shout and a trumpet signal His return (v. 16).
4. The "dead in Christ" (deceased generations of believers) rise first (v. 16).
5. Living believers are raptured ("caught up") with resurrected believers as one body of Christ (vv. 16–17).
6. All believers meet the Lord "in the air" at the Rapture (v. 17).
7. This promise is the basis of our present hope and comfort (v. 18).

First Thessalonians 4:13–5:11 can be outlined as follows:

IV. ESCAPE OF THE BELIEVERS IN THE RAPTURE (4:13–5:11)

A. Promise of the Rapture (4:13–14)
Questions about deceased believers are not new. The early Christians were looking for the Rapture to be imminent. As believers died,

some questioned, Where are the dead? Will we be left out of the Rapture if we die before it occurs? These are natural concerns of believers in every age.

Paul addressed these concerns about those who were "asleep" (dead). He reassures us that if we believe in the resurrection of Christ, we can be confident of the resurrection of dead believers as well. A Savior who has the power to come back from the dead has the power to raise us from the dead as well. When believers die, their spirits go to heaven to be with the Lord (see 2 Cor. 5:8). In the meantime, their bodies are buried in the dust of the earth. At the Rapture, those dead bodies will be resurrected to be reunited with the spirits of those God will bring with Him from heaven (v. 14).

B. Process of the Rapture (4:15–17)

The Bible makes it clear that the Rapture includes two groups—the living and the dead. The "dead in Christ" (deceased believers' bodies) will be raised first. Then, living believers ("we who are alive and remain") will be raptured ("caught up") with them, together to meet the Lord in the air.

Note that the Rapture takes place in the air, not on the earth. It is the "snatching" away of the bride of Christ to the marriage of the Lamb (Rev. 19:6–8). This is not the return of Christ with the bride at Armageddon. Rather, the Rapture precedes the Tribulation judgments, which culminate at Armageddon.

C. Power of the Rapture (4:18)

The significance of the Rapture is that it is a promise of deliverance from divine wrath. Therefore, we can comfort each other with this promise. If there is no rapture before the tribulation period, there is no promise of comfort and encouragement for the Church. The Rapture must come *before,* not during or after the Tribulation, if its promise is to be a "comfort" to believers who are alive today.

D. Purpose of the Rapture (5:1–11)

The Rapture will come like a "thief in the night" (v. 2). It will catch the unbelieving world by surprise and they will not escape (v. 3). By contrast, believers are not in darkness, but in the light (vv. 4–5). Therefore, we are to be watching and waiting with expectation for the imminent coming of Christ for His bride—the Church.

The fact that we are "not appointed unto wrath" (v. 9) indicates that believers will escape the Tribulation when the wrath of the Lamb is poured out (see Rev. 6:16). This promise is the basis of our hope and comfort. It is also the basis of our encouragement to one another. Believers need not fear the second coming of Christ in judgment on the world because it will be preceded by His coming to rapture the Church home to heaven.

Here is an ideal place in your study to observe the differences between the Rapture of the Church and the return of Christ as two distinct aspects of the second coming of Christ.

Rapture	Return
1. Jesus comes in the *air* (1 Thess. 4:17)	1. Jesus comes to *earth* (Zech.14:4; Acts 1:11)
2. He comes *for* His own (John 14:3; 1 Thess 4:17)	2. He comes *with* His own (1 Thess. 3:13; Rev. 19:14)
3. *Believers* are removed (1 Thess. 4:17)	3. *Christ* is revealed (Rev. 1:7)
4. *Saved* are *delivered* from wrath (1 Thess. 1:10)	4. *Unsaved experience* God's wrath (Rev. 6:12–17)
5. World is *deceived* (2 Thess. 2:3–12)	5. Satan is *bound* (Rev. 20:1–2)
6. Antichrist is *revealed* (2 Thess. 2:6–8)	6. Antichrist is *defeated* (Rev. 19:20)
7. Church at marriage of Lamb in heaven (Rev. 19:7–9)	7. Church rules with Christ in His kingdom (Rev. 20:1–4)

The first letter to the Thessalonians closes with Paul's encouragement to the believers to persevere in their walk with Christ (5:12–28). He urges them to respect their spiritual leaders, and to live at peace (v. 13) so that they might be "sanctified" in spirit, soul, and body and be found "blameless" when Jesus returns (v. 23). *Key words* in this section are generally in the form of imperative commands: *warn, comfort, support, follow, rejoice, pray, give thanks, quench not, despise not, prove all things,* and *abstain from all appearance of evil* (vv. 14–22).

First Thessalonians 5:12–28 can be outlined thus:

V. ENCOURAGEMENT OF THE BELIEVERS TO PERSEVERE (5:12–28)
  A. Respect Leaders (5:12–13)
     Leadership is the gift of God. He gifts some believers to lead others so that we might all be more effective in our service to Christ. It is the believer's responsibility to recognize those whom God has so gifted and follow their leadership. Spiritual anarchy will never build the Church nor evangelize the world. The mission of the Church must be clearly articulated if we are to cooperate together in the common task of world evangelization.
     Part of Christian discipleship is to recognize the value of Christian leaders. We ought to pray for them, support them, and encourage them in their labors for Christ and the gospel. As we learn to work together for the cause of Christ, we increase the Church's impact on the world. There is no place for pride, arrogance, competition, and selfishness in the ministry of the gospel of Jesus Christ.
  B. Rebuke Troublemakers (v. 14)
     Not all ministry is aimed at the gifted, the successful, and mature believers. Sometimes it is necessary to minister to the complainers, the failures, and the immature believers as well. Paul urges us to (1) "admonish" (confront) the unruly (disobedient), (2) encourage (comfort) the faint-hearted or feeble-minded, (3) support (help) the weak.
     This pattern of ministry reminds us that we must deal with the less glamorous aspects of the ministry as part of our responsibility to the whole body of Christ. Genuine Christian love motivates us to minister to the struggling so that they too might learn the victory that is ours in Christ.
  C. Receive Instruction (vv. 15–23)
     Some of the best advice in Scripture on practical matters of personal discipleship is found in the closing verses of 1 Thessalonians. We are told to "rejoice evermore," "pray without ceasing," in everything "give thanks," "quench not the spirit," "despise not preaching," "test all things," and "abstain from the appearance of evil" (vv. 16–22).

Practical theology is the capstone of systematic theology. It is not enough to *know* what you believe unless you are willing to *live* what you believe. Professing Christians whose disposition is negative, who don't pray, who resist God, despise preaching, and live as close to the world as they can, have good reason to examine whether they have ever been born again.

C. S. Lewis said, "The best argument for Christianity is Christians: their joy, their certainty, their completeness." But he also warned that Christians can be the "strongest argument against Christianity . . . when they are somber and joyless, when they are self-righteous and smug . . . when they are narrow and repressive, then Christianity dies a thousand deaths."[1]

PART THREE

Second Thessalonians
Commentary

■

CHAPTER ELEVEN

Paul's Greetings

I. PAUL'S GREETINGS (1:1–2)

> **1:1** Paul and Silvanus and Timothy to the church of the Thessalonians in God our Father and the Lord Jesus Christ:

Paul and Silvanus and Timothy to the church of the Thessalonians in God our Father and the Lord Jesus Christ. The wording of this verse is the same as in 1:1 in the first letter. Some have speculated that Paul used the same wording because this letter continues the "same song, second verse." Paul picks up his dialogue and simply continues with the concerns that this church is facing (see 1 Thess. 1:1).

Because Paul addresses the Thessalonians in the same way in both letters, it is apparent that his attitude about them has not changed by what had occurred in Thessalonica since the first letter was written and sent (Lenski). Some believe that between the first and second epistles, the Thessalonians had written Paul with some additional questions, especially about the Day of the Lord and the Antichrist. That such a letter existed cannot be proven. Nonetheless, something prompted a response. Maybe a traveler brought the questions from the assembly. "We know the fact that this information reached Paul, but we do not know how the information was carried" (Lenski).

Paul and his missionary party were in Corinth when word came of the concerns raised in Thessalonica. Probably no less than several months had passed since the first epistle had been sent.

1:2 Grace to you and peace from God the Father and the Lord Jesus Christ.

Grace to you and peace from God the Father and the Lord Jesus Christ.
This sentence is similar to the latter part of 1:1 of the first letter, except Paul adds "from God the Father and the Lord Jesus Christ." The sentence appears, too, in Romans 1:7, except there Paul adds "our" Father. The phrase actually reads in Greek, "from God Father and Lord Jesus Christ."

> As in so many places in the New Testament Epistles, Jesus Christ is placed on an equal level with God the Father. God is the Father of Christians individually, a revelation given first by Jesus Christ (Matt. 6:9). A church is an assembly of individuals who are in Christ by faith in His atoning death and are therefore the children of God. (*BKC*)

II. PAUL'S ENCOURAGING THOUGHTS ABOUT SUFFERING (1:3–12)

> **1:3** We ought always to give thanks to God for you, brethren, as is only fitting, because your faith is greatly enlarged, and the love of each one of you all toward one another grows ever greater;

We ought always to give thanks to God for you. Here the apostle is repeating what he said in the first letter (1:2). Despite problems in the assembly, Paul had great regard for these young believers, possibly because of the suffering they were enduring for the sake of the gospel.

Ought always comes from *opheilo* (present active indicative) and carries the idea "to owe, be obligated" (*EDNT*). As Paul uses the word, he is expressing gratitude to this assembly for their expanding fellowship and love shown to one another. *Opheilo* "expresses the duty of thanksgiving from its subjective side as an inward conviction" (Alford). Expressing appreciation is often lacking among believers. The "ought" brings out "the Apostles' sense of thanksgiving as actually a debt owing to God in view of their converts' rapid growth in spiritual things" (Milligan). He could have used the particle *dei* (it is necessary), but hard-pressed compulsion is not in view here. Spiritual matters call for a spiritual response, not one based upon some legalistic requirement.

To give thanks is a present active infinitive, that is, "to be continually giving thanks." *Eucharisteo* is used extensively in the Thessalonian letters (1 Thess. 1:2; 2:13; 5:18; 2 Thess. 1:3; 2:13). In Paul's other letters he uses the word nineteen times. Some of that thankfulness is directed toward God the Father (1 Cor. 1:4), through Jesus Christ (Rom. 7:25), for all things (Eph. 5:20) and, as Paul expresses in other letters, thankfulness for others. Paul is the "thankful" apostle.

Brethren. Again, here is the word *brethren,* much used in these two epistles. Paul must express often that family closeness he felt with the Thessalonians. He uses *adelphos* approximately 133 times in his epistles, with most instances referring to the family of believers. He was striving hard to create a close community among all Christians. History would tell us that the numbers of those coming to Christ was exploding, with pockets of the faithful scattered throughout various cities, villages, and ethnic communities and speaking in different languages. Yet Paul was looking at the miracle of the growth of the whole body of Christ, as fostered by the Holy Spirit. This fraternity of the faithful was most important to him.

As is only fitting. This little phrase is a bridge between what he has already said and the reason for his thanks as expressed in the next clauses. This phrase actually reads "as worthy is." *Worthy (axios)* is translated "to consider worthy, appropriate, fitting" (*EDNT*). "It is only worthy, right that thanks be given," or "to be thankful to God is due because . . ."

Because your faith is greatly enlarged. *Greatly enlarged (huperauxano,* present active indicative) is a compound verb, *huper* (above) and *auxano* (to grow, increase). As a present tense it could read "your faith is continuing to grow higher." "'Faith,' an area commended in the first epistle (1:3), was one where improvement was needed. The apostle's earlier prayer (1 Thess. 3:10) had in view a return visit to strengthen the believers in this respect" (*EBC*). That faith must have grown since Paul, Silas, and Timothy were there.

And the love of each one of you all toward one another grows ever greater. This growing love could not have made Paul happier. He is glad and thankful that their suffering has brought them closer to each other and to the Lord. Instead of stunting their growth, as trouble so often does, it has made them stronger. In the area of mutual love, their concern had not dried up. "Paul is proud of his friends, because suffering has not spoiled their characters, as suffering, especially when due to oppression and injustice, is too apt to do" (Nicoll).

Grows greater is the verb *pleonazo* (present active indicative) and can be translated, "cause to become rich, to multiply, become more" (*EDNT*). In 1 Thessalonians 3:12 it may read, "May the Lord make you rich in love." The love coming from the individual is continually growing explosively rather than "organically." "Hence [it] is fittingly used of *agape,* while this love is further characterized as not only individually manifested . . . but as extended to the entire Christian community at Thessalonica" (Milligan).

The text may actually read, "The love is multiplying each one of you, all of you, into one another [*allelous*]," or "the love of each one of all of you is growing for one another" (*NIGTC*). This is a most unusual construction for the New Testament. It is as if Paul began a phrase that he could find no end for—he just had to keep going! The wording is somewhat awkward but is appropriate because of the emotional feelings the apostle is displaying.

> Clearly in this entire passage—whether it be read in the original or in the translation makes no difference—the writers reveal themselves as men who are elated (see also on 2:13; 3:4) rather than reluctant, exuberant rather than hesitant. The presence in the congregation of a few members who were not living in accordance with the rules cannot be denied. . . . But in the jubilant passage which we are now discussing the disorderly persons are kept in the background for the moment. (*NTC*)

> **1:4** therefore, we ourselves speak proudly of you among the churches of God for your perseverance and faith in the midst of all your persecutions and afflictions which you endure.

Therefore, we ourselves speak proudly of you among the churches of God. The churches throughout Macedonia and Achaia had already heard of the Thessalonians' faith toward God (1 Thess. 1:8). Now Paul can add to that how this church, under siege, continues to persevere and endure under terrible afflictions. The apostle is not simply using hyperbole; he is sincere in proclaiming the truth of their struggles and victories.

Speak proudly. *Ekauchaomai* is a present active infinitive and is a compound verb, *ek* (out) and *kauchaomai* (to boast), meaning "to boast forth." Often used in the negative sense, Paul here makes it a legitimate word. This assembly has not given in to punishment for their belief in Christ. They have withstood it all and passed the test, and rightful honor and recognition is due them.

For your perseverance and faith in the midst of all your persecutions and afflictions. *Perseverance* (*hupomone*) is a compound noun, *hupo* (under) and *monos* (only, alone). The word "refers to steadfastness and perseverance 'under' certain circumstances, and also to remaining expectant in the face of passing time" (*EDNT*), or "to be under [it] along." Paul wants the churches also to hold the Thessalonians up in prayer that they might maintain their faith while suffering persecutions (*diogmos*) and afflictions (*thlipsis*). He uses *diogmos* in several other important passages (Acts 8:1; 13:50; Rom. 8:35; 2 Cor. 12:10; 2 Tim. 3:11). The word comes from *dioko*, "to chase, to pursue," a word used by Paul to describe his treatment at Corinth (2 Cor. 12:10). In all of his epistles Paul uses *thlipsis* a total of twenty-three times, often translated with the descriptive word "tribulation."

Faith (*pisteos*) in this context could be translated to mean a rare sense of "faithfulness." Paul, in a few places, does use the word this way (Rom. 3:3; Gal. 5:22; Titus 2:10). Tangible faith is not the idea here but the "visible fruit of faith—faithfulness" (*EBC*). And to demonstrate that kind of faithfulness is what the churches need reminding of.

Some commentators have confused the doctrine of the Tribulation (the seven-year period known as Daniel's Seventieth Week) with the daily tribulations and troubles that Christians may experience in this life. There is a vast difference in the two, and context—not simply how a word is used—determines what is being described (see 1 Thess. 5:9–10).

Paul writes "we also exult in our tribulations [*thlipsis*], knowing that tribulation brings about perseverance [*hupomone*]; and perseverance, proven character; and proven character, hope" (Rom. 5:3–4). Further, he asks the question "can tribulation separate us from the love of Christ?" (8:34). He answers that nothing "shall be able to separate us from the love of God, which is in Christ Jesus our Lord" (v. 39).

Which you endure. *Endure* (*anechomai*, present active indicative) means "to bear, have forbearance," even "to suffer." Some have taken "endure" as a command—"You endure." But that is not the thought here. The apostle wants all the congregations in the region to know how the Thessalonians have suffered and how they have endured through it all (see 1 Thess. 2:14). "The greater is the pity that a church so brave, . . . should have members that have wild, disorderly notions in another direction" (Lenski).

> **1:5** This is a plain indication of God's righteous judgment so that you may be considered worthy of the kingdom of God, for which indeed you are suffering.

This is a plain indication of God's righteous judgment. *Plain indication* is from one Greek word *endeigma,* which means "indication" or "a manifest token," thus "an open evidence or proof" (Ritchie). It is from the verb *endeiknumai* "to prove, show, demonstrate" (*EDNT*). *Endeigma* is a compound word, *en* (in, with) and *deiknumi* (to show"), or "to show or indicate" something. The word occurs only in the New Testament. In this case it has to do with the Lord's righteous (*dikaias*) judgment (*kriseos*). The "indication" is evidence or a token of God's judgment that honors the confident endurance and patient waiting of the Thessalonians: "God will vindicate these believers for their suffering."

This judgment might take place in the lifetime of the suffering Thessalonians. Part of the judgment could be temporal in the form of vengeance on the pagans who were tormenting the church. Judgment certainly refers also to the future when, before the great White Throne Judgment, the Lord will heap punishment on the tormentors of the righteous. In fact, Paul clearly has in view an eternal judgment when he writes that these persecutors face "an eternal destruction, away from the presence of the Lord" (v. 9). The Lord will have the last say!

May be considered worthy is from the compound verb *kataxiothenai* (aorist passive infinitive), *kata* (accordingly) and *axioo* (counted worthy). The believers will receive such a positive judgment because, in part, they have remained faithful in their stance for the gospel. The preposition *eis* comes before this verb, indicating a "purpose": "This righteous judgment is future and final (verses 6–10)" (Robertson). "The worthiness of the Thessalonian believers had already been established before persecution came. Their firm stand in the face of persecutions (v. 4) confirmed their relationship to God and was a pledge that their worthiness will be openly declared by God himself" (*EBC*). Notice that Paul does not say "worthy of heaven" but "worthy of the kingdom of God." Heaven is not this kingdom nor is the Church.

Of the kingdom of God. "The kingdom of God" and "the kingdom of heaven" are all references to the messianic and Davidic reign of the Christ. Both expressions are but two ways of describing the same thing—"the kingdom *from* God" or "the kingdom *from* heaven." Jewish interpreters point out that the Messianic Kingdom is clearly set forth in Daniel 7–9. The Messiah comes "to establish the world dominion of God, an everlasting kingdom— 'to perfect the world under the Kingdom of God'—a Kingdom of Heaven on earth."[1] The "Greek element," as the Jewish scholars label allegorical interpretation, as promoted by Origen and Augustine, destroyed the historical nature of that kingdom. It was later "spiritualized" by the Church, even down through the period of the Reformation.

Origen tended to "psychologize" away the eschatological imagery found in Matthew 24–25. He said the first and second comings of Christ symbolized "Christ's coming in the souls of the simple [the average Christian] when they receive the rudiments of Christian doctrine."[2] Though Origen did not openly deny prophetic expectations, such as the earthly kingdom of God, "he tended by psychologizing them to make them irrelevant. Although that was far from Origen's intention, the outcome of his work was to make the church feel distinctly more at home in the world."[3]

All of history is moving toward the historic and literal kingdom of God. But again, the Church is not that kingdom. (For more on the kingdom of God, see 1 Thessalonians 2:12.)

For which indeed you are suffering. The Thessalonians are *suffering* (*pascho,* present active indicative) for the sake of the glory of the kingdom that will someday come. Paul and his associates were also suffering, and that suffering was still going on (Robertson). Though it is not stated in the two Thessalonian letters, some of these believers later may have suffered even unto death.

Statistics show that the twentieth century was the greatest period of Christian martyrdom, more than any other time in history. The message of the Cross is foolishness to the Gentiles and a stumbling block to the Jews (1 Cor. 1:23), but it is the power of God to those who are being saved (v. 18). The Thessalonians "gladly endure tribulation in order that one day they may enter into the kingdom of perfection, in which God will be all in all, and his sovereign rule will be joyfully recognized and obeyed" (*NTC*).

> **1:6** For after all it is only just for God to repay with affliction those who afflict you,

For after all it is only just for God. *For after all* (*eiper*) introduces a conditional clause and could be translated "for although" or "since indeed" (*EDNT*). It is only right, just, or righteous (*dikaios*) that the Lord gives back: "If so be that it is a righteous thing with God." *Dikaios* is a first class conditional, with *eiper,* which shows fulfillment as absolutely true. "A righteous thing 'with God' means by the side of God (*para theoi*) and so from God's standpoint. This is as near to the idea of absolute right as it is possible to attain" (Robertson).

Repay (*antapodidomi,* aorist active infinitive) is derived "from the simple form *didomi,* [and] takes on by means of a prefixed *anti* the character of finality and irrevocability" (*EDNT*). "The idea of recompense is connected with the announcement of judgment. Second Thessalonians 1:6 promises terrible *retribution* to those who 'afflict' the Church" (*EDNT*).

The Lord keeps perfect and infallible records. Someday those records will be opened and the unsaved dead, including the pagan persecutors of Thessalonica, will be resurrected and "judged from the things which were written in the books, according to their deeds" (Rev. 20:13).

Who afflict. *Afflict* in the Greek is *thlibo,* a present active participle dative plural. The last part of the verse reads God repays "to the ones right now afflicting you, with affliction," or "to recompense affliction to them that afflict you." Upon these persecutors, "if not in this life, it is a certain thing that hereafter such shall have indignation and wrath, tribulation, and anguish; they shall be cast into outward darkness" (Gill).

> **1:7** and to give relief to you who are afflicted and to us as well when the Lord Jesus shall be revealed from heaven with His mighty angels in flaming fire,

And to give relief to you who are afflicted and to us as well. Relief will come when the Lord returns. With this verse and the next, Paul describes Christ coming from heaven to bring judgment and retribution. This coming should not be mistaken for the Rapture in which the Church saints are resurrected and the living saints are transformed and taken by the Lord to glory. Instead, in verses 7–8, Paul is saying that He deals out retribution to those who have not obeyed the gospel, and such dealings will take place during the seven years of tribulation.

To give is not in the Greek text but it is supplied from verse 6 and the word *antapodidomi* (to repay). The Lord will repay the wicked with affliction, and repay with relief the righteous who have suffered. "Though their domination is tolerated for the present, when the proper time comes, the roles will be reversed" (*EBC*). *Relief* (*anesis,* "rest, relaxation, refreshment") is rewarded in the future for the present affliction the church is enduring. Notice that Paul says "to us as well." He includes himself, the other apostles, and all who are persecuted for the gospel's sake. It is safe to say that all who suffer for Christ throughout the ages will be especially remembered when He brings forth judgment.

When the Lord Jesus shall be revealed. *Shall be revealed* is actually "in the revealing, revelation" (*en te apokalupsei*). The noun *apokalupsis* is a compound, *apo* (from) and *kalupsis* (hidden). The *apokalupsis* is the "uncovering of something which is hidden." Jesus is not now seen by earthlings in His glory, but He will be. But first the Rapture of the Church, followed by the Tribulation, and then the revealing of Him as the earthly King and Judge.

From heaven. Christ and the Church have been waiting out the Tribulation in glory, and "heaven" here could certainly be referring to the abode of the Father, where we will be with Christ. It could also simply be referring to the "sky." Jesus returns with the messianic title "the Son of Man coming on the clouds of the sky with power and great glory" (Matt. 24:30).

This is the Lord Jesus, the Man in heaven. He will exercise the power then; the Christians' persecutors do so now. . . . If the Rapture had occurred in Paul's lifetime, the enemies of the Thessalonian believers would have been judged shortly (seven years) thereafter, at Christ's second coming. (*BKC*)

With His mighty angels in flaming fire. This phrase is reminiscent of the words of Enoch as quoted by Jude: "Behold the Lord came with many thousands of His holy ones, to execute judgment upon all, and to convict all the ungodly of all their ungodly deeds which they have done in an ungodly way, and of all the harsh things which ungodly sinners have spoken against Him" (vv. 14b–15). The holy ones mentioned by Jude refer to the angelic host. They are clearly identified in Matthew 25:31: "But when the Son of Man comes in His glory, and all the angels with Him, then He will sit on His glorious throne."

In regard to the book of Revelation, questions have been raised about the angelic host. Some commentators think the armies from heaven, clothed in white linen, who follow Christ from glory, as mentioned in 19:14, is a reference to this same angelic army of Matthew 25:31. Others believe these are the righteous saints of all ages past, who accompany Him to earth to co-reign during the kingdom.

Mighty. This host is apparently His own company of angels who constitute His special forces when He returns. They must not be ordinary angels for they are called "mighty" (*dunamis,* "powerful, capable"). *Dunamis* comes from the verb *dunamai,* which can be translated "can do, able."

In flaming fire. Nothing was more frightening to ancient warriors than fire. Burning oil was poured from walls on invading troops below. Cannonball-like weights, soaked in oil, flamed down on attacking infantry. Arrows and firebrands rained heavily upon helpless soldiers. Fire is the ultimate picture of judgment and retribution. The apostle Paul paints such a terrifying scene to remind suffering Christians that a judgment day is coming. God is not slack concerning what He has said.

Though mockers say, "Where is the promise of His coming?" (2 Peter 3:4), that day is sure to come because He will keep His Word (v. 7a). "The day of the Lord will come like a thief in the night" (v. 10a; 1 Thess. 5:2). Fire is reserved for judgment and the destruction of ungodly men (v. 7b). The apostle's view of what the future holds is bleak. Vengeance is sure to come with eternal destruction, with unbelievers excluded from the glory of God. A day of wrath and judgment is certain (Rom. 2:5; 1 Thess. 1:10; 2:16) just prior to the revelation of the glory of the Messiah in the world.

> **1:8** dealing out retribution to those who do not know God and to those who do not obey the gospel of our Lord Jesus.

Dealing out retribution to those who do not know God and to those who do not obey the gospel of our Lord Jesus. *Dealing out* (*didomi,* present active participle) simply means "to give." Because it is a masculine singular verb, the subject is the Lord Jesus (v. 7). *Retribution* (*edikesis,* "punishment, vengeance") is a compound noun, *ek* (out, forth) and *dikaioo* (to judge righteously), and it comes from *ekdikos.* Jesus will "be giving forth righteous judgment." As mentioned, the context is His second coming, not the Rapture. This is full and complete punishment and vindication. The exact phrase "dealing out retribution" is not found elsewhere in the New Testament, but it occurs several times in the LXX (Ezek. 25:14). Isaiah 66:15–16 reads,

> For behold, the Lord will come in fire and His chariots like the whirl-wind, to render His anger with fury, and His rebuke with flames of fire. For the Lord will execute judgment by fire and by His sword on all flesh, and those slain by the Lord will be many.

The Lord adds, "For I know their works and their thoughts; the time is coming to gather all nations and tongues. And they shall come and see My glory" (v. 18).

To those who do not know God is almost the same grammatically as "to those who do not obey the gospel." *Know* (*oida*) is a perfect active participle dative plural and could read "to those who through a process have [not] come to a knowledge of God." *Obey* (*hupakouo*) is a present active participle dative plural and could be translated "to those who right now have [not] obeyed the gospel." With *know* in the perfect tense, one might infer that they had an opportunity to know but refused to respond. With *obey* in the present tense the sense is "right now they do not know the gospel and probably never will," or to put it another way, "those who never knew God, neither do they now obey the gospel."

Lightfoot believes that two classifications are meant here. One would be the Gentile who by his natural depravity refuses God; and the other is the Jew who distinctly and specifically has rejected the gospel and his own promised Messiah. Lenski agrees. But Milligan thinks otherwise and notes, "The two clauses . . . are often referred to the Gentile . . . and Jewish . . . opponents of the Gospel respectively. It is doubtful whether any such distinction was in the writers' minds at the time, nor can it be strictly applied, for Gentiles as well as Jews." Wanamaker agrees and notes, "'Those not knowing

God' and 'those not obeying the gospel of our Lord Jesus' form a synonymous parallelism."

Thomas believes two classifications are meant here—Gentile and Jew. He
then admits, "The immediate context does nothing to prepare for separate
allusions to Gentiles and Jews," and concedes, "When the wrath of God makes
itself felt at the revelation of the Lord Jesus, both classes of humanity will
face dreaded agonies."

It is better to refer to both clauses as pointing to the same general class,
that is, all who live willfully ignorant and disobedient to God and the gospel.
Not knowing God is, as spelled out in Romans 2:14–16, willful, guilty ignorance. Not accepting the gospel of Christ is to refuse what God has histori-
cally confirmed and testified with the first coming of His Son.

> **1:9** And these will pay the penalty of eternal destruction, away
> from the presence of the Lord and from the glory of His power,

And these will pay the penalty of eternal destruction. This clause may
prove Thomas's point made above. Both Gentile and Jew, if two separate classifications were in the mind of Paul, are here experiencing the same eternal
destruction. The reader is persuaded that, in Paul's mind, they are as one in
regard to their fate. In the dispensation of the Church, God is graciously waiting
for both Gentile and Jew to come to Christ. In regards to personal judgment,
their end is certainly the same.

Will pay (*tino*, future active indicative) is an old word that is used only here
in the New Testament. It means "to pay, settle up" a debt. Here, the apostle is
referring to the future judgment that leads to eternal punishment. John writes
of this terrible day when he says, "I saw a great white throne and Him who
sat upon it, from whose presence [face] earth and heaven fled away, and no
place was found" for those resurrected for judgment (Rev. 20:11). John sees
a book opened, the Book of Life, and a set of many books opened, which
apparently contain the works of the lost. The accused will be judged according to what they did while living on earth (v. 13), that is, if their names are
not written in the Book of Life. "And if anyone's name was not found written
in the book of life, he was thrown into the lake of fire" (v. 15).

The "penalty" (*dike*, punishment, condemnation) is only just and right. *Dike*
is used to describe a court case or the process of law (Robertson). The lost

are storing up disobedience that will receive such a legal response before the bar of God's justice. The penalty is "eternal destruction" or *olethros* (destruction) *aionios* (eternal). *Olethros* pictures "ruin as unto death," for "men who shall pay the penalty of eternal destruction" (Nicoll).

Destruction here is not, as some wrongly presume, implying annihilation but eternal separation from God. As the life that God gives the righteous is called "eternal life," so the lost receive "eternal punishment" (Matt. 25:46). The adjective *aionos* (eternal) is used here to describe both nouns, "life" and "punishment."

Away from the presence of the Lord and from the glory of His power. *Presence* (*prosopon*) is the most common word for "face," the opposite of what Paul expresses concerning the Thessalonians being brought before the presence (in front of) of God the Father and of Christ at His coming (1 Thess. 2:19; 3:13). Not only will the lost not experience the presence of the Father and of Jesus but they will be eternally banished from "the glory [*doxa*] of His power [*ischus*]."

Ischus implies His warlike power and strength. The apostle could be referring to Daniel 7:14, where Daniel prophesied concerning the coming Son of Man, "To Him was given dominion, glory and a kingdom, that all the peoples, nations, and men of every language might serve Him. His dominion is an everlasting dominion which will not pass away; and His kingdom is one which will not be destroyed."

When Christ comes to establish this kingdom there will be a number of judgments—a judgment of those who "did not understand" and who were all taken away (Matt. 24:39); a judgment upon the worthless slave (25:30) and upon the goats that are separated by the Messiah, the Shepherd (v. 32); a judgment that falls upon all those who followed the Beast during the Tribulation (Rev. 19:17–21). Then the Great White Throne judgment takes place after the millennial reign of Christ (20:11–15). In these various periods and stages of judgment, the lost are driven from the presence of Christ and His glory.

> By the manifestation of that power and glory the wicked will be driven away into eternal ruin. They will not be able to stand before it, and though they may see the majesty of the Redeemer in the last day, yet they will be driven away to witness it no more. (*Barnes*)

1:10 when He comes to be glorified in His saints on that day, and to be marveled at among all who have believed—for our testimony to you was believed.

When He comes to be glorified in His saints on that day. The thought of the glory of the Lord continues from verse 9. *When He comes* (*erchomai,* aorist active subjunctive), with *hotan,* is a future and indefinite temporal clause: "When He comes, and He will come at some point"; when this happens, "He will be glorified" (*endoxazomai,* aorist passive infinitive). *Endoxazomai* is an aorist infinitive of purpose (Ritchie). With the passive voice, the action comes upon Him: "The time is ripe for His glory to be seen." His glory will be seen here on earth only when He comes. His glory will not be displayed in the world when the Rapture takes place and He carries the redeemed away into heaven. In heaven, we will certainly see the glory of His deity. His earthly glory, although certainly related to His deity, has to do with His glorification when He comes as the reigning King, the Son of David.

This verse, then, is continuing to describe the second coming of Christ when His glory is established with His reign on earth. "On that day" clearly refers to the Second Coming, and it is here on earth that He will "be marveled at" among the believers. The glorification referred to here happens "with" (*en tois hagiois*) His saints, "the set aside ones" (see 1 Thess. 3:13). His glorification is not because of us, but we share and are party to this blessed event. The saints here are probably others besides the Church saints. The Old Testament saints, as well as the tribulation saints and the Church saints, return for His earthly glorious rule. Even the saints of the dispensation of the Church are told they "shall also reign with Him" (2 Tim. 2:12) and will be given "authority over the nations" (Rev. 2:26). What Paul writes here fits well with Daniel's vision: "Judgment was passed in favor of the saints of the Highest One, and the time arrived when the saints took possession of the kingdom" (Dan. 7:22). It is as if Paul is saying,

> The object of His coming is that He may be glorified in His saints; and yet from that glory the wicked, your persecutors, will be shut out. Thus have they hindered the high purposes of God, and been untrue to the end for which they were created. (Lightfoot)

To be marveled at among all who have believed. *Marveled at* (*thaumazo,* aorist passive infinitive) means "to be astonished, amazed, to wonder at"

(*BAG*). The believers will be overjoyed. All the longings and expectations of seeing Jesus and His glory will have come to pass. All the tears that have been shed washed clean the path for this moment. "That believed" (*pisteo,* aorist active participle) carries a sense of past tense because it looks back to the time when the redeemed trusted God, "to the ones who believed," or "looking back from that day on the past" (Alford). "Many sons made like unto His glorious Son; they shall come with Him having been perfected at the *Bema* [judgment], His glory shining forth in them" (Ritchie).

For our testimony to you was believed. The *testimony* (*marturion,* witness) to the Thessalonians was accepted. Here Paul goes from a general truth, that all will marvel, to a specific reference, that the Thessalonians believed because they accepted the witness of Paul, Silas, and Timothy. Therefore, this assembly is counted among the believers. For this Paul is extremely thankful because he will see them among the company of redeemed. Calvin believes that because the Thessalonians received the gospel witness, the apostles receive, in a sense, credit for their ministry. Calvin paraphrases Paul, "My preaching has obtained credit among you, Christ has already enrolled you in the number of his own people, whom he will make partakers of his glory."

> **1:11** To this end also we pray for you always that our God may count you worthy of your calling, and fulfill every desire for goodness and the work of faith with power;

To this end also we pray for you always. *To this end* actually reads in Greek "into which also" (*eis ho kai*). The apostle is developing a continuous thought and he has not yet finished with it. He is developing his thought, progressing from glory to what is happening now on earth, moving from positional truth ("your calling") to experiential truth ("God may count you worthy") of that calling. God's calling here is regarded by Paul as that sovereign decree that brings the elect to salvation (Rom. 11:29; 1 Cor. 1:26). *We pray* (*proseuchomai,* present active indicative) could better read "we are continually praying." He reinforces this clause with *for you always* (*pantote,* unceasing). In the New Testament, *proseuchomai* means "to make intercession, to petition." Though a common and much-used word, it expresses an important and personal practice in the early church.

The prayer of the primitive Christian Church, . . . lives by unqualified trust in the salvation given by God through Christ. This faith finds expression before God and in the community of believers in prayer, and at the same time prayer supports and strengthens that faith. (*EDNT*)

Our God. The literal interpretation is "the God of us all." With the pronoun *us* (*hamon*) "the Apostle once more asserts his fellowship with his converts" (Lightfoot). He sees himself and the other apostles as together in Christ with the saints. He identifies with their persecution and comes alongside to include himself with their experiences. Once more, he emphasizes the fraternity of believers who suffer as brothers for the sake of Christ.

May count you worthy. Some identify this as a *hina* clause with a causative verb, but it is merely a purpose clause in the classical sense: "We are praying *in order that* you might be counted worthy" (Lightfoot). The believer, in his or her experience of living out the Christian life, should be always aware that he or she was sovereignly called by the grace of God into the family of the redeemed. To be *counted worthy* (*axioo*, aorist active subjunctive) is to be considered living appropriately, as one's position calls for, as a slave who has been judged responsible by his master because of his faithfulness. The believer then is to be continually living up to his or her position of divine election and calling in Christ.

It is easy for Christians to forget from whence they came. It is easy to have tunnel vision or shortsightedness and lose spiritual perspective. Paul is praying that this church would show forth their calling in their moral and spiritual lives, and that God would aid them in this important function.

The walk of the Christian may be flawed and imperfect, yet the believer's eternal life is certain because of the completeness of the Lord's election and salvation and by his justification through faith in Christ (Rom. 8:28–30). Regardless, the walk of the believer needs the assistance of prayer. Temptations and failings are sure to come, though no one wishes this to be so. When such failings do come, however, other believers should rise to the occasion to restore the one tempted (Gal. 6:1–2). As well, confession of sins is vitally important to restore fellowship. The cleansing that comes with confession is not based upon our merit but on the shed blood of Christ, which is applied to our walk (1 John 1:5–2:2). "It is assuring to know that God's call is made effective quite apart from human merit (cf. Gal 1:13–15)" (*EBC*).

And fulfill every desire for goodness and the work of faith with power.
In regard to "and that you might fulfill," *fulfill* (*pleroo,* aorist active subjunctive) carries the thought here of "bringing to completion." As with *count worthy,* it is also a subjunctive that is tied to the *hina:* "In order that you might be
counted worthy . . . in order that you might fulfill." "Every desire for goodness" reads better in the Greek text—"every [all] good pleasure of goodness"
(*pasan eudokian agathosunees*). Paul concludes with the clause "the work of
faith done by means of power." This power (*dunamei*) is of course the power
given by the Spirit of God; it is not human ability.

Milligan paraphrases, "And now that all this may be brought to pass, our
earnest prayer is that our God will count you worthy of the heavenly rest for
which you are looking. To this end may He mightily animate [empower] you
with all delight in goodness, and with a wholehearted activity inspired by the
faith you possess."

The apostles' goals for the Thessalonians are that God would bring about
their every resolve for goodness and prompt every act they did for Christ by
faith. Goodness is a fruit of the Spirit (Gal. 5:22), and Paul had seen those
acts of faith in the Thessalonians before (1 Thess. 1:3), which was commendable but there was yet room for growth (3:10; 4:1). None of this can come
about except by His power and working in them.

> **1:12** in order that the name of our Lord Jesus may be glorified
> in you, and you in Him, according to the grace of our God and
> the Lord Jesus Christ.

**In order that the name of our Lord Jesus may be glorified in you, and
you in Him.** Paul brings all his arguments to this end: Christ must be glorified by what He does. This sentence, then, might read, "'Inside of you' [*en
humin*] the Lord is working! He sovereignly is causing all things to be." Adding to this thought, Paul writes elsewhere, "For it is God who is the One continually emerging inside of you [*en humin*] even to the willing and to the
working concerning His good-pleasure [*eudokias,* 'good will, degree')]" (Phil.
1:13 translation mine). On this Philippians passage, Kent notes, "Paul depicts
God as actively and continually putting forth his energy in believers to insure
the accomplishment of their task."

May be glorified (*endoxazomai,* aorist passive subjunctive), being in the
passive voice, means the action comes upon the Lord. What is happening

within the believer (which is actually God's own work) brings glory to Christ. In the Lord's mysterious providence He has designed a plan whereby He would use limited and weak clay to accomplish His work. He certainly does not need us. Concerning the message of the gospel Paul writes, "But we have this treasure in earthen vessels [clay pots], that the surpassing greatness of the power may be of God and not from ourselves" (2 Cor. 4:7).

By being "in Him" (in Jesus) we, of course, are also glorified, or we are set forth to receive honor. This honor is not self-generated but is given to us by our relationship with Him. "It stands to reason that Christians must share Christ's 'glory' . . . it is . . . a recognition that they were right and wise to follow Him" (Ellicott). Jesus spoke of this relationship and of the fruit it could bear: "I am the vine, you are the branches; he who abides in Me, and I in him, he bears much fruit; for apart from Me you can do nothing" (John 15:5); "Thou, Father, art in Me, and I in Thee, that they also may be in Us" (17:21a).

According to the grace of our God and the Lord Jesus Christ. "The glory which [believers] receive is not given according to the standard of human merit, for then there would be none. It is given according to the standard of 'the grace of our God and of the Lord Jesus Christ'" (*NTC*). Though Jesus is the God-man, His equality with the Father is not seen in this phrase, as set forth by the Greek grammar. It is seen in the fact that grace comes from both God and Christ. No mere human could impart something that must be divine in origin. In this fashion, the equality of Christ with the Father is here expressed.

In these two Thessalonian epistles grace always has a two-fold source, from the Father and from Jesus (see 1 Thess. 1:1, 2; 2 Thess. 1:2). Thus, since the fountain of grace is God the Father, and it is being mediated through the Lord Jesus, it may be said to also be derived from Him.

In praying thus, Paul was asking that God would fully glorify Jesus Christ in these saints. This is in keeping with and springs from the "grace of" God, personalized again by Paul as "our God," and linked with "the Lord Jesus Christ" as an equal. . . . Answers to prayers depend on and are traceable to God's grace. Such lofty requests as these can be fulfilled only by God's grace. (*BKC*)

In summing up, Milligan paraphrases, "Thus the full glory of the Lord Jesus will be displayed in you, as you in your turn derive your glory from Him in accordance with the gracious purposes of our God and the Lord Jesus Christ."

Study Questions

1. What is important about verse 1?
2. Are Paul's words about retribution encouraging to the suffering Thessalonians (vv. 4–9)? Would they be encouraging to you if you were struggling under such torment? How can we love the lost and yet be looking for a certain vengeance upon them for their mistreatment of Christians?
3. Explain in your own words what Paul means about being worthy "of your calling" (v. 11).
4. What is the apostle's great wish and desire (v. 12)?

CHAPTER TWELVE

Concern and Questions About the Day of the Lord

III. PAUL'S DOCTRINAL CORRECTION ABOUT THE DAY OF THE LORD (2:1–17)
A. "The Misunderstanding" (2:1–3)

Scholars have conflicting opinions as to why Paul and the other apostles wrote this chapter. Some argue that the Thessalonians were confused over Paul's teaching about the Day of the Lord (1 Thess. 5:2) and the Rapture, that they did not correctly perceive the order of events, and that they thought their current troubles proved that the Day of the Lord itself had arrived. Others, such as Walvoord, argue that false teachers had already come who were teaching aberrant doctrine. What Walvoord writes seems to be closer to the truth:

> The teaching that the Church would go through the Tribulation was already being advanced by certain teachers whom Paul opposed in this passage. It is sometimes assumed that in the early apostolic period only pure and accurate doctrine was taught. Nothing could be farther from the truth. Paul had to write his Epistle to the Galatians to correct the error of legalism. He wrote most of 1 Corinthians to correct doctrinal and moral errors in the Corinthian church. It seems quite clear that most of the heresies that later emerged in the second and third centuries had their small beginnings in the apostolic church.[1]

By the guidance of the Holy Spirit, Paul had told the Thessalonian church the meaning of their sufferings and its reward. He had carried them to the heights by explaining the coming of the Lord in the Rapture. He had told them about the resurrection of their loved ones and how together they would be transported to glory.

The Thessalonians had received the clear teaching about the Lord's coming. They were blessed by it, as the apostle had reminded them in 1 Thessalonians 1:10. Their hearts and minds had been occupied by it. Paul most likely had taught the truths contained in this letter when he was in Thessalonica. They should have known from 5:9 that they would not have to undergo the wrath of God, the Tribulation, that would someday come to the earth.

Since receiving the first letter, however, many had evidently become confused as to the order of events. Either traveling false teachers or the Judaizers of the city had sown doubt, claiming that they could prove the Messiah's coming by all of the Old Testament passages. With subtle propaganda, they preyed on the fears of the new converts concerning the darkness of the Day of Judgment and convinced them that this day of the Lord's wrath had come. Paul's present letter was written to correct the views of the false teachers and to reestablish the Thessalonian church in their hope, dispelling the fear that gripped them.

The apostle calms the new coverts (1) by explaining that they are not in the Day of the Lord, (2) by showing that the man of sin must also first be revealed, and (3) by using the certainty of the Rapture as the basis for removing their doubts. His purpose will be to show that grace will operate before judgment; the Rapture will take place before that "dreaded day." He states the truth with warmth, affection, and the assurance of the first verse, "our gathering together to Him."

Lenski summarizes the impact of false teaching upon the Thessalonian church:

Some imagined . . . , "that the day of the Lord is present," and sought to support this strange idea by supposed testimony of Paul's and his assistants' themselves. The writers inform the Thessalonians that all such alleged testimony is false, and that two dreadful things must precede the coming of the Lord, the great apostasy and the great Antichrist. . . . Now the writers correct those of the Thessalonians who were erring in regard to the date of the day of the Lord and were drawing dangerous conclusions from this error regarding their lives.

2:1 Now we request you, brethren, with regard to the coming of
our Lord Jesus Christ and our gathering together to Him,

Now. With *now* (*de*) the apostle radically changes subjects. "He now turns
aside (*de*) to correct any mistakes which his mention of this day may have
occasioned, to calm any feverish desires which it may have excited"
(Lightfoot). *De* is "used to connect one clause with another when it is felt
that there is some contrast between them" (*BAG*). Paul returns to the issue of
the Day of the Lord (v. 2), apparently because more assurance on the subject
was needed.

We request. Paul is using one of the most common words for *ask, request*
(*erotao,* present active indicative) in a more forceful way than is usual. *Erotao*
is more appropriate with exhortation and its urgency is heightened (Milligan).
While he is sympathetic with their confusion, he is urging them to consider
carefully what he has to say. "Paul begs his readers not to be thrown into con-
sternation or kept in a flutter of excitement over that matter of the Parousia,
or 'coming'" (*PCH*).

Brethren. *Adelphos* ("brother") in the New Testament denotes the same religious community, the fellowship of Christians. It probably has its common
origin from the Jewish community (Acts 2:29, 37; 3:17) (Milligan). Paul repeatedly uses it here in the Thessalonian epistles, because he felt such com-
radeship with these suffering believers. Their quick response to the gospel and
stability under pressure pleased Paul and made all his labors seem worthwhile.

With regard to the coming of our Lord Jesus Christ. *With regard* (*huper*)
to the "coming" (*parousia*) introduces the subject at hand. Soon after Paul
had written of the distinction between the Rapture and the Day of the Lord
(1 Thess. 4:13–5:10), false prophets began confusing the people by teaching
that they had missed the "catching up" (4:17) and were already in the hour of
terror. The apostle assured them that before the Day of the Lord arrives, the
falling away or the *apostasia* would come first.

Is the next clause, *and our gathering together to Him,* synonymous with
this first clause? "Our gathering together" fits with the Rapture, certainly not
the Second Coming, though some think that two distinct comings are in view
here: *The coming* would be referring to His kingdom reign and the *gathering*

together would be referring to the Rapture. Some have tried also to associate the Rapture with the Second Coming, speculating that the Rapture takes place and believers go up when the trumpet sounds, but then they return immediately with Him as He establishes the kingdom!

Both Alford and Robertson see "the coming" and "the gathering together to Him" as the same thing. The grammar probably well supports this by the use of the one preposition *huper* (concerning, regarding), which controls the two nouns "the coming" and "the gathering together." Thus it would read "With regard to the coming of our Lord Jesus Christ *even* our gathering together to Him." The gathering together refers to the meeting of the dead and the alive together as found in 1 Thessalonians 4:14–15, 17 (Ellicott). "Paul is referring to the Rapture, mentioned in 1 Thess. 4:15–17, and the being forever with the Lord thereafter" (Robertson).

Gathering together is actually three words (*episunogoge*) combined to make one—*epi* (upon), *sun* (together), and *ago* (to lead), or "to lead upon together." The word is used in Hebrews 10:25: "Not forsaking our own 'assembling together.'" *To Him* better reads "up to Him" (Alford).

Despite being momentarily confused about these events, the Thessalonians had been well taught. They knew that their suffering would be rewarded at Christ's coming for His Church. Their eyes would behold Him in the air as they are caught away from this sinful world. If they died before the Rapture, they still had hope of experiencing this event and receiving a new, eternal body. Paul

> . . . beseeches them by this event, for if their hearts could but grip the fact that their "gathering together unto him," their being taken to heaven, and thus being "for ever with the Lord" (1 Thess 4:17), meant they would be delivered from the coming wrath on earth, then all fear must vanish. (Ritchie)

> **2:2** that you may not be quickly shaken from your composure or be disturbed either by a spirit or a message or a letter as if from us, to the effect that the day of the Lord has come.

That you may not be quickly shaken from your composure. *May not be quickly* (*me tacheos*) can be translated "not be hastily, readily." Many of the believers seem to have been overwhelmed, thrown into shock. *Tacheos* could also be translated "after so short a time" (Lightfoot), that is, so quickly after Paul had taught them on these matters. Some false teachers must have tossed the assembly literally into a spin.

Be [*not*] *shaken* (*saleuo,* aorist passive infinitive) shows this emotional state coming upon the congregation, as in "to agitate, to cause to totter like a reed (Matt. 11:7), the earth (Heb. 12:26)" (Robertson). Their sober senses were shaken as a ship adrift from its moorings and tossed upon a troubled sea, that is, shaken "of the waves agitated by a storm" (Alford). In a sense they were helpless to stop the anxiety because what they were told by false teachers was so contrary as to what Paul had taught them.

From your composure actually means "from your mind" (*apo tou noos*). *Noos* refers to the "mind, reason, sober sense, composure" or "wit." They were losing their minds, their reasoning ability was shaken in regard to this particular subject. "This came as a shock to the mind and then left them in the greatest mental agitation. Note that Christians are to keep their heads against error and fanatic notions" (Lenski). The truth of God is sane and never unbalances the mind.

> Believers were behaving like ships that have become the victim of waves and winds and are being blown hither and thither. It seems that in the case of some the *Parousia* had become the main subject of conversation, the one important and ever-recurring theme for discussion. People were "losing their heads" over it, so that some decided to stop working altogether. (*NTC*)

Or be disturbed. This is the most emotional word Paul uses in this discussion. *Disturbed* (*throeo,* present passive infinitive) is a strong and powerful word in Greek that is used only here and in two other places in the New Testament (Matt. 24:6; Mark 13:7). It means "to cry aloud" as in pain or tumult. With the present tense and passive voice it can be translated "to be in a state of shock" as if the Day of the Lord is going on now (Robertson). They were continually disturbed, shaken, but they were not to be alarmed so easily (*NTC*). It is interesting that the word *throeo* is used in Matthew 24:6 and Mark 13:7 in the same context about the Tribulation or the Day of the Lord, with the same warning by Christ that Paul uses. "It seems fair to conclude that Paul is practically quoting Jesus" (Lenski).

Jesus warns a future generation of disciples, "You will be hearing of wars and rumors of wars; see that you are not frightened [*throeo*], for those things must take place, but that is not yet the end" (Matt. 24:6). "The end" would be the Day of the Lord or the seven-year period of tribulation. As Christ and Paul teach, some specific things will happen in the Tribulation, such as the revelation of the man of sin, the Antichrist. The Church, the body of Christ, will not see the events of that seven-year horror. The Church does not go through that terrible period. Yet someone in Thessalonica had spread the word that the Day of the Lord had come.

The aorist infinitive of *saleuo* followed with the present infinitive of *throeo* is very descriptive, the first expressing momentary shock to the mental state, the second expressing agitation that continues. The first is like the impact of a roaring wave, the second the awesome disturbance that comes after. When the Thessalonians thought that the Day of the Lord was already upon them, it came as a terrible, traumatic shock.

Despite their troubles (1:4) these new believers were not in the Day of the Lord as they thought and as they were told. To properly understand the expression *being gathered to Him* shows that they could not be so entangled with that awful period. "In fact, their 'being gathered to him' will be the event that signals the day's beginning" (*EBC*).

Either by a spirit or a message or a letter as if from us. *By* (*dia*) refers to the agencies that could have caused the shock of what the Thessalonians were hearing. *Dia* is used before each noun—"By means of a spirit, by means of a message, by means of a letter." *Pneuma* is not referring to the Holy Spirit as might be assumed, but probably refers to some ecstatic utterances, a false religious prophetic teaching, or demonic prophecies given by some of the charlatans so prevalent in Thessalonica. If the last is in view, Paul could be referring to spirits as demons. If this is the case, he is using strong language to emphasize how concerned he is over this false doctrine and its source.

Message (*logos*) could refer to those who claim the gift of knowledge (1 Cor. 13:8) or the gift of prophecy (14:29–32). These gifts, though important to the early church, were not infallible. The one uttering a revelation had to speak with two or three and then the message had to pass judgment (v. 29). The message could be analyzed since "the spirits of prophets are subject to prophets" (v. 32). In other words, the messages had to be checked and balanced and certainly they would have to conform to what the apostles teach. These "communication" gifts of prophecy, tongues, and knowledge would end (13:8–10) probably when the canon of Scripture was complete.

Letter (*epistolos*) may refer to the first epistle Paul wrote to this church, but this is probably not what is in view here. Paul's adding, "as if from us" (*hos di hemon*) can be taken three ways: the Thessalonians thought Paul either (1) instigated these forms of communication, (2) used other messengers, or (3) approved of the messages. Some may have said, "This is what Paul indeed said."

There must have been no end to the claims when the congregation assembled. "Interpreters" abounded and would be reporting inspired messages or prophetic voices. They would claim to have the truth and would assert that "Paul must mean this, for I heard the word from his own lips while he was here with us" (*NTC*). Others reported getting a letter from the apostle. The message of all of these "communications" was that the Day of the Lord had come. One can easily understand why God in His providence would settle His Word in scriptural form. The Holy Spirit controlled the writing of authorized prophets and apostles, and rumors have far less credibility than the written Word.

To the effect that the day of the Lord has come. *Has come* (*enistemi*, perfect active indicative) is a compound verb from *en* (in, with) and *histemi* (to stand, position). With the perfect tense, the thought is "the Day of the Lord 'has progressively come and is now at hand,'" or "be present" (*EDNT*), even "be imminent." Paul "does not deny that that day of the Lord may be near. He asserts that it is not imminent. Certain events must take place before it arrives" (Lightfoot).

> Paul's words should make us hesitate to affirm that Paul definitely proclaimed the early return of Jesus. He hoped for it undoubtedly, but he did not specifically proclaim it as so many today assert and accuse him of misleading the early Christians with a false presentation. (Robertson)

Some saints in Thessalonica had probably said, "How could the apostle speak of Christ's return as preceding the Day of the Lord?" (1 Thess. 1:10). "Did he not say we would in no way see the wrath of God?" (5:9). Without question Paul taught the pretribulational Rapture, but the confusion of the assembly was that they could not separate their own troubles from those anticipated at the Day of the Lord (*BKC*).

2:3 Let no one in any way deceive you, for it will not come unless the apostasy comes first, and the man of lawlessness is revealed, the son of destruction,

Let no one in any way deceive you. That is, "deceive you in thinking that
the Day of the Lord has arrived and that you are in it." *Deceive* (*exapatao*,
aorist active subjunctive) is a compound verb, *ex* (out) and *apatao* (to deceive),
and it means "to extremely deceive." It is translated "entice" when referring
to the deception of Eve by the serpent (1 Tim. 2:14). In Romans 16:18 "Paul
warns of some who *'deceive* the hearts of the simpleminded'* with pretty
words" (*EDNT*). With the aorist subjunctive the clause could read, "Just don't
let anyone really lead you astray."

In any way (*kata medena tropos*) or "according [*kata*] not at all [*medena*]
manner, way [*tropos*]*"* is a strongly stated prepositional phrase, which might
read, "*according to no way whatsoever,* 'do not let anyone deceive you,'" or
"whatever device they may adopt . . . do not be duped by them" (Ellicott).

For it will not come unless the apostasy comes first. Some commentators have thought the *apostasia* could refer to the Rapture in the sense of "the
departure." But almost all scholars agree it has to do with religious or spiritual departure. *Apostasia* is a compound word, *apo* (from, away from) and
stasia or *histemi* (to stand), thus, a "standing away from," or "positioning
oneself from." Apostasy has the article attached, which makes the word definite, *the* apostasy. Some have suggested that use of the article clearly indicates that Paul has spoken of apostasy before as a distinct and definite period.

Some think the apostasy actually comes about when the rebellion, with the
"lawless one," the Antichrist, comes on the scene. "This [theory] places the
rebellion and the revelation of the person of rebellion on a similar footing"
(*NIGTC*). Though this view is remotely possible, it still does not negate the
idea of an apostasy at the end of the Church dispensation. The New Testament is clear that such a departure takes place. Though a distinct period of
apostasy is coming, both Paul and John point out that the spirit of apostasy is
always present. Paul mentions it, in fact, when he writes "that in the last days
difficult times will come" (2 Tim. 3:1). He points to apostate leaders in his
day who held to a form of godliness but were denying the power: "avoid such
men as these" (v. 5). The apostle John concurs and writes that the spirit of
Antichrist is present with those who deny the actual physical nature of Christ

(1 John 4:2), but he notes that, although this spirit is already in the world, "you have heard that it is [also] coming" (v. 3).

> A parallel term is the Greek *aphistemi* (to withdraw, depart, or fall away). It is used in 1 Timothy 4:1 where it is translated "some shall depart from the faith." This apostasy is said to occur in the latter times. It results in the apostates giving heed to seducing spirits and doctrines of devils. Parallel expressions include: "go away," "turn away," "lead astray," "miss the mark," "suffer shipwreck." In Hebrews 3:12, *aphistemi* is used of those departing from the living God. It implies a deliberate abandonment of one's beliefs.[2]

Since apostasy is now with us in this Church Age, no one knows how much more intense it must become before Christ returns for His own. That indicators are now present in no way removes the hope of an imminent return of the Lord. The final apostasy will be an intensification of denials. Men will deny God (2 Tim. 3:4–5), Christ (2 Peter 2:6; 1 John 2:18; 4:3), and even faith itself (1 Tim. 4:1–2; Jude 3). They will deny the Lord's return (2 Peter 3:3–4), sound doctrine (2 Tim. 4:3–4), a separated life (2 Tim. 3:1–7), Christian liberty (1 Tim. 4:3–4), morals (2 Tim. 3:1–3, 13; Jude 18), and authority (2 Tim. 3:4).[3]

Even amillennialist Calvin agrees, though he anticipates a restoration of the Church in the final stage of history. He writes, "Paul, therefore, predicts a certain general revolt of the visible Church. 'The Church must be reduced to an unsightly and dreadful state of ruin, before its full restoration be effected.'"

Lightfoot thinks the apostasy will only be from within the Church and not from without. "It must arise either from the Jews or from apostate Christians, either of whom might be said to fall away from God. On the other hand it cannot refer to Gentiles." This is too restrictive. The passages above indicate belief that the revolt is also cultural and social. The Church simply falls in line with what is going on in the world. Signs are evident that, coupled with the explosion of communication and the rapid development of technology, humanity will feel it is divine and needs no other God. This could be driving the world rapidly into the full apostasy that will be both cultural and religious and even "Christian" in outward appearance.

In regard to "it will not come," *come* (*erchomai*, aorist active subjunctive) is a "negative condition of the third class, undetermined with prospect of determination [with] the aorist subjunctive" (Robertson). The third class subjunctive condition expresses that which is not really taking place but which probably will take place in the future. It is not happening now but it will happen if God permits. The apostasy will come when the conditions are met.

In "comes first," *first* (*proton*) here has in view the chronology of events. There is no way the man of lawlessness can appear before the apostasy begins. This apostasy is probably both cultural and spiritual. Organized religion will exist, "a form of godliness" (2 Tim. 3:5a), but its power and authority will be denied (v. 5b). A vacuum will be created for the son of destruction.

Some of the older amillennial or postmillennial writers view the apostasy as some event in the past. They also identify the Antichrist as being some famous personality of antiquity. These teachers of the Word of God do not believe that such prophecies could still be future. But if the book of Revelation is yet future, the matter is settled. The "Beast" is the Antichrist and all the events described in that prophecy are still to come.

It must be remembered that much that Paul and John wrote was already well known from the Old Testament. Jewish and early church interpretation of tribulation events were without a doubt premillennial and literal. The Holy Spirit gave additional revelation to these two apostles, but the essence was already proclaimed and understood by the Jewish people. It would not be until around the third century A.D. that both Jewish and Christian interpretation would become nonliteral. The earlier writings of the Jewish philosopher Philo and the Hellenistic idealist school of allegory would influence Origen and Augustine.

> The Jewish hermeneutic of a literal, futurist interpretation was followed by the Jewish writers of the New Testament, and Jewish views of the Antimessiah influenced both early Jewish-Christian interpretation and the interpretation of many of the early (ante-Nicene) church fathers. For example, Irenaeus (c. A.D. 185) wrote: "But when this Antichrist shall have devastated all things in this world, he will reign for three years and six months, and sit in the temple at Jerusalem; and then the Lord will come from heaven in the clouds, in the glory of the Father, sending this man and those who follow him into the lake of fire; but bringing in for the righteous the times of the kingdom."[4]

And the man of lawlessness is revealed, the son of destruction. The *and* could very well be translated *then.* After the apostasy *then* the man of lawlessness is revealed, the man who is without law (*anomias*), or above law, will be revealed. He will be a law unto himself, making his own laws and despising the laws of God. This is a man and not a religion or religious system,

> . . . the incarnation of evil, even as Christ is of all that is holy, and good, and true. The title "lawlessness" denotes his character. *Anomia* means without law, altogether, and this comes out in Daniel's description of him as "willful," indicating deliberate, arrogant perversity and self-will. (*NIGTC*)

Is revealed. *Revealed* (*apokalupto,* aorist passive subjunctive) implies that his identification had been hidden or certainly not known. The time must be right in God's providence to bring him into power. He will be a superhuman personality who will be hidden from view until the right moment, and then he will be suddenly manifested. "Both Christ and the adversary of Christ are revealed, there is mystery about each, both make divine claims (verse 4)" (Robertson).

Dozens of views have been offered about the apostasy and the Antichrist but twelve seem to be the most prevalent:

1. Because of early church persecution such as Paul is addressing in the Thessalonian letters, some believe the apostasy is the falling away from Christianity before the destruction of Jerusalem in A.D. 70.
2. The coming of the Lord refers to the destruction of Jerusalem by Titus. With this there would be a great apostasy.
3. The apostasy is a great defection from the faith that occurred between the Roman emperors Nero and Trajan.
4. Also before A.D. 70, the apostasy represents a return of Jews back to Judaism from Christianity.
5. The man of sin is identified as the evil Jewish nation characterized by wickedness for rejecting Christ.
6. The Gnostic Simon Magus is named by many as the man of sin.
7. Caesar Caius or the emperor Caligula is possibly the Antichrist; either man's evil represents the apostasy.

8. The man of sin is the Roman general Titus and the house of Flavian produced the evil line.
9. Mohammed is the man of sin.
10. Roman Catholics in the Middle Ages believed the apostasy was the falling away of Protestants from the papacy.
11. Napoleon Bonaparte is the man of sin.
12. To many of the Reformers, the Pope, the Roman Pontiff, is the man of sin and the world system he created is his evil kingdom.

That Caligula was the Antichrist has been one of the most popular views. Caligula is considered by history an immoral madman who stands out as one of the worst of the Roman emperors. Born in A.D. 12 to Germanicus and Aprippina, he lived with the older emperor Tiberius. In A.D. 37, at Tiberius' death, Caligula was named emperor. His name was actually Gaius Julius Caesar Germanicus, but by the Roman soldiers of the Rhine army, he was nicknamed "Little Boots," or Caligula.

Out of hatred for the Jews he attempted to have his statue placed in the Holy of Holies in the temple in Jerusalem. He had earlier decided to have himself declared a god and ordered the Romans and all other subjects, including the Jews, to worship him. This would, of course, have ignited the Middle East and threatened the Roman hold on Palestine. To avoid bloodshed, prominent Jewish leaders went to Rome in A.D. 40 to persuade Caligula to change his mind about the temple. Their success or failure became a moot point because the mad emperor died a year later, which averted disaster. His death by assassination ended a terrible period of cruelty and tyranny. His sadism and lurid life made him a candidate to be cast as Antichrist.

Antiochus Epiphanes, who was foreshadowed in Daniel 11:36, gave the earlier Jews a foretaste of such a personality. Many have thought that Paul used Antiochus and Caligula as examples of such an Antichrist. When Caligula attempted to place an image of himself in the temple many feel that he then projected for Paul a delineation of this future deceiver.

But Paul does not identify the final deceiver with the imperial *cultus,* which was far from a prominent feature when he wrote Thessalonians. Paul's point

. . . is that the last pseudo-Messiah or anti-Christ will embody all that
is profane and blasphemous, every conceivable element of impiety;

and that, instead of being repudiated, he will be welcomed by Jews as well as pagans. (Nicoll)

A sketch of the Antichrist is given in both Old and New Testaments, beginning in Daniel 7:20, where he is called the boastful "other horn," which has "larger appearance than its associates." In 9:26 he is identified as the prince whose people destroy the temple. By this, we know that he is aligned with the empire of the Romans who will rise again someday as a powerful nation in the end times. In a new context that begins in Daniel 11:36, this personality seems to be mentioned again. He will honor a god of fortresses and give great honor to those who acknowledge him (vv. 38–39). Many believe he is mentioned once more in the Old Testament where he is called "the worthless shepherd who leaves [abandons] the flock!" (Zech. 11:17). He is described as mutilated with a withered arm and his right eye blinded.

Jesus talks of him violating the temple (Matt. 24:15), Paul describes also this future desecration (2 Thess. 2:3–9), and John mentions him as Antichrist (1 John 2:22). But the most extensive description is in the book of Revelation with the main description of him as the Beast (Rev. 13). A terrible end awaits him and his followers who give him honor and worship. They will be tossed into the lake of fire and brimstone: "And the smoke of their torment goes up forever and ever; and they have no rest day and night" (14:11).

The son of destruction. The Antichrist is the son of *destruction* (*apolia*, "perdition"), that is, "the son who is due destruction and punishment," which is his "predominating quality" (Ellicott). *Apolia* is related to the verb *apollumi* and means "to destroy, lose, die, be lost" with the idea of "waste, annihilation" (*EDNT*). Judas was called by Christ the son of destruction (John 17:12), and Peter, more than any other writer, uses the word in regard to a future judgment (2 Peter 2:1, 2, 3; 3:7, 16). It is sometimes translated "damnation" (2:3).

The fathers of the early Church, for at least three centuries after the apostolic age, while differing on some minor details, seemed unanimous in understanding by the Man of Sin, not a system of deceit and wickedness, or a succession of individuals at the head of such a system, but some one man, the living personal Antichrist, the incarnation of Satanic craft and energy. (*PCH*)

B. The Man of Lawlessness (2:4–9)

2:4 who opposes and exalts himself above every so-called god or object of worship, so that he takes his seat in the temple of God, displaying himself as being God.

Who opposes and exalts himself above every so-called god or object of worship. *Who opposes* (*antikeimai,* present active participle) is a compound of anti (against) and *keimai* (lie, find oneself). The basic meaning of *keimai* is "to lie, be laid" and sometimes "to find oneself, appear, be destined, be put in place"; while *antikeimai* carries the thought "be opposite, oppose, be in conflict with" (*EDNT*). With the article *ho* and the present participle it might read, "the one who is opposing," or as the subject, "the adversary, the enemy," as describing Satan in 1 Timothy 5:14. Though *antikeimai* is a present participle, the time frame for such is not during the period of the apostle Paul. The Antichrist comes at some future time. Because this section is relating prophecy, it may be translated "the one who will oppose." Barnes thinks the Antichrist here is opposing the gospel. This is true, but the Antichrist will carry his opposition much farther. Although the Church is raptured out of the earth before the seven-year period of tribulation, the eternal gospel will be proclaimed during that terrible period (Rev. 14:6). Even under the wrath of God, the world can still find grace. Yet most of those who do accept Jesus during that time will probably die as martyrs. John the apostle was given a vision of those slain. He saw their souls under the altar before the Lord in heaven. They cried out, asking how long it would be before the "judging and avenging our blood on those who dwell on the earth?" (6:10). They then waited for the completion of the slaughter of the righteous, "their fellow-servants and their brethren who were to be killed even as they had been" (v. 11).

What religious system will be behind the Antichrist? Under the spiritual leadership of the "other beast" (13:11), it could be the system of Roman Catholicism that would be growing even more powerful during the Tribulation. The False Prophet (16:13) could be the Pope, who at this stage of the Tribulation "performs great signs, so that he even makes fire come down out of heaven to the earth in the presence of men" (13:13).

Other scholars think the Antichrist represents the Catholic system. What he is able to do on a worldwide scale of deception seems conclusive to Bible teachers like Barnes: "No Protestant will doubt that this has been the character of the papacy. . . . No one can reasonably doubt that all that is here affirmed may be found in the claims of the pope of Rome."

The Antichrist will also be opposing even other pretender gods and imitating the true God Himself (2 Thess. 2:4b).

Exalts himself (*huperairo,* present middle participle) is a compound form, *huper* (over) and *aireo* (take with the hand, overpower, entrap) (L&S), that is, "the exalter of himself" (Milligan). The thought is far stronger than exalt. A better connotation is the idea of being "overbearing" (*EDNT*). The Antichrist will himself (middle voice) "take over, take charge over, dominate, subdue" even other religions or gods. He will create an eclectic religion and spiritual domination that will unite all belief systems into one. At first he will not do this by brute force but through subtle salesmanship and persuasion.

It is interesting that the same article, *ho,* controls both participles with the *kai* in between. It could read, "the one opposing and himself taking over." "This spell[s] out the distinctive activity of the person of rebellion" (*NIGTC*), giving "a continued description of the lawless one in two participial clauses bound together under . . . a common article" (Milligan). "The literal rendering of the [first] participle gives a stronger sense of the character of the man of lawlessness, namely, 'the opposer (withstander, or adversary) who greatly exalts himself.' All the defiance, arrogance and willful pride of this opposer of God come out in this short description" (Ritchie).

Every so-called god (*panta legomenon theon*) is an interesting expression in the Greek text—*legomenon* (*lego,* present passive participle), "all being called god." *Being called* implies that they are only designated as gods but are not. The Lord makes it clear: "I am God, and there is no other" (Isa. 46:9a). In the depraved mind of humanity, however, millions of gods reign. The Antichrist will place himself above even these. "The expression includes the *true* God, as well as the false ones of the heathen" (Alford).

"Object of worship" is a good translation of the Greek *sebasma* (*BAG*), a religious term that expresses both heathen and Christian worship. It carries the thought of respect for the deity, and it is sometimes translated "devout" (Acts 13:50; 17:4, 17). Paul used the related verb when he wrote of how the Gentiles "worshipped and served the creature rather than the Creator" (Rom. 1:25). *Sebasma* is "comprehensive . . . denoting everything held in religious honour" (Milligan).

So that he takes his seat in the temple of God, displaying himself as being God. Literally, "to be seated," *kathizo* is an aorist active infinitive. The aorist usually "denotes that one definite act and not a series of acts is spoken of, but here, from the peculiar nature of the verb, that one act is the *setting himself down,* and the *session* remains after it" (Alford). Thus, the Antichrist will have stationed himself, planted himself in the seated position of authority. By this act, he is declaring himself to be God.

What temple (*naos*) is in view here? Paul actually writes *"the temple the of god."* The nature of the context, the use of such a local term as "seated," and the twice-repeated use of the definite article, "all point to a literal reference in the present instance" (Milligan). Milligan notes that "these words were understood of the actual temple at Jerusalem by Irenaeus . . . , but this view was modified by Chrysostom and the Antiochenes [scholars] who extended them metaphorically to the Church or Churches of Christ."

Over time, allegory replaced the literal or normal interpretation with obscure spiritualization, a position advocated by such teachers as Barnes, who writes about the temple reference here: "That is, in the Christian Church. It is by no means necessary to understand this of the temple at Jerusalem, which was standing at the time this epistle was written." It is true the Church is described sometimes as a temple (1 Cor. 3:16; 2 Cor. 6:16; Eph. 2:21), and the word may refer to the heavenly temple, the abode of God Himself (Heb. 8:1–4; 9:23, 24; Rev. 15:5), but with a normal interpretation applied in context, these references fall short of the literal meaning required by the passages. A man can take his seat in none of these other places mentioned. The article with "temple" is another indicator that the Jerusalem temple belonging to the God of Israel is in view.

The Scriptures highlight five temples:

- Solomon's temple. Begun in 966 B.C. and finally and completely destroyed by Nebuchadnezzar in 586 B.C.
- Zerubbabel's temple. Begun in 536 B.C. and finished in 516 B.C.
- Herod's temple. Begun in 20 B.C. and destroyed by the Romans in A.D. 70. This destruction is prophesied in Daniel 9:26: "The people [Romans] of the prince [the future Antichrist] will come and destroy the city and the sanctuary."
- Tribulation temple. "The prince" at some future date "will make a firm covenant with the many for one week, but in the middle of the week he

will put a stop to sacrifice" (v. 27). The Antichrist will sign a peace agreement with the Jews for this one week (seven years), which is the last distinct period of what is called Daniel's Seventy Weeks (v. 24). These seventy weeks (*heptads*), or 490 years, represent God's timetable of activity in dealing specifically and righteously with His people the Jews. This clock of years was stopped when Christ entered Jerusalem to be tried and crucified (A.D. 30, spring), that is, 483 years had passed since, in 444 B.C., Artaxerxes I granted permission for the rebuilding of the temple. The Antichrist will break that peace pact in three and a half years, or "in the middle of the week," at which time he will put a stop to sacrifice. This takes place when he enters the temple as Paul describes and turns and proclaims himself as God (2 Thess. 2:4), an event that Jesus, quoting Daniel 27b, referred to as the "abomination of desolation" (Matt. 24:15).

In these words we note Antichrist's intrusion into the special dwelling-place of God, his usurping session there, and his blasphemous and ostentatious assumption of divinity. The wildest excesses of pride and audacity cannot exceed this (*PCH*).

(For a scholarly comprehensive treatment of Daniel's Seventy Weeks, refer to Harold W. Hoehner, *Chronological Aspects of the Life of Christ* [Grand Rapids: Zondervan], 1977.)

• Millennial temple. The description of the millennial temple is given in detail in Ezekiel 40–48. The Messiah Jesus will grant that this temple be built after the Jews have fully returned from their worldwide scattering. Although this will take place at the end of the Tribulation, the Jews began, in various stages, returning to the land of promise—Eratz Israel (land of Israel)—throughout the twentieth century, a migration accelerated by World Wars I and II. The Lord says that just prior to the building of the millennial temple, . . .

When I bring them back from the peoples and gather them from the lands of their enemies, then I shall be sanctified through them in the sight of the many nations. Then they will know that I am their God because I made them go into exile among the nations, and then gathered them again to their own land; and I will leave none of them there any longer. (Ezekiel 39:27–28)

In 2 Thessalonians 2:4, the apostle is describing the Antichrist's desecration of the temple, something that must follow the apostasy. His blasphemy manifests itself in his "displaying himself as being God." *Displaying* (*apodeiknuo,* present active participle) is a compound, *apo* (from) and *deiknumi* (to show, allow to see, display, reveal). The present participle gives the force of "continually displaying himself" as God. The Antichrist's main role will be to preside over the spiritual darkness that falls on the world, this reign held in joint rule with the Beast out of the sea (Rev. 13:1ff.), who will lead the whole world in opposition to God. As the Lord's main opponent in Jerusalem, the Antichrist, whose ancestry is possibly Jewish (Dan. 11:36–37), will guide the world's leaders to dominate the entire nations of the earth (*EBC*).

2:5 Do you not remember that while I was still with you, I was telling you these things?

Do you not remember that while I was still with you, I was telling you these things? Some commentators have asserted that Paul is almost insulting the Thessalonians, or at least was chiding them because they had forgotten his teaching on the subject. But this is probably not so. He is but firmly reminding them of what he taught. He is trying to calm them down by bringing back to their remembrance such important teachings about the Day of the Lord and the Antichrist.

These doctrinal nuggets were not new, and Paul was now calling on the Thessalonians to apply those earlier lessons to calm their fears. That the apostle taught them personally is established in the clause, "I was telling you these things," here being one of the first times he uses this clause. He wanted them to take note that he was the chief spokesman on this important prophetic subject. "He believed it was a vital part of the whole counsel of God, so he taught it without hesitation or apology" (*BKC*).

2:6 And you know what restrains him now, so that in his time he may be revealed.

And you know what restrains him now, so that in his time he may be revealed. *You know* (*oida,* perfect active indicative) might better be translated "you have come to realize." Paul is saying that although those in the Thessalonian church had arrived at this conclusion (with the perfect tense), he is implying by the context that the knowledge had not been internalized. They are not acting upon what they know and believe to counter suggestions that they may be in the Tribulation and that the Antichrist has come.

Restrains (*katecho*, present active participle) is a compound verb, *kata* (down) and *echo* (have, hold) and means "to hold down, confine, restrain." *Restrains* is in the neuter gender and, being a present participle, could read "that which is restraining." But the same word *katecho* in verse 7, used also as a present participle, is in the masculine gender and could read "the Restrainer," or "the one who is restraining." "The Thessalonians know the thing now holding up the revelation of the Antichrist. . . . Paul had told them long before this time" (Lenski)—"Well now, you know what restrains him from being manifested (coming fully into play and sight) before his appointed season" (Nicoll).

A persuasive, although not popular, view is that the restraining influence is the Holy Spirit. *Spirit* (*pneuma*) in the New Testament is a neuter word but, when referring to the Spirit of God, often has the masculine pronoun. He is not simply a force or spirit but the third person in the Trinity. This seems to be the most sensible answer as to the identity of this restraining influence, though many other views have been more widely accepted.

Gill says the restrainer is the Roman emperor and other emperors who followed. Some say "restrains"—expressed as neuter—represents the restraining power, and "restrains"—expressed as masculine—represents the actual person of the Antichrist. With this view, the man of lawlessness would represent the imperial line of emperors with its rage for deification. It has been suggested, too, that the restraining power would represent the Jewish state and its opposition to the true gospel. Some say the restraining power is the godly influence of the Church or, as Calvin states, it is the gospel itself: "This, therefore, was the delay, until the career of the gospel should be completed, because a gracious invitation to salvation was first in order." But

> . . . the term "Church" has been deliberately avoided in this explanation, for not only is it the case that the Scriptures do not speak of the Church on earth, but by use of the word some have provided occasion to those who oppose this view, for "Church" is feminine (*ekklesia*) whilst the word for the restraint in this verse is neutral. (Ritchie)

Other views include the following: the power of well-ordered human rule; law as established by Roman rule; Michael or some other restraining angel; Satan, who is waiting for the right moment to step aside and allow the Antichrist to take over; the providence of God in which the appropriate moment will be realized for the man of sin to be revealed. (This last view is, of course, true within the big picture of God's sovereignty, but there is someone specifically in mind by the term "restrainer.")

That Paul had in mind Roman dominion and human government as the restrainer is unlikely. Paul confines his views about human government to that which sometimes was beneficial (Acts 17:6ff.; 18:6ff.) or he limits human government to its judgment upon evil doers (Rom. 13). To forecast the fall of the Roman empire (that it would be "taken out of the way," v. 7) is quite unlike Paul. Too, the Roman emperors sometimes precipitated anti-Christian activities rather than restrained them. The elimination of Roman influence as the restrainer is sealed when we remember that the Roman Empire has long since ceased to exist, and the appearance of Christ or the lawless one has yet to take place (*EBC*).

To designate "the restraining" as some powerful force or ordinary person who is hostile to God is contradictory, because the restrainer or restraining influence is limiting Satan (vv. 7–9), not helping or cooperating with him.

The Holy Spirit seems to be the only One who has the divine power to restrain the forces of evil.

> The Holy Spirit of God is the only Person with sufficient (supernatural) power to do this restraining. . . . The removal of the Restrainer at the time of the Rapture must obviously precede the day of the Lord. Paul's reasoning is thus a strong argument for the pretribulational Rapture: the Thessalonians were not in the Great Tribulation because the Rapture had not yet occurred. (*BKC*)

So that in his time he may be revealed. *May be revealed* (*apokalupto*, aorist passive infinitive) is used by the apostle three times in its verb form in this chapter (vv. 3, 6, 8) and once as a noun (1:7). Paul is telling us that the Antichrist will suddenly be made manifest. *Apokalupto* (to reveal that which has been hidden) is a word characteristic of Pauline vocabulary; he uses both the verb and noun forms some twenty-eight times in his epistles. Paul thus describes the revealing of Christ (2 Thess. 1:7); of righteous judgment (Rom.

2:5); of the sons of God (8:19); of the righteousness of God (1:17); of the wrath of God (v. 18); of the coming glory (8:18); and of Jesus to Paul (Gal. 1:16). *In his time* more accurately reads "in the season [*kairos*] of him." Antichrist is to come at just the right and appropriate period of world history. The iniquity of the Gentiles will be piled up, and judgment through his evilness will be due upon the nations. "As there was an exact season for Christ to appear, so also is there for Satan's false christ. He is but a man; God will determine his permitted season" (Ritchie).

2:7 For the mystery of lawlessness is already at work; only he who now restrains will do so until he is taken out of the way.

For the mystery of lawlessness is already at work. *Lawlessness* (*anomia*, see v. 3) is present now, and it is having an effect. By writing *mystery* (*musterion*), Paul refers to that which is "too profound for human ingenuity" (*BAG*), or that is mysterious or illusive in its nature and cannot be comprehended, though evidence for it can be seen. Lawlessness is a dark spiritual force that is inspired by Satan himself. It is a rebellion and is in conflict with all that God is and that He sets forth as truth. The man of lawlessness (v. 3), whose power is presently at work in the world, will someday be revealed.

Already (*ede*) and even now this attitude of confusion, this lawlessness, is *working itself* (*energeo*, present middle/passive indicative). The voice of the verb (middle or passive) is important for interpretation. If it is a passive voice, it tells us God is responsible for the activity of the mystery of rebellion. But if it is a middle voice, then it means that rebellion against God is going on now (*NIGTC*). Alford takes lawlessness as "ungodliness—refusal to recognize God's law." Since ungodliness is mysterious, going on now, and it cannot be manifested fully, "its real character and full scope are not yet disclosed" (Nicoll). Though rebellion was obvious in Paul's day,

> . . . it was not evident that one day this spirit of lawlessness would become incarnate in "the man of lawlessness." This was still a mystery (cf. Rom. 11:25; 1 Cor. 15:51; Eph. 5:32); that is, a truth unknown apart from divine special revelation. (*NTC*)

Only he who now restrains will do so until he is taken out of the way. The masculine article *ho* in front of the participle (*katecho*, present active participle) is definite—*"the* one who is restraining," or *"the* Restrainer"—supporting the idea that this is the Holy Spirit. Some dispensationalists believe that the Holy Spirit leaves the earth when the Church is raptured. Although the Spirit of God has a vital ministry with the Church during this present age of grace, He is still operative during the Tribulation. Men and women will still come to saving faith during this terrible period. =e Spirit applies the benefits of the New Covenant to those who trust Jesus during the Tribulation, but He does not place them into "the body of Christ" as happens now in the Church dispensation.

The Restrainer restrains sin *until (eos)* a certain time period comes about. Then the Restrainer "should become *(ginomai,* aorist active subjunctive) out of the middle *(ek mesou genetai)."* The passage may reveal that He simply moves over. The Spirit changes His work but He does not leave. The change has to do with His restraining work not His salvation work.

The Holy Spirit was hindering or restraining when this epistle was written, but He has continued to do so, and will "until He be taken out of the way," or probably more accurately "until He becomes out of the way." "The Spirit shall become out of one sphere into another," or "He that withholdeth disappear from the midst" (Ellicott), thus, "to be taken, removed."

Some say *ginomai* cannot be translated "to be taken," but evidence exists to the contrary that is well in line with Greek usage. "The phrase is used of any person or thing which is taken out of the way. . . . He that hinders shall be removed" (Alford). *Ek mesou* with the various verbs it uses can read, "removal out of the way, or midst." That there was someone in the way, the Holy Spirit, who would in the future be taken out of the way, is palpably the point (Ritchie). To be taken out of the way is not to be entirely removed.

As already hinted above, the middle voice of *ginomai* may prove helpful in fully understanding this passage. Since the verb *ginomai* is deponent in form it may not denote removal by an outside force but instead be indicating a determined act on the part of the subject, the Restrainer. "The Holy Spirit is going to move out of the way, He is not going to be taken out of the way."[5] Many commentators, however, miss this distinction.

The Holy Spirit is present in order to save the lost during the Tribulation, but He will no longer restrain sin; His restraining activity will but cease.

2:8 And then that lawless one will be revealed whom the Lord will slay with the breath of His mouth and bring to an end by the appearance of His coming;

And then that lawless one will be revealed. *And then (kai tote)* is what is called an emphatic note of time—"Now this will certainly take place." Not until the Restrainer is taken out of the way will (Robertson) the revelation of the lawless one (v. 3) take place, but "then" it will no longer be delayed (Milligan). "'And then' denotes an emphatic point in time, and is in relationship to 'now' (*arti,* just now) in v. 7 and not to the 'now' of v. 6. It would seem to indicate that immediately after the hindrance and the Hinderer are taken out of the way, the revealing of 'the Wicked' will take place. It is a matter for wonder how each of these future events is in the calendar of God's timing; God is sovereign" (Ritchie).

Will be revealed (apokalupto, future passive indicative) is here used similarly as is parsed in verse 3 (aorist passive subjunctive) and in verse 6 (aorist passive infinitive). In all of these passages the passive voice is used, implying that some outside force is bringing about this revelation. The Lord Himself, of course, will bring about that revelation. From the dark unknown the lawless one will be brought to light, so that he may be finally destroyed. As related here, Paul is compressing the timetable, but in the book of Revelation, it becomes a process that takes several years to accomplish.

Whom the Lord will slay. *Will slay (anaireo,* future active indicative) does not mean the Antichrist will be annihilated out of existence. This diabolical individual is very human with a soul and spirit that will be judged and eternally punished. He is thrown into the lake of fire where he is joined later by the lost of all generations to experience the fires of torment forever and ever (Rev. 20:10).

The breath of His mouth. The Lord but speaks and the doom of the Antichrist is sealed. His breath is sufficient to bring forth this judgment. In Revelation 1:16, 19:15, 21 we are told that "a sharp two-edged sword" comes out of His mouth, thus, His command is cutting and final. These concepts are the fulfillment of what the Branch, the Messiah will do when he comes. "He will strike the earth with the rod of His mouth, and with the breadth of His lips He will slay the wicked" (Isa. 11:4). It cannot be denied that these words speak strongly of the second advent of Christ (*Barnes*).

In the drama of the book of Revelation, it seems as if the Antichrist may win. "Who is like the beast, and who is able to wage war with him?" (13:4). His activities are declared to be limited in that he is given authority "over every tribe and people and tongue and nation" (v. 7), and he is allowed to speak arrogant words "for forty-two months [three and a half years]" (v. 5b). With a host of evil kings of the earth, the Beast comes up against Christ when he comes forth "to make war against Him" (19:19). This military confrontation against the Messiah, the Son of David, is short lived because "the beast was seized, and with him the false prophet [the world religious ruler], . . . these two were thrown alive into the lake of fire which burns with brimstone" (v. 20).

And bring to an end by the appearance of His coming. That is, the Antichrist and all his evil will be brought to a climax so that he and all his forces of rebellion might be destroyed. *Bring to an end* (*katargeo,* future active indicative) is a compound verb, *kata* (down) and *argeo* (to be useless, to make ineffective) and can be translated "to render idle or inactive" and thus "to abolish" or "to bring to nothing" (Milligan). Habakkuk 3 mentions Christ's second coming and Christ's war against the nations. Verse 3 seems to refer to the head of the confederacy of the nations, the Antichrist: "Thou didst strike the head of the house of evil to lay him open from thigh to neck." "This, too, is a reference to his death at the Second Coming, and it is the Old Testament corollary to 2 Thessalonians 2:8."[6]

Appearance (*epiphaneia*) is a compound noun, *epi* (upon, above) and *phaino* (to shine, appear) (*EDNT*). The verb form can "refer to the illumination and shining of various sources of light, such as the sun, the moon, lamps, and fire" (*EDNT*). Sometimes in the New Testament it refers to the shining of a lamp. "And so we have the prophetic word made more sure, to which you do well to pay attention as to a lamp *shining* in a dark place, until the day dawns and the morning star arises in your hearts" (2 Peter. 1:19, italics mine).

Epiphaneia is used to describe both the Rapture (Titus 2:13) and the second coming of Christ (2 Tim. 4:1). Both happenings will be an illumination, a brightness, a shining. Simply as a verb, *epiphaino* may be used to refer to an appearance without some form of a glorious apparition, as "God our Savior and His love for mankind *appeared*" (Titus 3:4, italics mine).

Here in 2:8 the reference is to the second coming (*parousia*) of the Lord to reign and rule over the earth. "'The splendor of his coming' is his other means of conquest. . . . This 'appearance' phase of the *parousia* differs from the 'gathering' phase (v. 1). It concludes and climaxes the Tribulation instead of beginning it. The visible presence of the Lord Jesus in the world will put an immediate stop to an accelerated diabolical program" (*EBC*). "Christ will by his Spirit blow a blast upon antichrist and his kingdom, which he shall never recover again" (Gill).

> **2:9** that is, the one whose coming is in accord with the activity of Satan, with all power and signs and false wonders,

That is, the one whose coming is in accord with the activity of Satan. The subject is the lawless one in verse 8. "Whose coming *is* (*eimi*)" can be translated as a prophetic present with certainty that it will happen (*NTC*).

As with Christ, the Antichrist also has a "coming" (*parousia*), a glorious appearance that appears to be for the good but turns out for evil. This passage makes it clear that the word *parousia* can be used differently in various contexts. Some say that the expression, "the coming," always refers to Christ's second advent and therefore could not refer to the Rapture. Nevertheless, context demonstrates the difference and, in the case above, shows that even the Antichrist can have a "coming." "How terrible is the thought in the use of this word, as also of 'revealed,' in respect of the man of lawlessness, for it shows that Satan will bring in 'his man' in mimicry of the coming of Christ. This would mark the event as being in the matter of evil and unrighteousness what the Lord's coming [is] in the holy purpose of God" (Ritchie).

Activity (*energia*) means the "energy," "activity," or work of Satan, his master plan and strategy to attempt to defeat the purposes of God. The Lord also has a plan, a work that He is carrying out through His mighty power (Eph. 1:19; 3:7). Satan is trying to counterfeit and subvert God's sovereignty, but the end has already been determined. God has written the final chapter.

With all power and signs and false wonders. Again, this phrase is full of descriptions that also define the workings of God Almighty. The obvious difference is found in the word *false* (*pseudos*). "When the devil 'tells *lies*' (John 8:44), he functions as the eschatological opponent of Jesus, who 'has told the truth' . . . The devil counters the truth, i.e., God's revelation, with falsehood as a kind of anti-revelation" (*EDNT*).

These nouns *power* (*dunamis*), *signs* (*semion*), and *wonders* (*teras*) are also used to describe the workings of the Lord, but they also show how He worked through the apostles to verify His authority (2 Cor. 12:12). In the New Testament, these words are used independently, together, or in various combinations. Sometimes the words *dunamis* and *teras* are translated as "miracles."

Dumamis can mean "capability, strength, might, force." *Semion* may carry the idea of "genuineness, distinguishing mark, signal, miracle." And *teras,* used only in the plural in the New Testament, can be translated "omen, portent." It is always combined with "sign" (*BAG*).

Signs and wonders is first used in Deuteronomy 4:34 when the Lord asks Israel "has a god tried to go to take for himself a nation from within another nation by trials, by signs and wonders and by war and by a mighty hand and by an outstretched arm?" The Lord did this for the Jews "that you might know that the Lord, He is God; there is no other besides Him" (v. 35). The instrument the Lord used was Moses (Acts 7:36). From Deuteronomy 4 and forward into the New Testament these English words are used to describe the open and historic miracles that the Lord would perform to prove Himself.

As the Lord did in the Old Testament, Jesus while on earth performed signs and wonders, such as the healing of the son of a royal official at Capernaum (John 4:48). Such miracles were done because the Jews without such evidence "simply will not believe." Peter reminded Israel that by God the Father, Christ carried out "miracles and wonders and signs" in their midst and that what was then taking place at Pentecost were additional proofs that Jesus was "delivered up by the predetermined plan" of the Lord Himself (Acts 2:22–24).

In Acts, all the apostles were performing miracles and doing signs and wonders (v. 43; 5:12), and these were being done "through the name of Thy holy servant Jesus" (4:30). Stephen, though not one of the twelve apostles, was "full of grace and power . . . performing great wonders and signs among the people" (6:8). Paul was also given such "power of signs and wonders, in the power of the Spirit; so that from Jerusalem and round about as far as Illyricum I have fully preached the gospel of Christ" (Rom. 15:19).

In the Olivet Discourse, Jesus predicted false christs and false prophets would someday come who would "show signs and wonders, in order, if possible, to lead the elect astray" (Mark 13:22). This would take place during the "Great Tribulation" that is so bad, "unless those days had been cut short, no life would have been saved; but for the sake of the elect those days shall be cut short" (Matt. 24:21–24).

In the book of Revelation we are told the "other beast," the False Prophet, or religious leader, will perform "great signs, so that he even makes fire come down out of heaven to the earth in the presence of men" (13:13), by which he deceives those who dwell on earth "because of the signs which it was given him to perform in the presence of the beast [the Antichrist]" (v. 14).

Yet, as though this is not enough, as the Tribulation moves forward in its intensity, demonic deception accelerates. "Spirits of demons" come forth from the mouths of the dragon (Satan), the Beast, and the False Prophet. These spirits go about "performing signs" that influence the world's leaders to gather together "for the war of the great day of God, the Almighty" (Rev. 16:13–14). This is the battle of *Har-Mageddon* (v. 16). Their evil seduction is so great that even those in the Tribulation who have accepted Christ are susceptible to being fooled. The Lord warns them to stay awake and keep their "spiritual" garments of protection "lest he [they] walk about naked and men see his [their] shame" (v. 15).

> Antichrist as the masterpiece of Satan will be endowed with extraor-
> dinary qualities. The Devil will tax his prodigious abilities to the ut-
> most in making this great adversary . . . as potent for mischief as
> possible. . . . And how easy it is for Satan, with his vast knowledge
> and resources to delude thousands with his simulations of the miracu-
> lous! The advent of Antichrist is to be a fiendish caricature and auda-
> cious mockery of the glorious coming of the Son of God! (*PCH*)

C. The Delusion of the Unbeliever (2:10–12)

> **2:10** and with all the deception of wickedness for those who
> perish, because they did not receive the love of the truth so as
> to be saved.

And with all the deception of wickedness. With verses 10–12 Paul focuses on the results of the signs and wonders by the lawless one. A vast number of people will be fooled by blatant wickedness. In this dispensation of
the Church Age, as for millions in the Tribulation, the gospel is veiled to those
who are *destroying themselves* (*apollumi,* present middle participle) (2 Cor.
4:3, translation mine). The great, lost crowd of the world is not sad about rejecting the gospel. They do it willingly and gladly. Spiritually, people become
futile in their speculations (Rom. 1:21) and they profess themselves wise but
become fools (v. 22). Paul addresses "those without excuse" (2:1) and writes
"because of your stubbornness and unrepentant heart you are storing up wrath
for yourself in the day of wrath and revelation of the righteous judgment of
God" (v. 5). In every dispensation in history, humanity has no excuse. By works

(v. 6) and selfish ambition the world does "not obey the truth, but obey[s] unrighteousness, wrath and indignation" (v. 8).

Deception (*apate*) comes from the verb *apatao,* which means "to cheat, mislead." The word can also mean "to entice." In this passage *"seduction* is understood as a sign of the end time with all its destructive consequences" (*EDNT*). It must be kept in mind that the context is the Tribulation. This seduction grows worse as the kingdom of the Antichrist becomes darkened and begins to disintegrate (Rev. 16:10). Circumstances so deteriorate that bad men will gnaw their tongues because of the pain, but they will also blaspheme "the God of heaven" (v. 11a). In all of this they will "not repent of their deeds" (v. 11b). Those who have received the mark of the Beast, the Antichrist, will worship him (13:8) and also his image (v. 15). Besides, the people of earth "worshiped the dragon [Satan], because he gave his authority to the beast; and they worshiped the beast, saying 'Who is like the beast, and who is able to wage war with him?'" (v. 4).

"Wickedness" is not the best definition for *adikia.* The word is better translated as "wrongdoing, unrighteousness, injustice" (*EDNT*). The phrase might better read, "with enticing unrighteousness" or with "all the different kinds of deception which unrighteousness employs"—"any act which disturbs the moral balance" (Lightfoot), or "every sort of evil that deceives, . . . every deceit of unrighteousness" (*EBC*).

> The thought is that by means of all this deceit this unrighteousness palms itself off as righteousness. As all this power, these signs and wonders are necessary, so all this deceit is necessary to make the Antichrist appear as the true exponent of Christ, rightfully sitting in the sanctuary of God. (Lenski)

For those who perish. This is a participle with the dative case of personal interest (Robertson) and is the identical word and grammatical construction the apostle uses in 2 Corinthians 4:3 (*apollumi,* present middle participle). The middle voice "makes it clear that those who are perishing chose the path of destruction for themselves" (*NIGCT*). "They are destroying, ruining themselves" thus "the dreadful process goes on" (Robertson). They are "on their way to perdition" (Alford). "The apostle holds that the refusal to open one's mind and heart to the gospel leaves life a prey to moral delusion" (Nicoll). *Apollumi* is a "'perfective' verb marking out those so described as having already ideally reached a state of" dark and tenacious destruction (Milligan).

Because they did not receive the love of the truth so as to be saved. Their rejection will be a conscious reaction against the gospel and the truth of the only path to salvation. The Bible strongly teaches two important messages: (1) the absolute sovereignty of God, but also (2) the total responsibility of man to respond to truth or to reject it. These are two inscrutable doctrines of Scripture that cannot be reconciled, at least on this side of glory. In this verse, the lost are responsible as to how they will treat the truth of the gospel. It would be wrong to assume that their deception has made them amoral and irresponsible. Even Calvin writes,

> Lest the wicked should complain that they perish innocently, and that they have been appointed to death rather from cruelty on the part of God, than from any fault on their part, Paul shews on what good grounds it is that so severe vengeance from God is to come upon them—because they have not received in the temper of mind with which they ought [to receive] the truth which was presented to them, nay more, of their own accord refused salvation.

Receive (*dechomai,* aorist active indicative) implies that the gospel will be available in the Tribulation. The eternal good news about Christ will, in fact, be preached miraculously and dramatically by an angel flying in midheaven "to those who live on the earth, and to every nation and tribe and tongue and people" (Rev. 14:6). The majority living in that period will have already been duped to accept the lie. The earth will have become ripe for judgment and Christ will, with a sharp sickle, reap the earth with wrath (14:14–20).

It is noteworthy that the world will have rejected not only the truth that would have saved them, but the love (*agape*) of the truth (*aletheia*). The people of earth will be buying into a diabolical and satanic system, a religious philosophy that they will hope is correct. They will do this only for personal survival because they cannot buy or sell or survive without the mark of the Beast on their right hands or on their foreheads (Rev. 13:16–17).

By their own choice men will bring upon themselves their own condemnation. In spite of the attractive nature of the gospel, unbelievers will refuse it, because the gospel truth contrasts with the life of the man of sin. To love the truth of the gospel is to adhere to it and claim it as one's own. The results of believing this truth are salvation and eternal life. "One's response to the gospel must be a matter of the heart (love), rather than simply of the head" (*BKC*).

So as to be saved (*sozo,* aorist passive infinitive) is the main point of Paul's argument. The act of being saved would have come upon them, but evil reigns supreme through the "activities" of Satan and his puppet slave the Antichrist. The great issue of existence is at stake: to know God and enjoy Him forever, or to be cast into outer darkness and forever separated from His blessed presence. A great war in heaven is in its final stage here on earth and it climaxes with the horrors of the seven-year tribulation.

The purpose of the unbelievers' accepting the love of the truth would "have been 'that they might be saved.' . . . Here what is stressed is *man's guilt.* When man is lost, it is ever his own fault, never God's" (*NTC*).

> **2:11** And for this reason God will send upon them a deluding influence so that they might believe what is false,

And for this reason God will send upon them a deluding influence. *And for this reason* (*kai dia touto*) might better read, "and because of this." Since those in the Tribulation reject the love of the truth, God will respond by compounding the deception. In all dispensations humanity can harden their hearts so that additional blindness takes place. In the early history of the race, as God attempted to restore people to Him, they continued to turn away from the truth. The knowledge of God in nature was "evident to them" (Rom. 1:19), but they continued rejecting revelation and were "without excuse" (v. 20b). Therefore, as the apostle writes three times in Romans 1, God gave them over to "the lusts of their hearts to impurity" (v. 24), "to degrading passions" (v. 26), and "to a depraved mind, to do those things which are not proper" (v. 28). "Here is the definite judicial act of God who gives the wicked over to the evil which they have deliberately chosen" (Milligan).

But here in the Tribulation God adds even more to humanity's wretched state of depravity. *Will send* (*pempo,* present active indicative) is continual action: "God will be continually sending." *To them* (*autois*) is a personal pronoun dative plural, "directly toward them." Thus, the rejecters are targeted with this strong deluding influence.

Deluding influence (*energeian planes*) is better translated "energizing deception." Barnes translates it as "energy of deceit" and calls it a Hebraism, meaning strong deceit, or "a working of error" that is a "terrible result of willful rejection of the truth of God" (Robertson). The judgment of God is a frightening thing. Although we cannot understand it, the Lord may blind those who continue stubborn in the rejection of truth. Christ spoke of this blindness concerning His generation of Jews when He quoted Isaiah 6:9–10, wherein the Lord prophesied concerning Israel that they will hear and see but not understand nor perceive (Matt. 13:14–15), lest they should "understand with their heart and turn again, and I should heal them." In anger at the Jewish elders of the city of Rome, Paul also quotes this Isaiah passage. He tells them in so many words that the Lord is passing them by because they have rejected the sacrifice of their own Messiah for their sins. "Let it be known to you therefore, that this salvation of God has been sent to the Gentiles; they will also listen [whereas you would not]" (Acts 28:28).

So that they might believe what is false. These words speak for themselves. The passage is clear, and the truth of it is heavy on the heart. Believing what is false relates to the terrible judicial act by which, according to the constant teaching of Scripture, God gives the wicked over to the evil which they have deliberately chosen (Milligan). *Might believe* sounds like a subjunctive but is actually an aorist active infinitive of *pisteuo*. The clause better reads that "God will be sending an energy of deceit *to believe, or cause them to believe, what is false [pseudos]*," or "to the end that they should believe the lie." The word *lie* has an article before it making it definite, *"the* Lie," in contrast to *"the* Truth" in verse 10. "Because they had not cared for truth, . . . the presence of the Man of Sin, which could not even imperil the truth-lovers, would for them be full of special marvels and frauds by which they might be misled" (Ellicott).

> That is why God uses Satan as His instrument in punishing them, visiting them with a fatal delusion in believing this (great) Lie. False belief becomes thus the proof of falseness, and sentence is passed upon all who refuse to believe the truth, and made evil their good. (Milligan)

2:12 in order that they all may be judged who did not believe the truth, but took pleasure in wickedness.

In order that they all may be judged. The reason for the strong delusion is so that the doubters in the Tribulation may believe what is false (v. 10) and

SECOND THESSALONIANS COMMENTARY

also that they might be *judged* (*krino,* aorist passive subjunctive). Lightfoot paraphrases the verb as "called to account" and thus condemned. As the book of Revelation describes this judgment, it could be classified twofold. The first is certainly the temporal or physical judgment by Christ at His second coming that will fall on all those who have followed the Antichrist and have received his mark and who worshiped his image (19:20). Upon His glorious return they are killed with the sword that comes out of His mouth (v. 21). They will "drink of the wine of the wrath of God, which is mixed in full strength in the cup of His anger" (14:10), and they will suffer "the smoke of their torment" that "goes up forever and ever; and they have no rest day and night" (v. 11).

Second, with all unbelievers of all dispensations, the Tribulation wicked must face the Great White Throne judgment that takes place at the end of the one-thousand-year kingdom reign of Christ. All those not found written in the Book of Life are to be resurrected, the great and small, and will be judged out of the books that have recorded all the deeds they committed in life (20:12). Being cast into the lake of fire for eternity is the second death (spiritual) and constitutes an eternal state of separation from the God of the universe. There is no more terrible and awful picture painted in all of the Word of God.

Despite all the judgment spoken of in the Scriptures, the Lord God still declares "I take no pleasure in the death of the wicked, but rather that the wicked turn from his way and live" (Ezek. 33:11).

Who did not believe the truth, but took pleasure in wickedness. Both *did* [*not*] *believe* (*pisteuo*) and *took pleasure* (*eudokeo*) are aorist active participles. With the participle, the subject and the action is tied together—"*The ones who did not believe* the truth are *the ones who took pleasure* in wickedness." As aorists, the two participles are not expressing past action, but are simply indicating the facts of the matter (Lenski). As in verse 10, *wickedness* is actually the Greek word *adikia* meaning "unrighteousness" (v. 9). *Eudokeo* is a compound verb, *eu* (good) and *dokeo* (to think, believe, to will). It might read "they had good thoughts toward unrighteousness," or "they looked at unrighteousness in a good light," or possibly, "they found pleasure in iniquity" (Alford). (More on *eudokia* in 1 Thess. 2:8; 3:1; 2 Thess. 1:11.) "See here the fearful consequences of a hatred toward and rejection of the truth! The soul takes delight in sinning—has 'pleasure in unrighteousness.' It is, then, not only abandoned to its iniquity, but its delusions are intensified so as to embrace the most palpable falsehoods as truth" (*PCH*).

D. The Security of the Believer (2:13–17)

This section forms a transition from Paul's teaching about the Day of the Lord (2:1–12) to his exhortations for daily living in view of those times (3:1–15) (*BKC*). These verses are meant to uplift and encourage the Thessalonians to stand firm (v. 15) in the midst of all that was happening to them.

> **2:13** But we should always give thanks to God for you, brethren beloved by the Lord, because God has chosen you from the beginning for salvation through sanctification by the Spirit and faith in the truth.

But we should always give thanks to God for you, brethren beloved by the Lord. This wording is almost identical in construction to that found in the opening of this letter in 1:3. It might be said that Paul, by using these identical statements of warm encouragement, placed bookends on this letter. This construction has a regular verb (*opheilo,* present active indicative) and a present infinitive (*eucharisto*), working together to give one thought. *We should* (*opheilo*) has a stronger sense than is seen in this translation. The word means "to be indebted, to be obligated, to owe." It is a financial term used as a euphemism for doing a duty in many other areas (*BAG*). Here, it might read, "we really continually owe it to God to be giving thanks for you," or "we are obligated to give thanks to God always concerning you, brothers" (*NIGTC*).

Give thanks is a compound verb, *eu* (good) and *charizomai* (to grace, to freely give) and may be literally translated "to good grace" someone, in this case, God the Father. This instance, too, is one of twenty-four times the apostle has addressed the Thessalonians as brothers (*adelphos* in the plural) in these two letters. Paul has strong spiritual family ties with these young believers, and here he wants them to feel this sense of closeness in the common bond in Christ.

"Beloved by the Lord" are these Thessalonians, "though hated and persecuted by their godless neighbors" (*BKC*). Paul wants them to be aware of what the Lord did for them in Christ, and *beloved* (*agapao,* perfect passive participle) indicates how God saw them when He redeemed them. Using the perfect passive participle gives an unusual twist to this thought: "The Lord began in the past deeply loving you and that still remains today." This is "precisely the same phrase as in 1 Thess. 1:4, except for the substitution of 'the Lord' for 'God,' which shows the concurrence of the Eternal Son in His Father's predestinations" (Ellicott). God has a great love for the entire world (John 3:16), but the love spoken of here is a sovereign redemptive and efficacious love for His chosen. This love brought forth salvation but also keeps the child of God in His loving favor.

Because God has chosen you from the beginning for salvation. Here, Paul points out that the Thessalonians are *beloved* because of the Lord's intimate calling and choosing of them for salvation. He made them His own by a sovereign act of wooing them to Him by the Holy Spirit. *Hoti* (because) gives the reason for His love toward them.

Has chosen (*aireo,* aorist middle indicative) can be better read "He Himself chose." Although *aireo* is found in Philippians 1:22 and Hebrews 11:25, it does not occur with this meaning anywhere else in the New Testament. It generally expresses the sovereign call of the Lord or His predestination (Lightfoot). It is a rare word and not common in the LXX. "In the present instance the reference would seem to be to the *eternal* choice or purpose of God (1 Cor. ii.7, Eph. i.4, 2 Tim. i.9)" (Milligan). This thought is specifically expressed in Deuteronomy 10:15 and elsewhere in the Old Testament: "Yet on your fathers did the Lord set His affection to love them, and He chose their descendants after them, even you above all peoples, as it is this day" (also, Deut. 26:18; 7:6).

From the beginning (*aparche*) gives the time of this choosing and calling. "In addition to indicating a specific time [the beginning] and being the formal term for a birth certificate, [the word] is used in secular Greek primarily as the expression for *firstfruits* and *firstlings for sacrifice*" (*EDNT*). The Word of God makes believers into a new humanity, or a new creation. "These are sanctified by the Spirit and blessed with faith in the truth" (*EDNT*). By using *aparche* Paul goes back into eternity past when God designated those chosen for redemption. "They were chosen and given a birth certificate for salvation," or "God chose you *as first-fruits*" for salvation (*NTC*).

For salvation through sanctification by the Spirit and faith in the truth. Though *salvation* (*soteria*) is the bedrock of all of Paul's thinking, *soteria* is used only five times in the Thessalonian epistles. The verb *sozo* (to save) is used six times. God's choosing is the cause of salvation, but the means comes about by the sanctifying work of the Spirit and the verbal proclamation of faith in the truth. Salvation "becomes your possession through the work of the Holy Spirit, that is, *through sanctification*—a process of causing you to become increasingly detached from the world and attached to Christ" (*NTC*).

Divine election is proclaimed throughout the Scriptures. God chose or decreed before the ages (1 Cor. 2:7), from the ages (Col. 1:26), and "before the foundation of the world" (Eph. 1:4). Election is clearly Pauline revelation, that is, that God called men to a salvation to which He had before chosen them. "This is both logical and Pauline (Rom. 8:30)" (*NTC*). Paul's revelation of election reminds one of Deuteronomy 7:7–8a: "The Lord did not set His love on you nor choose you because you were more in number than any of the peoples, for you were the fewest of all peoples, but because the Lord loved you."

> Thus we must contemplate the judgments of God upon the reprobate in such a way that they may be, as it were, mirrors to us for considering his mercy toward us. For we must draw this conclusion, that it is owing solely to the singular grace of God that we do not miserably perish with them. (Calvin)

The Spirit of God is the agent for this sovereign calling and redemption (John 3:5; Titus 3:5). Faith is exercised in time by the one who has been awakened by the Spirit. Faith itself is not self-generated. All humans are said to be dead in sin and children of wrath by nature (Eph. 2:1, 3) and cannot come to salvation without faith that in itself is a gift of God (2:8). That faith will grab hold of the truth that Paul speaks of so much in this context (2 Thess. 2:10, 12) and that truth has to do with the gospel (1:8).

By using the word *sanctification* (*hagiosmos*), Paul refers to "the setting aside" work of the Spirit, who made holy (*hagios*, "special," "unique") that which was profane. Thus, with the preposition *en* Paul emphasizes that "sanctification [is] wrought by the Holy Spirit" (Robertson). The cleansing power that brings about sanctification is, of course, the blood of Christ that was shed on the cross. The child of God is redeemed "with precious blood as of a lamb unblemished and spotless, the blood of Christ" (1 Peter 1:19), who died "that He might sanctify the people through His own blood, suffered outside the gate" (Heb. 13:12). Not only does salvation come *by means* (*en*) of the sanctifying work of the Spirit and *by means* (*en*) of faith in the truth but *through the agency* (*dia*) of the gospel (v. 14).

To summarize,

> The Spirit must first set apart for God, awaken those initial faint desires after God, convict of sin, lead to Christ, bring faith to the heart. Being under the influences of the world, the flesh and the devil, the natural man needs as an essential pre-requisite in new birth, this action of the Holy Spirit; without it there would be no salvation. (Ritchie)

2:14 And it was for this He called you through our gospel, that you may gain the glory of our Lord Jesus Christ.

And it was for this He called you through our gospel. In Greek, the first part of the verse reads "into which also He called you." In *into which* (*eis ho*), the *ho* is the neuter relative pronoun with *into* in the accusative case. The pronoun is conforming to *salvation* (*soteria*), which is also in the neuter case. It can be translated "whereunto," or "'to which state,' referring to the whole expression," *salvation through sanctification by the spirit* (v. 13) (Lightfoot).

He called (*kaleo*, aorist active indicative) would indicate a once-for-all efficacious calling that brings the elect to salvation. Paul is saying, "The Gospel preached by us was the instrument whereby He accomplishes His purpose" (Lightfoot). Christ taught this sovereign work in salvation when He said "No one can come to Me, unless the Father who sent Me draws him; and I will raise him up on the last day" (John 6:44). Although God is at work sovereignly in salvation, the means of that redemption comes through (*dia*) the gospel, as well as the sanctification of the Spirit and belief in the truth (v. 13).

Kaleo is used of God's sovereign calling forth of events in history: He "calls [*kaleo*] into being that which does not exist" (Rom. 4:17). The word so often is used to describe the divine calling to be a child of God: "Whom He predestined, these He also called; and whom He called these He also justified; and whom He justified, these He also glorified" (8:30). Here Paul uses a series of aorist tenses that indicates completed action in the salvation process. This verse is like an unbroken chain—whom He calls, He glorifies, that is, in God's timeless viewpoint of things, we are already in heaven; we are glorified.

That you may gain the glory of our Lord Jesus Christ. Believers in the Lord partake in His glory. *May gain the glory* is actually a prepositional phrase, *eis peripoiesin doxes,* "into the *acquisition, possession* of the glory of the Lord

Jesus Christ" (*EDNT*). The Lord completed His foreordained work by calling the chosen to salvation "through our gospel." At a particular moment in time, Paul's preaching the gospel of divine truth was the way through which the Father called these Thessalonian new believers. What He had determined in time past was carried out in history that the future might grant them a share "in the glory of the Lord." The apostle had already written to the Thessalonians about this divine act when he penned "God who calls you into His own kingdom and glory" (1 Thess. 2:12). "As God's purchased possessions, they will be granted this matchless privilege. They do not earn it or in any way acquire it for themselves. It is accomplished solely by God, as is all else referred to in this context (2 Thess. 2:13, 14)" (*EBC*).

Some may ask, "If God has chosen sovereignly for salvation, why does one then even have to believe?" God has ordained the means as well as the ends of what He does. The Lord is the author of history and time and we are marching through it as He sees fit. No one can understand this because human wisdom is far too finite. "God has chosen you to salvation from eternity, and has made the gospel as preached by us the means of carrying that eternal purpose into effect" (*Barnes*).

> **2:15** So then, brethren, stand firm and hold to the traditions which you were taught, whether by word of mouth or by letter from us.

So then, brethren, stand firm and hold to the traditions which you were taught. *So then* (*ara oun*) can read "accordingly then" (Robertson). An important conclusion has been reached as the apostle ties together for the Thessalonians God's eternal calling to salvation with how they are to live presently in time. Paul is again connecting *positional truth* with *experiential truth,* and returning to practical application. He adds *brethren* in order to approach them in a warm fashion about the way they should walk.

The Thessalonians are to *stand firm* (*steko,* present active imperative) and *hold* (*krateo,* present active imperative) to the traditions. *Krateo* means "to seize, grasp, take hold of, hold fast, keep" (*EDNT*). It is most important that the Thessalonians keep standing fast and hanging tightly to what they have been taught by Paul, Silas, and Timothy. "Both imperatives are present tense and thus durative" (Lenski): "Keep on standing firm and holding on to the traditions."

Courageous, manly standing, combined with masterful, strong holding, both of which are wrought by the grace received, constitute the response of the Thessalonians, there is to be no letting themselves be shaken or disturbed (v. 2). (Lenski)

Traditions (*paradosis*) are often thought of as man-made rules that are not inspired and that may be out of touch with the truth. They are often thought of as legalisms that conflict with revelation. Such a view may picture traditions as "that which is handed down from generation to generation with an authoritative demand for compliance and is received accordingly" (*EDNT*). *Paradosis* is a compound noun, *para* (alongside) and *dosis* (a giving), thus "a laying down or giving" of principles or rules that must be kept or acknowledged as binding.

Jesus spoke in a negative way of the traditions of the elders (Matt. 15:2) and the traditions of men (Mark 7:8) that keep people from finding the truth. In this same negative sense Paul spoke of the "traditions of men" that negated the truth "according to Christ" (Col. 2:8). Before his conversion to Christ, he himself had been trapped in the legalism of Judaism and saw nothing wrong with following such a path. He wrote "I was advancing in Judaism beyond many of my contemporaries among my countrymen, being more extremely zealous for my ancestral traditions" (Gal. 1:14).

Paul also writes of traditions that have value and do not contradict biblical revelation. Some traditions are, in fact, built from important scriptural doctrines and should be maintained and kept. For example, Paul urges the Corinthian church to "hold firmly to the traditions, just as I delivered them to you" (1 Cor. 11:2). He then writes that women should have a head covering, not based on social or cultural conformity but based on doctrine: "Indeed man was not created for the woman's sake, but woman for the man's sake" (v. 9). As well, he will urge the Thessalonians not to live unruly lives that are "not according to the tradition which you received from us" (2 Thess. 3:6).

Which you were taught would include Paul's directives concerning work and the laziness of some of the believers there in Thessalonica (3:6–12). *Traditions,* then, as Paul uses the word in the positive sense, has to do with additional commandments that he or others gave that are given for the benefit of the body of Christ. They are tantamount to spiritual commands that bring peace and spiritual healing to the individual saint and to the collective assembly. "The beneficiaries of God's saving work cannot afford to lapse into lethargy, but must respond with loyal steadfastness ('stand firm') and keep a firm hold on the traditions ('teachings') taught them by Paul and his associates" (*EBC*).

Whether by word of mouth or by letter from us. This phrase further adds to the authority set forth in this verse. It does not matter how they received his words or the words of the other apostles. What they teach is coming from the Lord for the good of the Thessalonian congregation. "For some years after the ascension of Christ, there was no written gospel or epistle. The truth was taught orally by those who were living witnesses of the facts on which the doctrines—or traditions—were based" (*PCH*).

This verse may imply that some in the Thessalonian church were in danger of slipping away from what they had been taught. They "were in danger of loosening their grip on the apostles' teachings which they had received (cf. 2 Thess. 3:6) in person from the missionaries and from their letters. They were in danger of slipping backward in their Christian experience" (*BKC*). With great diplomacy and persistency, Paul is trying to prevent backsliding.

> **2:16** Now may our Lord Jesus Christ Himself and God our Father, who has loved us and given us eternal comfort and good hope by grace,

Now may our Lord Jesus Christ Himself and God our Father. This opening line goes to verse 17, wherein lie the verbs *"comfort* and *strengthen"* your hearts, two optative mood verbs that indicate strong contingency and possibility. Optative is sometimes called the mood of "wishing" (D&M, p. 172), and this phrase might be better described as *emphatic contingency* that could read, "Oh, may it be that God will *comfort* and *strengthen.*" "These optatives are voluntative in force, and this is why the prayer is referred to as a wish-prayer" (*NIGTC*).

The subjects of this desire are Christ and God the Father. When Paul finally gets to the main verbs in verse 17, however, he writes in a singular not a plural. Thus, it is "God, He might comfort and strengthen." Wanamaker assumes that "Paul forgot that he had used a plural subject because of the long intervening participial phrase related to God alone" (*NIGTC*). But the apostle knew exactly what he had in mind.

Paul makes the persons of the Godhead very close and intimate by emphasizing *our* (*hamon*). By placing *our* after God (*Theos*) and Father (*pater*) in the Greek text, the apostle emphasizes the relationship of spiritual children to their heavenly Father. Although Paul may not be stressing here that Jesus is God, he certainly is placing Son and Father on the same plane. Paul's desire is that the Father comfort and strengthen the Thessalonian believers, though the Lord Jesus is placed first because He is the mediator between man and God (Alford).

Who has loved us and given us eternal comfort and good hope by grace. Before Paul even gets to the verbs (v. 17), he gives a vivid description as to what the Father has done for the Christian. The first verb *loved* (*agapao*) is an aorist active participle, but it is in the masculine singular, therefore, it must be referring to the last antecedent, *God our Father.* With the participle, the subject is closely bound to the idea of the verb, "the one who is characterized as having loved" us.

The Father not only loved us but *gave* (*didomi,* aorist active participle) "*eternal [aionios,* 'forever'] comfort." *Aionios* is used in the LXX to represent the Hebrew *olam* "and thus infuses a statement which referred originally to a distant time . . . with the dimension of the 'eternal'" (*EDNT*). Not only does the word imply a timeless state, but it often relates to God and the quality of the divine realm. For example, *eternal* life

> . . . is the fruit of the Spirit (Gal 6:8) and thus confirms the authenticity of the life of those who believe. Integral to this is the knowledge that the royal reign of grace, which has eternal life as its goal, will finally reveal its superiority over sin's reign of death (Rom 5:21; cf. 2:7). (*EDNT*)

But here in this verse, God the Father is giving us eternal "comfort" (*paraklesis,* "consolation, counseling, exhortation"). By using the adjective *aionios* Paul may be thinking of the quality of the comfort, though the basic meaning of timeless cannot be ignored either. "This means 'an ever present source of comfort,' of which no persecution can rob us" (Ellicott). This comfort originates from God, it is divine and reflects His loving care for His own who are suffering here on this earth. This "consolation" will also be felt into the eons of eternity to come. (For other examples of how *paraklesis* is used in the New Testament, see 1 Thess. 2:3, 11; 3:2, 7; 4:1, 10, 18; 5:11, 14; 2 Thess. 2:17; 3:12.)

The Father has also given us "good hope" (*elpida agathes*), or "hope good," or "a good kind of *anticipation.*" This hope or anticipation is right. It lifts the believer up and out of a painful and unjust culture that cares not for spiritual things. This anticipation prevents the child of God from caring too much for this generation and all the temptations it has to offer. It gives perspective and balance to the glamor of the material and temporal world. "These words must be closely joined. God gave us not only a consolation under present trials, but a sweet prospect in the future" (Ellicott). It is a kind gift that carries with it great spiritual benefits. This good hope is fired and fueled "by means" (*en*) of grace (*karis*) or with God's graciousness, that is, the hope is "graced" or "gifted" to us by a wise and loving heavenly Father for comfort in this world; "for the world to come all hope is encouragement, but not vice-versa" (Nicoll).

2:17 comfort and strengthen your hearts in every good work and word.

Comfort and strengthen your hearts in every good work and word. *Comfort and strengthen* are the verbs in the singular number that are tied back to the singular noun of action, "God our Father." *Comfort* (*parakaleo,* aorist active optative) here is the same word *paraklesis* in verse 16. The optative thought continues: "Oh, may He comfort." The One who gives us eternal comfort (v. 16) is now called upon to give us immediate comfort because of the situation and stress. He is also called upon to *strengthen* (*sterizo,* aorist active optative) or "to establish firmly, make firm" (*EDNT*).

Your hearts (*kardia*) probably refers to the feelings of the Thessalonians, who are under terrible emotional stress from their pagan neighbors and the jealous Judaizers who were so fearful of Christianity. They are to remain emotionally buoyed and confident in continuing to give forth a good work and a truthful word no matter what the response from the unbelievers around them.

In the previous letter Paul told the Thessalonians that he had sent Timothy "to strengthen and encourage you as to your faith" (1 Thess. 3:2). God often uses human agencies to accomplish His plans. Although Timothy would be used of the Lord to lift up the spirits of this congregation, Paul had also warned them that we all are destined for afflictions (v. 3b), and "so it came to pass, as you know" (v. 4). Spiritual stability "will show itself 'in every good deed and word,' in all that we do and say, in all our daily activity of life. We will act as though our life belongs to heaven" (Lenski).

Study Questions

1. Why would the expression "our gathering together to Him" (2:1) be indicative of the Rapture of the Church?
2. Why were the Thessalonians so shaken and frightened (2:2)?
3. Discuss the definition, meaning, and implications of the word *apostasy* (2:2).
4. Some think the term *antichrist* is just an expression of some evil power or influence. How would it be shown that the man of lawlessness is not simply an evil force but an actual human personality (2:3–9)?
5. What coming of the Lord is Paul writing about in 2:8?
6. What are some of the main reasons for God's retribution as described in 2:10–12?
7. Using a concordance, list all the references to "chosen" and "called" in these two epistles. Discuss what the doctrine of "election" means.
8. How does the apostle use the word *traditions* here in chapter 2?

■ Chapter Thirteen

Paul's Concluding Remarks

IV. PAUL'S ENCOURAGEMENT AND WORDS OF DISCIPLINE (3:1–18)
    A. The Request for Prayer (3:1–5)

In this chapter, Paul concludes his thoughts to this church that he loved so well. He asks the congregation to pray for his work and that of Silas and Timothy. He also issues an order to those who are unruly and lazy—they must work or be put out from the body (v. 14). He closes with a positive prayer that this assembly be continually granted peace "in every circumstance" (v. 16).

> **3:1** Finally, brethren, pray for us that the word of the Lord may spread rapidly and be glorified, just as it did also with you;

Finally, brethren, pray for us. *Finally* (*to loipon*), with the article, is an adverbial accusative and may logically read *"now, thus, therefore."* Here, it has a classical, purely temporal sense, introducing a conclusion (*EDNT*). Robertson calls it an accusative of general reference. It could read "the remaining thought."

Paul again makes a direct address to the Thessalonians, using the vocative case, *brethren.* As has already been noted, in the two Thessalonian epistles Paul uses *adelphos* in the plural as a warm family greeting, almost more than in any other place in his writings. In his first Corinthian letter, he uses the expression somewhat more often, but that epistle is much longer than the two Thessalonian letters put together. Because of Paul's continual use of this term of endearment, no one can accuse him of being cold or uncaring for the flocks under his charge.

The apostle adds *"be praying [proseuchomai,* present active imperative] continually"* for us. This is the third time in these two epistles Paul has asked the Thessalonian church to pray (1 Thess. 5:17, 25). In all of his letters, Paul urges prayer. He believes God moves in response to and answers godly petitions. Paul prayed in groups (Acts 12:12); fasted and prayed (13:3); prayed and sang songs while in prison (16:25); knelt and prayed on the sea shore to give thanks for protection on his journey (21:5); prayed in the temple (22:17); prayed while laying hands on the sick (28:8).

That the word of the Lord may spread rapidly. *The word (logos)* is singular and with the article, making the idea definite (see 3:14). The Word is the entire body of truth about God, but it focuses on the knowledge of Christ and the gospel. The word of the Lord came to the pagan world in limited form through the Jewish synagogues. Before Christ came, many pious Jews demonstrated a meaningful testimony to the lost Gentiles, and this paved the way for the new message of Christ's sacrifice for sins. More than likely the gospel would not have spread so rapidly had not the way been opened through the synagogue system. Paul's desire is to see the gospel move even more rapidly, maybe because he knows his own time is short.

May spread rapidly (trecho, present active subjunctive) means "to run, strive forward" *(EDNT).* The next verb [*may*] *be glorified (doxazo,* present passive subjunctive) is also tied to the subject *the word of the Lord.* Both are subjunctives controlled by the *hina.* This is the usual construction of the *hina* after the word *prayer,* in what is called the sub-final use, combining content and purpose (Robertson). The passage can read "may the word of the Lord keep on running and being glorified" (Robertson), and also conveys "the sense of continuous action, 'keep on running' and 'go on being glorified'" (Ritchie).

"'May spread rapidly' (may run) is . . . emphasizing the living, active nature of the word in the Apostles' eyes, and their ardent desire that it may speed ever onward on its victorious course: . . . The figure, which falls in with St. Paul's well-known fondness for metaphorical language from the stadium (Rom. ix. 16, 1 Cor. ix. 24 ff., Gal. ii. 2, v. 7, Phil. ii. 16, 2 Tim. iv. 7)" (Milligan).

And be glorified. Why does Paul desire to see the word of the Lord glorified? Because he is aware of its great eternal value and worth, and, because its glory reflects back upon the God of mercy who wishes to save and bless all humanity. The Word is glorified when it is heard with respect and honor and when it is reverenced and highly esteemed. It is lifted up when it is accepted with love and greatly prized. "It is glorified when sinners are converted by it, and the lives of the professors of it are agreeabl[e] to it" (Gill). Calvin adds, "*Glory* means something further—that his preaching may have its power and efficacy for renewing men after the image of God. Hence, holiness of life and uprightness on the part of Christians is the glory of the gospel."

Just as it did also with you. The Thessalonians are the great proof of the power of the gospel. They apparently received the word quickly and also began to grow rapidly in the faith. They were almost unmovable when persecution overtook them, and other Christians throughout the regions heard of their faith.

Paul's great desire was "to see the results in Thessalonica (Acts 17:4; 1 Thess. 1:9–10) repeated in Corinth from whence he was writing" (Ritchie). But Paul experienced initial difficulties in Corinth; the assembly there seems to have been more deeply immersed in the pagan culture. Thus, they had difficulty breaking the bonds of sin and wickedness.

> **3:2** and that we may be delivered from perverse and evil men; for not all have faith.

And that we may be delivered from perverse and evil men. By writing *we,* Paul includes himself, Silas, and Timothy, but he may also be including the believers in the Thessalonian church. Most commentators, however, do not believe that is the case. A stronger sense is conveyed here that he is talking about his evangelistic team, which includes mainly Silas and Timothy. Those opposing them could possibly be the heretics Hymenaeus and Alexander (1 Tim. 1:20) or other hypocrites and false teachers in general. More than likely the opposition consists of unbelieving Jews in Corinth, where Paul was encountering difficulties as he wrote (Acts 18:5, 6, 12, 13). They also persecuted him in Thessalonica (17:5) and Berea (v. 13).

Delivered (*ruomai,* aorist, active, subjunctive) means "to rescue, save." *Ruomai* is used in several interesting contexts, such as "*saved* from the jaws of the lion" (2 Tim. 4:17) or "*delivered* from the power of darkness" (Col. 1:13). The deponent form *ruomai* comes from the Classical Greek word *eruo* (with the *e* dropped in *Koine*), and it is translated in the Classical Greek as "to drag, to draw away" (L&S) (see 1 Thessalonians 1:10). Paul's desire is that the apostles may be dragged away from *perverse* (*atopos*, "wicked") and *evil* (*poneros*, "worthless, malicious") men. "'Wicked' labels them as capable of outrageous and harmful acts against others. 'Evil' speaks of persons not only themselves thoroughly corrupted but intent on corrupting others and drawing them into their own slide toward perdition" (*EBC*). The word *atopos* signifies "out of place," and therefore "impracticable, perverse, irregular, outrageous" (Lightfoot).

For not all have faith. *Faith* (*pistis*) actually has an article, making this *the faith*. Paul is saying that the people he is talking about have not become believers; they are not walking in *the faith*. Although they may, to a degree, seem religious, they are, in fact, anything but members of the body of Christ. Their actions and intentions are continually evil and malicious. In Greek, the passage actually reads, "For not all, *the faith*" or "for not all have [true] faith." "The meaning is: 'Most people have and show in their conduct the very opposite of faith, namely, unbelief, vicious opposition to the truth.' Lack of faith explains the hostile attitude to Christ, his gospel, his ambassadors" (*NTC*).

> **3:3** But the Lord is faithful, and He will strengthen and protect you from the evil one.

But the Lord is faithful. The Greek text places *faithful* (*pistos*) in the emphatic position. It might read "Faithful exists [*eimi*] the Lord." The Lord is continually doing things for us, and in this case, He is strengthening and protecting. He is always working with us and has our best interest in view. Paul is reminding the Thessalonians that God was neither asleep nor unaware of their plight. "But whether men have faith or not, the Lord is faithful. . . . This characteristic of God is named because God stands pledged to all who believe in Him" (Ellicott).

He will strengthen and protect you. Both verbs here are future active indicatives. Paul uses *will strengthen* (*sterizo*, "to fix firmly, establish") several times in these letters (1 Thess. 3:2, 13; 2 Thess. 2:17). Through troubling circumstances the Lord will harden the believers that they may be able to endure what is coming. By using the future tense, the apostle may be saying that "the worst is yet to come," that more hardship is certain.

Will protect (*phulasso*, "to guard, watch over, preserve") is a word used to describe guarding a prisoner. It is related, in fact, to *phulake,* which means "a prison, dungeon" (*EDNT*). However, God will in the future serve as a prisoner's security and protection. Because Paul uses a future tense does not imply that they were at that moment unprotected, but he clearly has in mind something coming upon the believers at some specific time that is imminent.

How can it be reconciled that the Lord promises such protection and yet thousands in the early church would perish as martyrs for the name of Christ? Is this protection absolute or does it serve a certain season with the possibility that it can be removed at a time when God has other plans for His own?

In truth, an ongoing daily protection is rendered for the child of God, but the Lord may remove it for certain purposes. His temporal protection is real but it is not guaranteed forever. Paul, in fact, points out the limitation of physical protection: "For though we walk in the flesh, we do not war according to the flesh" (2 Cor. 10:3). He reminded the Corinthians that his life was given to Christ but that physically, "I will most gladly spend and be expended for your souls" (12:15). The apostle had no problem reconciling this protection with the reality of martyrdom if God saw fit: "For we who live are constantly being delivered over to death for Jesus' sake, that the life of Jesus also may be manifested in our mortal flesh" (4:11). He adds, "Therefore we do not lose heart, but though our outer man is decaying, yet our inner man is being renewed day by day" (v. 16). "The people of God do not perpetuate themselves. He perpetuates. His faithful guardianship gives persistency to His people" (*PCH*). "This *guarding* will prevent the Thessalonian believers from falling into the snares of the evil one, such as fanaticism, loafing, meddlesomeness, neglect of duty, defeatism (see verses 5–8)" (*NTC*).

From the evil one. It is not certain in the Greek text whether from *tou pomerou* is neuter or masculine. If neuter it would read "from the evil thing" or simply "from the evil" but if masculine, "from the evil one." The latter seems most likely because this is what Christ said in Matthew 13:38–39, where He is clearly speaking about the Devil. The evil one is also mentioned in other passages (Matt. 13:19; Eph. 6:16; John 17:15; 1 John 2:13).

3:4 And we have confidence in the Lord concerning you, that you are doing and will continue to do what we command.

And we have confidence in the Lord concerning you. *We have confidence* (*peitho,* perfect active indicative) likely is intended to give the majority in the Thessalonian church a spiritual lift. Paul is commending them but also states how much he trusts them. His trust does not, of course, extend to all of them, because he will bring up some debilitating moral failures in verses 6–15. *Peitho* means "to persuade, convince, trust, believe in" (*EDNT*). With the perfect tense Paul is saying "we became persuaded concerning you and that persuasion is still with us," or "we have arrived at a conclusion," or "we are in a state of trust" (Robertson). "Thus the sentence becomes almost equivalent to '[our] trust in you comes from the Lord'" (Lightfoot). *In* (*en*) *the Lord* carries the idea of "in relation to what the Lord is doing with you."

By adding, *concerning you* (*epi humas*), says Alford, these clauses can read "in reference to you—the direction of [Paul's] confidence." On this, Barnes gives a somewhat different explanation:

> Not primarily in you, for you have hearts like others, but in the Lord. It is remarkable that when Paul expresses the utmost confidence in Christians that they will live and act as becomes their profession, his reliance is not on anything in themselves, but wholly on the faithfulness of God.

That you are doing and will continue to do what we command. The *doing* and *will continue to do* are derived from the verb *poieo,* the former a present tense and the latter a future tense. The apostle is expecting action, accomplishing of tasks, doing of things that honor God, and witness of the Lord Jesus Christ. Christianity is a belief, but it is not meant to be lived passively. Believers are not saved by works, but works are to be the results of salvation by faith. We are created for good works (Eph. 2:10), and faith should produce a response of service. James says, "You will see that faith was working with his [Abraham's] works, and as a result of the works, faith was perfected [matured]" (James 2:22), and he adds, "faith without works is dead" (v. 26).

Command (*parangello,* present active indicative) is a compound verb, *para* (alongside) and *angelos* (message, commission, announce) (*EDNT*). The word might read "to command, instruct as to commission" you to a task. The apostle is not simply giving them an idea of what to do, nor is he pushing them in a harsh manor. He is speaking affirmatively and saying in so many words, "this is what we want you to do." "Note [the] apostolic authority here, not advice or urging, but command" (Robertson). With the present tense Paul may be saying, "We are saying this as an ongoing commission that you are doing." The *what* (*ha*) is a plural of the relative pronoun *hos,* thus *"the things* that you are doing." These commands were indeed from the Lord, thus the believer must put confidence in Him day-by-day and find rest for his or her soul by doing what the Lord says.

What are the commands? Part of them are what the apostles spoke when they were with the Thessalonians (1 Thess. 4:2, 11); they could be instructions passed on by Timothy, as well as what is said in this letter. In striving toward godliness, the Christian life is complicated. Our lives can have many deficiencies that need to be addressed by life principles from God's Word.

> **3:5** And may the Lord direct your hearts into the love of God and into the steadfastness of Christ.

And may the Lord direct your hearts into the love of God. *May direct* (*kateuthuno,* aorist, active optative) is a wish for the future. Paul had a similar thought in 2:17 and in 1 Thessalonians 5:23. The word *kateuthuno* is a compound, *kata* (down, through, thoroughly) and *euthuno* (to make straight, as the one steering straight the boat). The force of the thought could be "May the Lord *steer thoroughly straight* your hearts into the love of God."

Kateuthuno further carries the idea "to make a straight, smooth, and direct way, by removing all impediments; it is [so] used in 1 Thess 3:11." That Paul "has complimented them (v. 4) does not imply that they are self-sufficient. Therefore he requests the Lord to direct them into a fuller appreciation of God's love for them" (*EBC*). As previously shown, by writing *hearts* (*kardia*) Paul is thinking of their emotions. The thought here "expresses the desire that the Lord might remove anything which would interfere with their hearts' affections" (Ritchie) (see 1 Thess. 2:4, 17; 3:13; 2 Thess. 2:17).

Into [*eis*] *the love* [*agape*] *of God* means "into the realm of God's love" for us, "as the love which is God's special characteristic, and which He has displayed towards us" (Milligan). Some think Paul no longer entertains the hope of soon revisiting the Thessalonian church. He is possibly preparing them to depend upon God's love only and letting them know, in so many words, they cannot always count on his presence (Nicoll).

Into the steadfastness of Christ. *Steadfastness* is the standard word for "patience." It is a compound, *upo* (under) and *monos* (only, alone), which carries the idea "to be under [it] along." Here, the word is reflective of what Christ is and therefore the word *steadfastness* is appropriate. *Of Christ* is *tou christou* and may be in the genitive or ablative cases. If genitive, it would read, "the steadfastness that *belongs to* Christ, if the ablative, it would read, "the steadfastness that *comes from* Christ." In either sense, the believer in the Lord receives from that source. Lightfoot says it is the steadfastness "in which the believer participates."

B. The Resolve to Discipline (3:6–15)

> **3:6** Now we command you, brethren, in the name of our Lord Jesus Christ, that you keep aloof from every brother who leads an unruly life and not according to the tradition which you received from us.

Now we command you, brethren, in the name of our Lord Jesus Christ. *Command* is the same word, with the same grammatical structure, used in verse 4. Again, it carries the weight of apostolic authority. Paul again adds *brethren* because he feels so close to this church. He identifies with their suffering, and he is a companion with them in their state of persecution.

In the name of our Lord Jesus Christ means "with His authority, with His stamp of approval" and "strengthens" Paul's command (Alford). Thus, the apostle "commands, he does not simply advise. Moreover, he speaks 'in the name of our Lord Jesus Christ.' This is at once a reminder of the very authority that Paul exercised, and of the seriousness of any refusal to obey. Paul was not giving some private ideas of his own when he spoke 'in the name'" (*NIC*).

That you keep aloof from every brother who leads an unruly life. Paul is urging that the entire congregation (you, plural) stay away from each brother who is out of step with what is right. *Keep aloof* (*stellomai,* present active infinitive) is an unusual word used only here and in 2 Corinthians 8:20. The word means "to withdraw," but in the middle voice or deponent form—as here in Thessalonians—it can be translated "to avoid" (*EDNT*). With the present tense the apostle is saying "be avoiding every brother who . . ."

With *every brother* (*adelphos*) Paul again relates to the family of believers. Yes, his words will sting those who are not adhering to a proper way of living. By addressing them in the singular *every*, Paul personalizes the command to keep aloof and makes the censure very specific for a particular individual. One might gather that when keeping aloof, the Thessalonians must consider individually what each person was omitting in their Christian walk.

Unruly life is actually expressed in one Greek word, *ataktos* (in a disorderly manner). *Ataktos* is used exclusively by Paul only in his Thessalonian epistles. He uses the noun *ataktos* (disorderly) in 1 Thessalonians 5:14 and the verb *atakteo* (to be idle) in this chapter, verse 7. Here in 3:6 the thought is "living in an irresponsible manner" (*EDNT*), but it can also carry the thought "to be insubordinate" (1 Thess. 5:14). In Classical Greek the word can mean "to be undisciplined, to fail to discharge an obligation, to neglect one's duty." When used militarily, the word describes troops "not in formation in battle order," or "to not be at one's post" (L&S). In the language of strategy, *ataktos* is used as a metaphor for a cautious general shrinking from an encounter and timidly drawing off under cover (Ellicott).

By using *ataktos*, Paul is thinking of the witness reflected by every member of the assembly. As well, he is concerned that the needs of the group are met equally. He wants no loafer taking advantage of the others.

Not according to the tradition which you received from us. *Tradition* (*paradosin*) has already been mentioned (see 2:15). "The word must imply systematic and definite teaching; and we see here again that a clear code of ethics was part of the apostolic catechism" (Ellicott).

Paul's saying *from us* is important. This third person plural verb has considerable significance, emphasizing that the segment of the community that was out of step with Paul's instructions are isolated from the mainstream of the community. Paul probably intended the whole phrase "not according to the traditions that they received from us" as a warrant for the responsible members of the community to withdraw from those living in an idle and irresponsible fashion (*NIGTC*).

> **3:7** For you yourselves know how you ought to follow our example, because we did not act in an undisciplined manner among you,

For you yourselves know how you ought to follow our example. *Yourselves* is the plural of *autos*. Its first meaning is *self* and it is intensive, setting

SECOND THESSALONIANS COMMENTARY

the individual off from everything else, emphasizing and contrasting (*BAG*). Paul is really pointing a finger at the entire congregation and placing responsibility directly on them in this matter. The apostolic example carries spiritual authority and cannot be ignored. Paul's example here is how they should not do things, specifically in living an undisciplined life.

The apostle punctuates this matter by adding *you know* (*oida*, perfect active indicative). The other common word for *know* is *ginosko*, which generally carries the idea of "knowledge of information," whereas *oida* carries the thought "to understand, to become acquainted with, to stand in a close relationship with, to recognize, to experience" (*BAG*). The Thessalonians understood they were to follow the apostles' example.

How you ought to follow . . . example in Greek is *pos dei mimeisthai,* which literally reads "how it is necessary to be always imitating" us. *Mimeisthai* is a present active infinitive of *mimeomai,* "to emulate, follow after," or with the example of the apostles in view, "to be in obedience to" (*EDNT*). *Mimeomai* comes from an old Greek word, *mimos,* that has in mind a *mime,* an actor, or mimic (Robertson).

Dei is almost always translated "it is necessary," or it can be counted on to convey that thought. *Dei* "designates an unconditional necessity; sentences with this verb have fundamentally an absolute, unquestioned, and often anonymous and deterministic character" (*EDNT*). "Here his 'ought' is a strong expression. It is often translated 'must.' The imitation of the Apostles is not optional, but Paul regards it as imperative on the converts" (*NIC*). "It is imperative" might, in fact, be a more appropriate translation in this context.

Because we did not act in an undisciplined manner among you. *Act in an undisciplined manner* comes from the verb *atakteo* (aorist active indicative), but is found as an adjective in verse 6: "The way some of you are acting there in Thessalonica is not how we disciples presented ourselves to you."

> Truly, what the disorderly persons were doing was the very opposite of what the missionaries had done. The latter had been preaching the gospel and working at a trade besides! The former did not do a stitch of real work in either direction. They were loafers and spongers! Instead of being a help they were a hindrance to the progress of the gospel. (*NTC*)

3:8 nor did we eat anyone's bread without paying for it, but with labor and hardship we kept working night and day so that we might not be a burden to any of you;

Nor did we eat anyone's bread without paying for it. Now the apostle gets specific, because it is possible that some were saying Paul, Silas, and Timothy were moochers who were living off the financially struggling Thessalonians. Paul reminds them that they even paid for their own bread. They refused to accept free meals so that no one could call them freeloaders.

> "Eat bread" is a Semitic idiom for eating any kind of food. It should probably not be broadened to include one's total living. . . . Paul claims nothing regarding his living accommodations with Jason (Acts 17:7) beyond payment for his own meals. What the apostle did for housing is not stated here. (*EBC*)

But with labor and hardship we kept working night and day so that we might not be a burden to any of you. Paul was not seeking sympathy when he said this, but pointing out that they could testify that he was telling the truth. *Labor* (*kopos*) and *hardship* (*mochthos*) express the struggle the apostles endured to bring the gospel to the Thessalonians (see also 2 Cor. 11:27; 1 Thess. 2:9).

Burden (*epibareo*, aorist active infinitive) is a compound verb, *epi* (upon) and *bareo* (to burden, to oppress). *Bareo* is from *baros,* which means basically "weight." The word *barometer* comes from *baros,* and a barometer measures the weight of air. Thus, *epibareo* can be translated "to weigh down." The apostles refused to weigh down the Thessalonians with their daily needs. They were in Thessalonica to bless the people with the truth of the gospel. Money or financial issues, at least in this instance, would cloud the pure presentation of the grace of God.

Paul "does not simply mean that his example should be regarded by them as a law, but the meaning is, that they knew what they had seen in him that was worthy of imitation" (Calvin). "Paul was not saying that they never accepted a gift or a meal from others, but that they were self-supporting. They earned the bread they ate (cf. v. 12)" (*BKC*).

3:9 not because we do not have the right to this, but in order to offer ourselves as a model for you, that you might follow our example.

Not because we do not have the right to this, but in order to offer ourselves as a model for you. Here the apostle notes that it was certainly fitting that the missionaries could have asked for support while serving and ministering to the Thessalonians, but Paul sets this aside in order that no false accusation might be made. *We have* (*echo,* present active indicative) can be translated "we continually possess" this right (as apostles).

The Jewish community would have been the ones who accused the apostles of taking advantage of the people. *Right* is actually the Greek word for "power" (*exousia),* or it can mean "authority." As apostles of the Lord, Paul and his companions may have been able to demand such support while ministering the gospel, but the negative aspect of human nature would likely have been aroused. A demand for material support would have offended and caused suspicion against the apostles and then ultimately against the gospel itself. It is interesting that this is the only place in the Thessalonian letters that *exousia* is used.

Model (*tupos*) can mean "type, foreshadowing, representation, an example" (*EDNT*). By using the verb *didomi* (aorist active subjunctive, "to give") with *hina,* and using the reflexive pronoun *heautous,* the sentence might read "in order that we ourselves might give an example to you."

That you might follow our example. *Example* is the same word used in the same grammatical form as in verse 7 (*mimeomai,* present active infinitive). The sentence also has *eis to* (into the), the preposition *eis* "point[ing] to the end of the action" (Lightfoot). The entire thought might be

> "But in order that (*hina*) we might give . . . ourselves an example . . . to imitate" (same word as v. 7). . . . "Ourselves," as the gift, is emphatic by position; the sense from this is: we have the authority (from the Lord, 1 Cor 9:14) to receive from you of what you have, but in reality we give, not only of what we have, but our very selves. (Ritchie)

3:10 For even when we were with you, we used to give you this order: if anyone is not willing to work, then he is not to eat, either.

For even when we were with you, we used to give you this order: if anyone is not willing to work, then he is not to eat, either. *We were* (*eimi,* imperfect active indicative) and *give . . . order* (*parangello,* imperfect active indicative), both verbs being imperfect, refer to the time when Paul, Silas, and Timothy were with the Thessalonian believers. With the imperfect tense the sentence could read "when we were with you, we used to give you this command" (*NIGTC*). The problem of Christians being idlers and not pulling their full weight was one that Paul had seen previously and that now had to be addressed again. "The evil of which the apostle here complains had begun to operate even when he was with them" (*Barnes*). An unwillingness to work may have been a social weakness, and the new Christians carried it over into their way of living as children of God.

Because this matter was so important, Paul had to be adamant in his orders, which is why he used *parangello,* generally translated "to command." The word is used four times in this chapter (vv. 4, 6, 10, 12) and once in 1 Thessalonians 4:11.

Some have called Paul's orders here "a workshop morality" that was obviously needed. It must be remembered that the believers in Christ were at war in Thessalonica; they were being besieged. Under these circumstances, any Christian not helping to bear the burden became a detriment to the well-being of the whole church. Those not working were not handicapped and were well able to share the work load, but habits of laziness made them a concern for others.

If anyone is not willing to work, then he is not to eat, either. *Will*[*ing*] is from *thelo* (present active indicative) and "work" is from *ergazomai* (present active infinitive). When *thelo* is used of the human will, it refers to human volition, determination, or the desire to act (*EDNT*). One can be stubborn and refuse to do what is obvious. "The vice consists in the defective *will*" (Ellicott). Self-centeredness can rule and reign. When the apostle adds "then he is not to eat, either," he implies that there were communal meals in which everyone was partaking. The freeloaders were eating but contributing nothing for the support of the assembly. Apparently, the church was being strangled socially and financially by the ungodly and cruel culture. People were losing their jobs, and every able-bodied person was under moral obligation to attempt to provide some sustenance.

"No work, no eat" was a maxim among the Jews, Barnes writes, "and is founded in obvious justice, and is in accordance with the great law under which our Creator has placed us; Gen. iii. 19"; "by the sweat of your face you shall eat bread."

The law here laid down by the apostle extends to all who are able to work for a living, and who will not do it, and binds us *not* to contribute to their support if they will not labour for it. . . . In no possible circumstances are we to contribute to foster indolence. (*Barnes*)

3:11 For we hear that some among you are leading an undisciplined life, doing no work at all, but acting like busybodies.

For we hear that some among you are leading an undisciplined life. News had come back to Paul from the bearers of the first epistle. It is interesting that Paul waited until the end of this letter to address this disturbing problem. Since not everyone was behaving in an undisciplined manner, the apostle waited until the end of the epistle to address the problem. *Leading* (*peripateo,* present active participle) could be translated "going [walking] about." With the participle, the indication is strong that lack of discipline characterized the idlers' daily lives. They must have done the same in the past and they now continue living this way in the present.

Paul has used *ataktos* before to describe the idle or disorderly life-style (1 Thess. 5:14; 2 Thess. 3:6–7). It is unusual that such a specific word is used so often in such a narrow context—Paul could not ignore this problem; he had to address it head-on. Since Paul uses the present tense, the *hearing* (*akouo,* present active indicative) may suggest that he was told of the problem many times, although he already admitted having spoken about this concern when with them. The Christian community seems to have been forced to feed the indolent who were not working. The apostle does not imply that the entire congregation sent him word about the problem, but that someone passing through the city of Thessalonica or who was from another church in the area may have brought this bad news (*NIGTC*).

Doing no work at all, but acting like busybodies. He has written about the "no work" several times, but the matter of "busybodies" is just now mentioned. *Acting like busybodies* (*periergazomai,* present active participle) is a compound verb, *peri* (around) and *ergazomai* (to work, to accomplish). *Periergazomai* is used only here and can mean "to go around performing" useless things. As a participle the action is tied closely with the noun and may imply "these are characterized as those who go about doing useless activities," possibly, "doing nothing but doing around" (Robertson), or "doing no business but being busy bodies" (Ellicott). "These theological dead-beats were too pious to work, but perfectly willing to eat at the hands of their neighbours while they piddled and frittered away the time in idleness" (Robertson).

> The law of Christianity is both stern and gentle: unbending in prin-ciple, and flexible only in manifold persuasions to translate the prin-ciples into actual living practice. It rouses man from yielding to a sinful listlessness and helps him to develop a robust Christian man-hood. (*PCH*)

3:12 Now such persons we command and exhort in the Lord Jesus Christ to work in quiet fashion and eat their own bread.

Now such persons we command and exhort in the Lord Jesus Christ. By writing *such persons* (*toioutos,* masculine, plural) Paul creates a classifi-cation, an identifiable kind. The word means "such as this, such a kind" (*EDNT*). "Now people who act like this, this kind," these *we command* (*parangello*) and *exhort* (*parakaleo*) (on *parangello,* see 1 Thess. 4:11; 2 Thess. 3:4, 6, 10; on *parakaleo* see 1 Thess. 2:11; 3:2, 7; 4:1, 10, 18; 5:11, 14; 2 Thess. 2:17).

Command and *exhort* are in the present tense and can read "we are con-tinually commanding and exhorting." "In [*en*] the Lord Jesus Christ" signi-fies the relationship of all Christians to Him, that is "on the strength of our union in the Body of Christ" (Ellicott). In the experiential position of these saints they are walking carnally (1 Cor. 3:3) and pampering their flesh with laziness. They were a disgrace to the local assembly and to the larger body of Christ as well.

To work in quiet fashion. This phrase begins with a *hina* clause (in order that), followed by the prepositional phrase *meta* (with). *Quiet fashion* (*hesuchia*) means "to be at rest, be still, conduct oneself quietly" (*EDNT*), or "to be without agitation or stress, steadily and calmly going about one's busi-ness." This is "the opposite of bustling, and of idleness" (Ellicott). "It is not enough that they should not be disorderly, they must also work, and that too 'with quietness' for their own maintenance" (Milligan). Nicoll suggests three reasons for the unrest with those who would not work:

. . . (a) the disturbing effect of persecution, (b) the tension produced by the thought of the advent of Christ, and (c) as an outcome of the latter, irregularity and social disorganization in the community.

By saying *work* (*ergazomai*, present active participle) the apostle stresses what they must be doing. "The tense of the verb implies that they were to work steadily, not occasionally or spasmodically" (*EBC*). The harmony within the congregation is dependent upon everyone pulling his or her own weight and no one taking advantage of another.

And eat their own bread. This phrase (*esthio*, present active subjunctive) emphasizes that within the community each still had to exercise personal responsibility. Paul is not espousing communism, as some have suggested. He is arguing for community spirit but also personal responsibility and self-reliance. This could read "Literally, *that working with quietness they keep on eating their own bread*" (Robertson). The present subjunctive conveys the thought clearly that "this is what they ought [must] be doing." "Paul undoubtedly intended the practice of 'working with quietness' as an alternative to the indolent members' tendency to meddle in other people's business (v. 11)" (*NIGTC*).

3:13 But as for you, brethren, do not grow weary of doing good.

But as for you, brethren, do not grow weary of doing good. With all the pressures facing the Thessalonian church, it would be expected that some would simply give up the struggle. Paul urges them on by again appealing to the "brethren," to the family relationship and responsibility. *Grow weary* (*egkakeo*, aorist active subjunctive) can better be translated "to become tired, lose heart, to despair" or even "to be afraid (*BAG*). The word is a compound, *ek* (out) and *kakos* (bad, worthless, harmful), the idea being that "you should start now putting away the despairing" thought.

With *doing good* (*kalopoieo*, present active participle) Paul has coined a word that is used only here in the New Testament. It is a compound of *kalos* (good) and *poieo* (to do, perform), that is, "doing well, living diligently, and uprightly" (Alford). *Kalos* is the opposite of *kakos*. "Over against the irregular conduct of the few, Paul urges the many to persist in doing whatever is excellent: . . . They must not *begin to behave badly* or *become weary* . . . in the matter of *well-doing*" (*NTC*).

The rest of the members of the church, who were diligent and indus-
trious in their callings, minded their own business, and did not trouble
themselves, and their families, and were beneficent to others. . . . For
though the idle and lazy should not be relieved, yet the helpless poor
should not be neglected. (Gill)

3:14 And if anyone does not obey our instruction in this letter,
take special note of that man and do not associate with him, so
that he may be put to shame.

And if anyone does not obey our instruction in this letter. Paul goes
from an appeal of the heart, to obligation, to using his apostolic authority. He
wishes to be gentle, but he is not afraid to exercise the spiritual oversight given
him by the Lord. The apostle walks a fine balance in his dealing with human
personalities. No one could ever label him a pushover. He did not mind standing up for what was godly, spiritual, and correct. *Obey* (*hupakouo,* present
active indicative) is a compound, *hupo* (under) and *akouo* (to hear), thus "to
listen under" or "to pay attention." As a present indicative, Paul stresses the
fact that he wants those who will pay attention to be continually following
apostolic instruction. If they do not, they are to "be put to shame."

Instruction is the simple Greek word *logos* in the singular. The "instruction" certainly includes much of what he has just previously written, but it
could also refer to all the commands and directives he has given about those
who are not doing right. Since this word or instruction is found written in
Paul's letter, and carries such authority, the doctrine of the inspiration of Scripture is alluded to. What the apostle writes must be heeded because it is not
just the word of a man, but the Word of God (1 Thess. 2:13) (see 3:1).

The words *in this letter* (*epistole*) "are added, because the Apostle feared
that the unruly members might presume on his absence. . . . His written commands, he would say, are of equal authority with his personal commands"
(Lightfoot).

Take special note of that man and do not associate with him. *Take special note* (*semeioomai,* present active imperative) is used only here in the New
Testament. It is related to the noun *semeion,* which means a "distinguishing
mark, a sign." Paul is saying that man is "to be marked out, spotted, taken
note of," or "set your mark on" (Lightfoot).

[Do not] associate (sunanamignumai, present active infinitive), is "refer-ring to any member of the congregation who does not obey the apostolic message" (*EDNT*). In any context, this is strong language similar to what Paul writes in 1 Corinthians 5:2 about the man who has sexual relations with his stepmother. Paul chides the congregation that they had not mourned over the matter and grieved "in order that the one who had done this deed might be removed from your midst."

So that he may be put to shame. The man should be *put to shame (entrepo,* aorist passive subjunctive) before the church in order to bring him to his senses. With the *hina* clause, Paul is looking for results from the church not associat-ing with him. Using a seemingly harsh punishment and prohibition, the pur-pose is to drive the wayward believer back to the fold but changed in his behavior. In a metaphorical way in Classical Greek, *entrepo* carries the thought of shaming one to "make one turn, to turn about" (L&S). The apostle does not wish to leave the individual in a state of rejection, but he is seeking a spiri-tual response. With the passive, the thought might be " 'to be turned in (upon oneself).' It is this process of reflection on the enormity of one's actions that Paul wishes to see effected in the unruly" (*NIC*).

> The treatment is primarily intended to bring him back to his rightful position. At the same time it is a punishment. He is one who has ig-nored the teaching originally given by word of mouth, then the in-junctions of the First Epistle, and now those of the Second. Clearly this shows a measure of obduracy. It is no longer possible to regard such a person as being in good standing with the church. He must be disciplined. (*NIC*)

> **3:15** And yet do not regard him as an enemy, but admonish him as a brother.

And yet do not regard him as an enemy, but admonish him as a brother. The apostle "immediately adds a softening of his rigour; for, as he elsewhere commands, we must take care that the offender be not *swallowed up with sor-row,* (2 Cor. ii. 7) which would take place if severity were excessive" (Calvin). *Regard (hegeomai,* present active imperative) means "to believe, think, consider" (*EDNT*). With the present tense Paul indicates he does not want a negative attitude about the offender to persist indefinitely. He does not want the man who is so ostracized to be treated hatefully as an enemy (*echthros*) or with hostility (*echthra*). The Church of the Lord should not be in combat against itself, though there are moral guidelines that all must adhere to.

In *but admonish him as a brother,* the word *but* (*alla*) gives a strong contrast to what he has said. Paul wants to make sure no one is mistreated. Though judgment and punishment are painful in the experience of the believer, such wounds are meant for the good.

Admonish (*noutheteo,* present active imperative) is a compound of *nous* (mind, understanding) and *tithemi* (to place, to position). *To admonish* is to "establish the mind" or intellectually bring one about to a new way of thinking (see 1 Thess. 5:12, 14). Again, by using a present tense, Paul indicates that he perceives the acquisition of a new way of thinking as a process. Rarely does anyone, even a Christian, change instantly. When, however, the believer changes his or her habits or mind set, a higher reason must be in view. The change must first be spiritual, then moral, and finally practical and observed in the daily experience. Others will know if that change is superficial or genuine.

As a brother punctuates again the family relationship. The camaraderie in the body of Christ begins with mutual salvation in the Savior, and this closeness must not be permanently damaged. The Thessalonians are to "withdraw, to refuse fraternal association until shame results. But they are not to turn their back upon [the offender] and at once to abandon him as being hopeless" (Lenski).

Barnes warns, "There is great danger that when we undertake the work of discipline we shall forget that he who is the subject of it is a brother, and that we shall regard and treat him as an enemy. Such is human nature." The believers must receive the offender back with open arms when he or she gives evidence of repentance. Paul's words in Galatians 6:1 are appropriate: "Brethren, even if a man is caught in any trespass, you who are spiritual, restore such a one in a spirit of gentleness, looking to yourself, lest you too be tempted."

C. The Reminder of the Lord's Presence (3:16–18)

3:16 Now may the Lord of peace Himself continually grant you peace in every circumstance. The Lord be with you all!

Now may the Lord of peace Himself continually grant you peace in every circumstance. This letter closes with a wish-prayer, a final greeting, and a benediction. "This is Paul's fourth prayer for the Thessalonians in this

epistle (cf. 1:11–12; 2:16–17; 3:5). From correction Paul turned to intercession" (*BKC*). *May . . . grant* (*didomi*, aorist active optative) is a longing desire on Paul's part. In the Greek, *Himself* (*autos*) is actually placed at the
beginning the sentence: "Now Himself the Lord of peace may He grant to
you the peace." The thought implies, "Yet without the help of the Lord all
your efforts [for peace] will be in vain" (Lightfoot). The apostle stresses that
only the Lord may give peace and contentment in the midst of strife and tur-
moil. He points out that only the Son of peace can give genuine inner peace.
It must be remembered that one of the names for the Messiah is "Prince of
Peace" (Isa. 9:6), although the Isaiah reference is looking first at the subject
of world and international peace when the king and the kingdom arrives. "May
the Lord, from whom all peace comes, Himself give you His peace" (Milligan).

In every circumstance in Greek is *dia pantos en panti tropo* or "at all times
and in all ways" (Milligan). *Tropos* means "way, manner."

> "At all times" would give them a sense of proportion as to their ex-
> pectations of the Lord's coming, without imposing any suggestion
> of its remoteness, whilst "in every way" would exclude any circum-
> stance for alarm. His peace is unbroken as to time, and unbreakable
> as to conditions. The world may inflict tribulations, but did He not
> say, "I have overcome the world"? (Ritchie)

The Lord be with you all! By this the apostle probably has in mind His
presence as the Thessalonians experience additional persecution. Things will
not get better but worse. By writing *with* [*meta*] *you all* Paul includes even
those who are walking carnally and contrary to his instructions. The church
was full of both faithful believers and the wayward with whom he was so
concerned. But even these would have the Lord's closeness.

> Considering the dissensions that disturbed the harmony of the
> Thessalonian Church, this epistle appropriately closes with a prayer
> for peace. First, and most important of all, peace with God and the
> individual conscience; then mutual peace and concord one with an-
> other. (*PCH*)

> **3:17** I, Paul, write this greeting with my own hand, and this is a
> distinguishing mark in every letter; this is the way I write.

I, Paul, write this greeting with my own hand, and this is a distinguishing mark in every letter; this is the way I write. *This greeting* (*aspasmos*) has an uncertain etymology. "Perhaps a connection exists with *spao*, 'attract' . . . , as an expression of affection or friendly reception" (*EDNT*). Paul is making sure that the Thessalonians know that he personally penned this epistle. Since some wanted to claim that he was a pretender or fake, such demonstration of a personal touch was important. Paul even alludes to a *distinguishing mark* or sign (*semeion*) that he must have used regularly to authenticate his letters. Or he is simply saying that he has a distinct handwriting that imprints all his epistles. Whichever, the writings of Paul were well identified by those receiving them.

Most believe that Paul had a specific style to prevent his letters from being forged. "The practice was customary in ancient times" (*EBC*). Notice that he writes *in every letter.* He is not simply referring to letters past, but he will follow this habit in later writings also. Since we know that he wrote other letters (1 Cor. 5:9) that were not preserved by the providence of the Holy Spirit, he did the same with them as well. "The handwriting furnished a key by which his Thessalonian readers could recognize a spurious Epistle bearing his name" (*EBC*). Many believe that Paul mentions the identifiable mark because someone may have earlier sent "a letter as if from us" (2:2).

3:18 The grace of our Lord Jesus Christ be with you all.

The grace of our Lord Jesus Christ be with you all. This benediction also closed the first Thessalonian epistle (5:28). It is used in some form in all of his letters. Sometimes he even places such words as a greeting at the beginning of his epistle: To Timothy, "Grace, mercy and peace from God the Father and Christ Jesus our Lord" (1 Tim. 1:2). As noted in 1 Thessalonians 1:1, such a mention of *grace* (*charis*) is not simply a polite courtesy; the apostle desires that such grace operate in the every day affairs of the believer's life. We are saved by grace (Eph. 2:8) and we must be blessed in the Christian walk by grace. As Paul wants the Lord to be with all in Thessalonica (v. 16), in like manner he desires that this grace be with all.

Paul was the great apostle of grace; it is only fitting that his letters end with grace.

Study Questions

1. List all of the positive and encouraging thoughts that Paul sets forth in verses 1–5.
2. Why do you think Paul waited until the end of this letter to address the unpleasant matter of the undisciplined believers?
3. Review the relevant passage and explain why the apostle had to use harsh words for those he calls busybodies (v. 11).
4. Why did Paul, Silas, and Timothy take special precautions not to take food from the Thessalonians when they were ministering to them? (vv. 7–10).
5. What was the purpose of shaming the wayward brother? (v. 14).

CHAPTER FOURTEEN

Bible Study Outline of 2 Thessalonians

Edward E. Hindson

PAUL'S SECOND LETTER to the Thessalonians was written to correct their misunderstandings regarding the return of Christ (2:2). He explains in detail the series of coming events in their proper sequence. More than any New Testament letter, this epistle addresses the second coming of Christ. Like 1 Thessalonians, the second letter to the church at Thessalonica emphasizes *key words* like *glory, tribulation, gospel, coming,* and *thanksgiving.*

The letter opens with Paul's assurance that those who trouble them will be judged when Jesus comes again (1:4–10). Then he answers their concerns about the order of events relating to the second coming of Christ (2:1–12). Paul assures them that the "day of Christ" (His return in judgment) will not come until after a series of events that will precede it:

1. Falling away first (2:3)
2. Man of sin revealed (2:3)
3. He opposes God (2:4)
4. He sits in the temple of God (2:4)
5. He claims to be God (2:4)

In the meantime, Paul assures us that the Antichrist (man of sin) cannot be identified until the "restrainer" is removed (2:6–7). Assuming the removal of the restrainer is a reference to the Rapture (see commentary), the following sequence would also apply:

1. Rapture of the Church (2:6–7)
2. Rise of the Antichrist (2:8)
3. Antichrist empowered by Satan (2:9)
4. Antichrist's identity revealed (2:8)
5. Antichrist destroyed at the coming of Christ (2:8)

Chapter 2 is a very important section of Scripture for preaching and teaching. This chapter makes it clear that believers do not need to fear the rise of the Antichrist or the coming Day of the Lord. Both of these events will not occur until after the "restrainer" is removed. This means that born again Christians are looking for the coming of Jesus Christ, not the rise of the Antichrist. We are listening for the trumpet, not looking for the Tribulation.

The outline of 2 Thessalonians is, in general, as follows:

   I.   DESIRE OF THE LORD: GLORY OF HIS SAINTS (CHAP. 1)
  II. DAY OF THE LORD: REMOVAL OF HIS SAINTS (CHAP. 2)
III. DISCIPLINE OF THE LORD: ADMONITION OF HIS SAINTS (CHAP. 3)

Chapter 1 is written to encourage believers who are suffering for their faith in Christ (vv. 4–5). In contrast to the trouble they are experiencing at the hands of unbelievers, Paul promises that when Christ returns (vv. 6–9) God will "trouble" those who trouble them. This judgment of tribulation will be both severe and extensive. By contrast, Jesus will come to be glorified in those who believe (vv. 10–12).

The passage in 1:7–9, provides a vivid discussion of what will happen to unbelievers who are left behind after the Rapture. Their deliberate rejection of the gospel will result in a fiery judgment and ultimately in eternal punishment. In many ways verses 7–9 are a picture of the tribulation period in microcosm (cf. Rev. 6–19).

Chapter 1 can be outlined as follows:

   I.   DESIRE OF THE LORD: GLORY OF HIS SAINTS (CHAP. 1)
     A. Their Troubles (v. 1–6)
        Suffering for the sake of Christ was a badge of honor for the early Christians. They expected it. Therefore, they handled it by God's grace in ways that are almost beyond our comprehension today. The Christians at Thessalonica were no exception. They were counted

"worthy of the kingdom of God" because they suffered for the cause of God. In contrast to their present sufferings, Paul promised their eventual triumph at the return of Christ.

B. Their Triumph (vv. 7–12)

Paul looks ahead beyond the Rapture to the return of Christ when He will be "revealed from heaven in blazing fire" (v. 7). His return to the earth will involve the punishment of those who do not know God. As tragic as that day will be for unbelievers, it will mark the triumph of the Church when we return from the marriage supper in triumph with Christ (see Rev. 19:11–18). This triumphal return will mark the end of the tribulation period and will usher in the millennial kingdom of Christ on earth (see Rev. 20). The ultimate realization of God's kingdom on earth will only occur when the King is reigning on earth.

Chapter 2 is written to correct the Thessalonians' misgivings about the return of Christ. Several key doctrines are taught in this chapter: coming apostasy, the restraint of the Holy Spirit, the rapture of believers, the rise of the Antichrist, his false miracles and spiritual deception, and his ultimate destruction. The chapter ends with Paul's words of assurance to the believers whom God has chosen, called, and sanctified (vv. 13–14). They are to "comfort" each other by the hope of the return of Christ (vv. 15–17).

Chapter 2 can be outlined thus:

II. DAY OF THE LORD: REMOVAL OF HIS SAINTS (CHAP. 2)

A. Assurance of Christ's Coming (vv. 1–2)

Concerns about the timing of Christ's coming are as old as the Church itself. Apparently some of the believers at Thessalonica were concerned that those Christians who had already died would miss out on the benefits of the Second Coming. As persecution intensified against them, their expectation of the Rapture increased. But as time wore on, some began to wonder if they had missed it.

Paul sets the record straight in this chapter. He points out that the return of Christ cannot take place until after the revealing of the Antichrist (v. 3). The rise of the Antichrist, in turn, cannot take place until after the Rapture of the Church—the removal of the restrainer (v. 6).

Therefore, this section of Scripture clearly indicates a sequence of events:
1. Increase of apostasy
2. Rapture of the Church
3. Rise of Antichrist
4. Return of Christ

B. Explanation of Christ's Coming (vv. 3–12)
   1. Man of Sin (vv. 3–6)

The Antichrist is described in these verses as the "man of sin" (or literally, lawless one) who is destined to perdition, or "destruction." Here is one of the most important passages in the Bible about the character and career of the Antichrist. He is described as (1) opposing God, (2) exalting himself as God, (3) demanding worship as God (v. 4).

While the "mystery of iniquity" (the "spirit of antichrist," 1 John 4:3) is always at work resisting the person and work of Jesus Christ, it cannot culminate in the arrival of the Antichrist until the removal of the restrainer (v. 6). Then the Antichrist will be indwelled and empowered by Satan and revealed to the world. But he will eventually be destroyed by the glory of Christ at His second coming.

   2. Mystery of Iniquity (vv. 7–8)

Satan is pictured as the real power behind the throne of the Antichrist. He is the one who is waiting for the Rapture to pass so that he can empower a human being to fulfill this role. Satan's desire, however, is limited by the sovereignty of God, for only God, not the angels (and certainly not Satan) knows the timing of the Rapture. Therefore, Satan is left waiting, guessing, wondering, and speculating like everyone else. His evil quest is a restless search to find the right candidate for Antichrist, but he must wait until the restrainer is removed.

   3. Mighty Deception (vv. 9–12)

After the Rapture, the vast majority of people left behind will be deceived regarding the identity of the Antichrist. They will believe "the lie," presumably some official explanation regarding the disappearance of the true believers. This deception will be so widespread that it will affect the whole world.

We must urge people under the sound of our teaching not to gamble with their eternal souls. Chances are that most of those who are left behind will be lost. If a person will not receive Jesus as his or her Savior now, why would they then—when most are deceived and those that do believe are martyred for their faith (Rev. 6:9–11).

C. Hope of Christ's Coming (vv. 13–17)

In contrast to those who will be deceived, Paul expresses assurance for those who believe. They will not be deceived because they have believed the truth. God has chosen them to salvation and sanctified us through the Spirit. The destiny of true believers is clearly spelled out: (1) called by the gospel, (2) chosen to salvation, (3) sanctified by the Spirit, (4) believes the truth, (5) destined to glory.

We do not dread the coming of Christ. Rather, we look forward to the Rapture of the Church. We are not looking for the rise of the Antichrist, but the return of Jesus Christ. We do not fear the future because we have the hope of heaven. True Christians know who we are, where we are going, and how we are going to get there. We are confident of our relationship to Christ and are sure of our destiny in Christ.

Chapter 3 shifts to a more personal note as Paul asks the believers to pray for him that he might be delivered from "unreasonable men" (v. 2). In turn, he encourages them to exercise church discipline over those who walk "disorderly" among them (vv. 6–15). The apostle's instructions sound harsh but must be viewed in light of his statement that disobedient believers are to be admonished as brothers, not enemies (v. 15).

One cannot teach effectively on this chapter and avoid the subject of church discipline. Questions will naturally arise about how these policies might be enacted in the local church today. Therefore, one would be well advised to make sure the local assembly has a clearly stated policy regarding such matters. If that is the case, studying this chapter will enhance the spiritual character of the local body.

Chapter 3 can be outlined in the following manner:

III. DISCIPLINE OF THE LORD: ADMONITION OF HIS SAINTS (CHAP. 3)

A. Apostle's Request: Pray for us (vv. 1–2)

Paul emphatically urges the believers to pray for him that he may
be free to preach the gospel. His hope is that the Word may be "glorified" as people see what it does in the lives of those who believe
it. Paul's request reminds all of us that the success of any ministry
for Christ is dependent upon the prayers of God's people. Prayer
support is necessary for public success in the work of God.

B. Apostle's Advice: Discipline the Disorderly (vv. 3–15)
    As in all of Paul's letters, he turns to the practical matters of church
    life and discipline. He reminds us that the "love of God" and "pa-
    tience of Christ" are essential for the work of the ministry. Servants
    of Christ ought to (1) imitate a godly example, (2) work hard, (3)
    be an example to others, (4) discipline the lazy and the disorderly,
    (5) work quietly and humbly, (6) take care not to wear out in the
    process.

C. Apostle's Blessing: Grace and Peace (vv. 16–18)
    The closing benediction reminds us that peace comes from the Lord
    of peace. When He is with us, we can rest assured that our lives are
    under His sovereign control and loving grace. We are saved by His
    grace and sustained by His grace. We have made peace with God;
    therefore, we can be at peace with ourselves and others.
    We are both the recipients of His grace and the receptacles of His
    love. What He has done for us, He desires to do through us as we
    share His grace and peace with others.

■

Endnotes

Part 1: INTRODUCTION TO THE THESSALONIAN LETTERS

Chapter 1: The Importance of the Thessalonian Letters

1. Charles A. Wanamaker, "The Epistles to the Thessalonians," in *The New International Greek Testament Commentary,* ed. I. Howard Marshall and W. Ward Gasque (Grand Rapids: Eerdmans, 1990, p. 14).
2. John F. Walvoord, *The Rapture Question* (Grand Rapids: Zondervan, 1981, p. 200).
3. Ibid.
4. Paul N. Benware, *Understanding End Times Prophecy* (Chicago: Moody, 1995, p. 86).
5. Mal Couch, ed., *A Bible Handbook to the Acts of the Apostles* (Grand Rapids: Kregel, 1999, p. 35).
6. R. C. H. Lenski, *The Interpretation of St. Paul's Epistles to the Colossians, to the Thessalonians, to Timothy, to Titus, and to Philemon* (Minneapolis, Minn.: Augsburg, 1964, pp. 255–56).
7. William Hendriksen, *New Testament Commentary: Thessalonians, Timothy, and Titus* (Grand Rapids: Baker, 1983, p. 68).
8. Lenski, *Interpretation of St. Paul's Epistles,* p. 306.

Chapter 2: The Canonicity, Authorship, and Date of the Thessalonian Letters

1. Henry Clarence Thiessen, *Introduction to the New Testament* (Grand Rapids: Eerdmans, 1958, p. 189).
2. Everett F. Harrison, *Introduction to the New Testament* (Grand Rapids: Eerdmans, 1974, p. 263).

3. William Hendriksen, *New Testament Commentary: Thessalonians, Timothy, and Titus* (Grand Rapids: Baker, 1983, pp. 20–25).
4. Harrison, *Introduction to the New Testament*, p. 263.
5. George Milligan, *St. Paul's Epistles to the Thessalonians* (Minneapolis, Minn.: Klock & Klock, 1980, p. lxxiii).
6. Thiessen, *Introduction to the New Testament*, pp. 195–96.
7. Harrison, *Introduction to the New Testament*, pp. 265–66.
8. Ibid., p. 266.
9. Ibid.
10. R. C. H. Lenski, *The Interpretation of St. Paul's Epistles to the Colossians, to the Thessalonians, to Timothy, to Titus, and to Philemon* (Minneapolis, Minn.: Augsburg, 1964, p. 215).
11. James L. Boyer, *New Testament Chronological Chart* (Chicago: Moody, 1968).
12. Albert Barnes, *Notes on the New Testament*, 14 vols. (Grand Rapids: Baker, 1983, 12:vi).
13. A. T. Robertson, *Word Pictures in the New Testament*, 6 vols. (Nashville: Broadman, 1931, 4:xv–xvi).

Chapter 3: Background to the Thessalonian Letters

1. Merrill C. Tenney, *New Testament Times* (Grand Rapids: Eerdmans, 1965, p. 260).
2. Ibid., p. 261.
3. W. J. Conybeare and J. S. Howson, *The Life and Epistles of St. Paul* (Grand Rapids: Eerdmans, 1980, p. 257).
4. Merrill F. Unger, *Archaeology and the New Testament* (Grand Rapids: Zondervan, 1975, p. 227).

PART 2: FIRST THESSALONIANS COMMENTARY

Chapter 5: Paul's Commendation of the Thessalonians

1. Merrill F. Unger, *Unger's Commentary on the Old Testament*, 2 vols. (Chicago: Moody, 1981, 2:1248).

Chapter 6: Paul's Care for the Thessalonians

1. Gerhard Kittel, ed., *Theological Dictionary of the New Testament*, 10 vols. (Grand Rapids: Eerdmans, 1987, 5:859).

Chapter 8: More on Christian Living and the Rapture of the Church

1. John F. Walvoord, *The Rapture Question* (Grand Rapids: Zondervan, 1981, p. 35).
2. Ibid., pp. 175–76.
3. Mal Couch, ed., *Dictionary of Premillennial Theology* (Grand Rapids: Kregel, 1996, p. 337).
4. Everett Ferguson, *Backgrounds of Early Christianity* (Grand Rapids: Eerdmans, 1993, pp. 232–33).
5. Couch, *Dictionary of Premillennial Theology,* p. 342.

Chapter 9: Reason for the Rapture

1. Arnold Fruchtenbaum, "Day of the Lord," in *Dictionary of Premillennial Theology,* ed. Mal Couch (Grand Rapids: Kregel, 1996, pp. 87–88).
2. J. Dwight Pentecost, *Things to Come* (Findlay, Ohio: Dunham, 1961, p. 235).
3. Paul N. Benware, *Understanding End Times Prophecy* (Chicago: Moody, 1995, p. 247).

Chapter 10: Preaching from 1 Thessalonians

1. *The Complete C. S. Lewis* (New York: Macmillan, 1963, p. 101).

PART 3: SECOND THESSALONIANS COMMENTARY

Chapter 11: Paul's Greetings

1. Michael Avi-Yonah and Zvi Baras, eds., *The World History of the Jewish People: Society and Religion in the Second Temple Period,* vol. 8 (Jerusalem: Massada, 1977, p. 159).
2. Joseph Wilson Trigg, *Origen* (Atlanta, Ga.: John Knox, 1983, p. 212).
3. Ibid., pp. 212–13.

Chapter 12: Concern and Questions About the Day of the Lord

1. John F. Walvoord, *The Rapture Question* (Grand Rapids: Zondervan, 1979, p. 238).
2. Mal Couch, ed., *Dictionary of Premillennial Theology* (Grand Rapids: Kregel, 1996, p. 56).
3. J. Dwight Pentecost, *Things to Come* (Findlay, Ohio: Dunham, 1961, p. 155).

4. Couch, *Dictionary of Premillennial Theology,* pp. 49–50.

5. Ibid., p. 175.

6. Ibid., p. 51.

■

Glossary of Theological Terms

Antichrist. Paul does not use this title in the Thessalonian letters; he does , however, use other descriptions for the historic character who will openly oppose God and proclaim himself as "messiah" in place of Christ during the Tribulation. After the Rapture of the Church and the apostasy, then comes the Day of the Lord (2 Thess. 2:2), and the "man of lawlessness," the "son of destruction" (v. 3). He opposes God, exalts himself, and displays himself "as being God" (v. 4). He is called "that lawless one" (v. 8) whose coming is instigated by Satan (v. 9), but who will be slain by the arrival of the Lord, who comes to establish His kingdom (v. 8). Many other passages from Daniel to Revelation describe the powerful and deceptive activities of this evil personality.

apostasy. *Apostasia* is used twice in the New Testament. Paul was accused of apostatizing from the teachings of Moses (Acts 21:21), and in 2 Thessalonians 2:3, Paul writes that the Day of the Lord will not come "unless the apostasy comes first." The word is a compound of *apo* (from) and *histemi* (to stand), thus, "to stand away from" or "to fall away." Another related noun (*apostasion*) means a certificate of divorce. There are many contexts that teach the concept or doctrine of the apostasy, such as 2 Peter 3:3: "In the last days mockers will come with their mocking, following after their own lusts."

apostle. Paul mentions his apostleship only once in this letter, but he also includes Silas and Timothy as holding such a position (1 Thess. 2:6). With Paul, they also asserted some authority over the Thessalonian Christians. Paul is considered on the same level as the first twelve apostles, "the most eminent apostles," the "true apostles" (2 Cor. 12:11–12). The word *apostolos* is a compound of *apo* (from) and *stello* (to journey), as in "to set forth on a journey" as a courier or ambassador with a message. Paul had a special calling that Silas and Timothy could not claim (Rom. 1:1; 1 Cor. 1:1; Gal. 1:1).

called. A family of words speak of God's sovereign calling to salvation (*eklegomai,* "to chose, to call out"; *eklektos,* "chosen"; *kaleo,* "to call"; *klesis,* "calling"; *kletos,* "called"). In Thessalonians the apostle writes of the believer's election by God Himself (1 Thess. 1:4); of their being worthy of His calling (2:12); of their being called in sanctification (4:7). He reminds them that they were called by the One who is faithful (5:24), chosen from the beginning (2 Thess. 2:13), and called to salvation by the gospel message itself (v. 14).

church. Paul writes of the *ekklesia* (the called out) as the body of Christ— "you in Christ Jesus" (1 Thess. 5:18)—but he also mentions that the suffering of the Thessalonians was known among "the churches of God" (2 Thess. 1:4). Paul probably has local churches in mind when he writes that their faith had gone forth throughout the regions of Macedonia and Achaia (1 Thess. 1:8) (see "In Christ," 1 Thess. 1:1; 5:18; 2 Thess. 1:1).

dead in Christ. These have died and fallen asleep in Jesus (1 Thess. 4:13–14). God will bring their souls with Jesus when He returns (v. 14), which are united with new bodies that are then caught up to heaven to meet the Lord in the air (v. 17). When the Rapture trumpet is sounded these dead in Christ will rise first, then the living are changed (given a glorified body) to join the raised dead in the clouds (v. 17). This doctrine is to give comfort to the living (v. 18).

Day of the Lord. This is the technical phrase that describes the seven-year tribulation that comes suddenly upon the world (1 Thess. 5:2). "They," the world, will be caught up in terrible destruction while saying "peace and safety!" (v. 3). The Tribulation is a time of darkness that overtakes like a thief (v. 4) and a night of fear and wrath (vv. 5, 9). A period of apostasy will come first, followed by the man of sin, the Antichrist (2 Thess. 2:3). The saints understood the doctrine of the Day of the Lord and did not need to be told about it (1 Thess. 5:2). It is mentioned about twenty-five times in the Old Testament.

eternal destruction. "Eternal destruction" (*olethron aionion*) is the retribution (2 Thess. 1:8) for disobeying the gospel. It is a penalty paid (v. 9) that carries the unbeliever away from the presence of God and from the glory of His power. This destruction is initiated at the second coming of

Christ (v. 7), but certainly would include the final Great White Throne judgment of the lost before eternity begins (Rev. 20:11–15). There is a special penalty for those who follow the Antichrist during the Tribulation. The Lord sends to them a deluding influence "so that they might believe what is false in order that they all may be judged who did not believe the truth, but took pleasure in wickedness" (2 Thess. 2:11–12).

Gentiles. The Gentiles (*ethnos*) are those who do not know God (1 Thess. 4:5), in contrast to the Jews who were given the revelations of God (Rom. 9:4). Yet God is the God of the Gentiles also (3:29) and salvation has come to them (11:11) through the gospel (Gal. 2:2). The Jews in Thessalonica tried to stop Paul from speaking to the Gentiles about Christ in order that they might be saved (1 Thess. 2:16), although in this dispensation of the Church, both Gentile and Jew are to believe on Christ as Savior. But because of the Jews' blindness to their own Messiah, it is mainly Gentiles now who are accepting Christ.

glory. This word (*doxa*) refers to the divine splendor, brightness, and purity of both God the Father and the Lord Jesus Christ. At His second coming, Jesus is glorified in His power He displays as the Lord's reigning king (2 Thess. 1:9), and He is glorified with (*en*) "His saints on that day" (v. 10; John 17:22). Paul further adds that we are called into His kingdom and glory (1 Thess. 2:12). Referring to the preview of the coming kingdom at Christ's transfiguration (Matt. 17:1–6), Peter says he was a partaker of "the glory that is to be revealed" (1 Peter 5:1), i.e., the future kingdom glory. The Thessalonians are also called the apostles' glory and joy (1 Thess. 2:20). The glory of the Father and the Son is one of the major doctrines of the New Testament.

gospel. The "good news" (*euangelion*) includes the death, burial, and resurrection of Christ for our sins (1 Cor. 15:1–8). Paul writes of "our gospel," meaning that he and the other apostles were responsible for witnessing of this message of grace and salvation (1 Thess. 1:5). The gospel did not come to the Thessalonians simply by word but in power and in the Holy Spirit, and with full conviction with those who responded (v. 5). The gospel is to be obeyed (2 Thess. 1:8), and God calls the elect through (by means of) "our gospel," "that you may gain the glory of our Lord Jesus Christ" (2:14).

Holy Spirit. When Paul warns the believers to avoid sexual immorality, he reminds the Thessalonians that his words really are those of the Holy Spirit given directly to them (1 Thess. 4:8). Likewise, the Spirit was not to be quenched or extinguished in His convicting work with the saints (5:19). And, though facing terrible persecution, it is the Holy Spirit who imparts to the saints His joy in the midst of such troubles (1:6). The Spirit saves (v. 5), and in that process of salvation, sanctifies those providentially chosen (2 Thess. 2:13).

in Christ, in God. In the mysterious workings of the Lord in salvation, believers are said to be placed into (*en*) Christ (1 Thess. 1:1; 5:18). As well, they are said to be placed into God the Father (2 Thess. 1:1). This is the Scriptures' way of showing the new relationship we have with the persons of the Godhead because of our salvation secured through Christ. Jesus spoke of this coming new position when He prayed to the Father before His death, "Thou, Father, art in Me, and I in Thee, that they also may be in Us" (John 17:21).

kingdom. This is the messianic reign mentioned so often in the Gospels. There the gospel writers speak of "the kingdom of God" or "the kingdom of heaven." Both refer to the millennium and the Davidic earthly reign of Christ. "The kingdom of God" can be translated with a genitive, "the kingdom belonging to God," or with the ablative, "the kingdom coming from God as source." Paul writes of the messianic reign, saying the Lord calls "you into His own kingdom and glory" (1 Thess. 2:12). In their suffering, writes Paul, believers are "worthy of the kingdom of God" (2 Thess. 1:5).

prayer. In the Thessalonian letters, Paul mentions prayer often, but he also uses another expression that means a form of praying. He uses the subjunctive mood that often places a "may" with the verb. This is a "wish" or "desire" that God would respond and do something specifically requested. The apostle writes, "May our God and Father Himself and Jesus our Lord direct our way to you; and may the Lord cause you to increase and abound in love" (1 Thess. 3:11–12). This construction is used often by Paul. As well, he uses the common word for prayer, *proseuche,* and its verb. Besides using "may the Lord . . . ," Paul saturates these letters with prayer requests: He mentioned praying specifically for them (1 Thess. 1:2; 2 Thess. 1:11); he urges them to pray for him, Silas, and Timothy (1 Thess. 5:25; 2 Thess. 3:1); he urges them to simply be believers who are prayer warriors (1 Thess. 5:17).

Rapture. Though there are many verses in the New Testament that give us the doctrine of the Rapture, the most important passage is 1 Thessalonians

4:13–18. However, other verses in both these letters also teach this truth. Paul writes of the believers waiting for the Son from heaven and being delivered from the wrath to come (1:10); of being transported into the very presence of Christ (2:19); of being before our God and Father (3:13). He writes that we are not destined for wrath, but for obtaining salvation (deliverance) through Christ (5:9), and he desires that we be sanctified, without blame at the "coming of our Lord Jesus Christ" (5:23). He writes also that the Rapture is "our gathering together to Him" at His coming (2 Thess. 2:1).

In the central Rapture passage Paul says those asleep in Jesus go before those who are alive (1 Thess. 4:14–15). At the trumpet of God the dead in Christ rise first, "then we who are alive . . . shall be caught up together with them in the clouds to meet the Lord in the air" (v. 17). These verses lead us to four important points about the Rapture: (1) It could have happened to that early New Testament generation; (2) It involves a resurrection for those who have died and a transformation (change) for those yet alive (1 Cor. 15:51–52); (3) The saints are caught up to Christ—He does not come down to reign; (4) The Rapture is for removing Church saints (those "in Christ") from earth before the impending wrath falls (1 Thess. 1:10; 5:9).

Resurrection. *See* **Rapture.**

resurrection of Christ. Though Paul mentions the resurrection of Christ only once (1 Thess. 4:14), this truth is still central to all he writes about in these letters. The Thessalonians knew that some day they would see Christ in His glory. They were comforted by the fact that their loved ones were already with Him: "God will bring with [Christ] those who have fallen asleep in Jesus" (v. 14). The resurrection of Christ is the most important of all doctrines throughout the rest of Paul's epistles.

sanctification. The word comes from *hagios* (holy) and other related words. In both the Old and New Testaments these words mean "to set [someone, something] aside, to make special or unique." The thought is that someone or something that is holy is not to be profaned; it is kept or declared clean and undefiled. Positional sanctification is part of the work of salvation itself. One is declared holy because one is "in Christ" and receiving His righteousness to their account. "God has chosen you from the beginning for salvation *through* sanctification by the Spirit and faith in the truth" (2 Thess. 2:13, italics mine). Experiential sanctification has to do with the progressive spiritual growth and maturity of the believer. God's will is the sanctification of the believer in which he or she is to "abstain from sexual immorality" (1 Thess. 4:3), for God has called His own to live a sanctified life (4:7). Paul prays for the saints in Thessalonica to be entirely sanctified and kept complete, "without blame at the coming of our Lord Jesus Christ" (5:23). Finally, the apostle urges this church to "stand firm and *hold*" by keeping what he has said and written (2 Thess. 2:15, italics mine). No one can be sanctified without the inner work of the Holy Spirit.

Satan. Many names are used in Scripture to describe this evil personality. Though he was once the highest of the archangels, he now opposes God to the fullest extent of his power. Paul uses two descriptions in two passages in the Thessalonian letters—*Satan* and *the evil one. Satan* is an Aramaic word meaning "adversary." The Antichrist is said to come "with the activity of Satan, with all power and signs and false wonders" (2 Thess. 2:9). Paul adds that "the Lord is faithful, and He will strengthen and protect you from the *evil one*" (3:3, italics mine).

Second Coming. The Bible predicts the dramatic coming (*parousia*) of Christ to establish His kingdom reign. The word *second* is a theological usage to distinguish between the first coming of Jesus to die for sins, over against His Second Coming to reign. The Rapture of the Church is not the Second Coming in that Christ does not come to the earth to reign. Instead, the saints ascend and are caught up to be with Him. The word *second* is used once in Hebrews, however, to describe the Lord's coming earthly reign: "So Christ also, having been offered once [at His first coming] to bear the sins of many, shall appear a second time [to establish the kingdom] not to bear sin, to those who eagerly await Him" (9:28). The context of 2 Thessalonians 1:6–10 describes in part that return to earth to begin the Davidic reign. Relief will be given to all who suffer for Christ's sake "when the Lord Jesus will be revealed from heaven with His mighty angels in flaming fire" (v. 7), and "when He comes to be glorified in His saints on that day, and to be marveled at among all who have believed" (v. 10). (See the commentary on these verses.)

walk. The apostle describes throughout these two letters how the believer is to walk. Paul mentions that he, Silas, and Timothy walked "devoutly and uprightly and blamelessly" before the assembly (1 Thess. 2:10). Paul urged the congregation to "stand firm" (3:8), to walk as to please God

(4:1), to lead a quiet life (v. 11), and "behave properly toward outsiders" (v. 12). He pleads that believers not fall asleep (5:6) and live soberly (v. 8). This Christian walk is spelled out in detail in 5:12–21 with many practical moral and spiritual imperatives. Paul's desire for this church was that "the Lord direct your hearts into the love of God and into the steadfastness of Christ" (2 Thess. 3:5). Paul is concerned not only with what the believers know, but also how they live.

word. To Paul, the Word of God reflects not only the Lord's commands but also His authority as to what is to be believed and how the saint is to live. The word (*logos*) is referred to in the sense of an authority to be adhered to and believed (1 Thess. 4:15). And the Thessalonians did just that. Going through many tribulations, the assembly still received the word with the joy of the Holy Spirit (1 Thess. 1:6). To make sure the church understood that when the apostles spoke, they taught with that authority given from the Lord, he often said "we command you, brethren, in the name of our Lord Jesus Christ" (2 Thess. 3:6), yet, as "apostles of Christ," they instructed without harshness and forcefulness (1 Thess. 2:6). Finally, Paul is grateful and writes to the congregation that "when you received from us the word of God's message, you accepted it not as the word of men, but for what it really is, the word of God, which also performs its work in you who believe" (2:13).

wrath. This word (*orges*) is used in several places to describe the Seventieth Week of Daniel, the Day of the Lord, the Tribulation. In some contexts, *orges* is sometimes used to define the persecution by the unbeliever against the saints. The apostle speaks of those in Christ being delivered "from the wrath to come" (1 Thess. 1:10), but the ungodly have the wrath hanging over them. This "wrath has come upon them to the utmost" (2:16). But the child of God is not destined for this wrath (5:9). Although not using the word *orges,* in the second Thessalonian epistle Paul describes this wrath as "God's righteous judgment" (1:5) and a "repaying" of those who persecute believers (v. 6), as well as a divine "retribution to those who do not know God and to those who do not obey the gospel of our Lord Jesus" (v. 8).